CHURCH
HISTORY
for
Latter-day
Saint
Families

CHURCH HISTORY

for
Latter-day
Saint
Families

─────── GENERAL EDITOR ───────
Thomas R. Valletta

─────── ASSOCIATE EDITORS ───────

Bruce L. Andreason	Richard O. Christensen	Brian D. Garner	Dennis H. Leavitt
Randall C. Bird	John L. Fowles	Gordon B. Holbrook	George R. Sims

─────── ILLUSTRATORS ───────

Robert T. Barrett	Gary Kapp	Greg Olsen	Clark Kelley Price
Ted Henninger	Tom Lovell	Del Parson	Scott Snow

DESERET
BOOK

SALT LAKE CITY, UTAH

Dedicated to President Joseph F. Smith, who saw "the hand of the Lord . . .
in every hour and in every moment of the existence
of the Church" (Conference Report, April 1904, p. 2).

Library of Congress Cataloging-in-Publication Data

Church history for Latter-day Saint families / Thomas R. Valletta, general editor.
     p. cm.
  Includes bibliographical references.
  ISBN 1-59038-327-3 (hardbound : alk. paper)
  1. Church of Jesus Christ of Latter-day Saints—History. 2. Mormon
Church—History. I. Valletta, Thomas R.
  BX8611.C575 2004
  289.3'09—dc22   2004012043

Printed in the United States of America   42316
Inland Press, Menomonee Falls, WI

10 9 8 7 6 5 4 3 2 1

CONTENTS

INTRODUCTION

TO THE YOUNG READER

Welcome to *Church History for Latter-day Saint Families!* This book, like *The Book of Mormon for Latter-day Saint Families* and *The New Testament for Latter-day Saint Families,* is designed especially for families with young readers. It will help you read, understand, and think about the early history of The Church of Jesus Christ of Latter-day Saints in exciting new ways.

You will notice right away there are many beautiful pictures and drawings to help you understand what you are reading.

In addition to the pictures, several other kinds of help can be found on every page. You will often see small numbers that are a little higher than the rest of the line (like this⁵). These are called superscript numbers, and they tell you that there are the following kinds of helps at the bottom of the page:

• Many words that may be hard to understand are colored blue in addition to having a superscript number next to them. That means you will find help for those words at the bottom of the page next to that same number and this picture: 📖 In some cases the word helps are definitions of hard words, but most often they are replacement words to help you understand what the sentence means.

• Sometimes you will find a superscript number next to an idea in a paragraph that is worth a closer look. Next to that same number at the bottom of the page you will see the picture of a magnifying glass 🔍. There you will find helpful explanations about the background, history, or meaning of that idea that make it interesting.

• Often we can gain a better understanding of an event or story in Church history by comparing it to verses of scripture that talk about the same truths. Prophets, apostles, and other Church leaders in our day have also taught us many things that help us understand these stories better. When the superscript number in the paragraph matches a number at the bottom of the page with a picture of a sun ☀ next to it, you will find more light on that story from modern scripture and Church leaders. (Note that whenever a non-scriptural source is given in the text, the full publication information for that source can be found in the "Sources Cited" section at the back of the book.)

• Sometimes the best way to understand the truths in these stories is to ponder them. To *ponder* means to stop and think and pray about what you are reading so Heavenly Father can help you learn what he wants you to learn. When the superscript number in the paragraph matches a number at the bottom of the page with this picture 🔄 next to it, you will find some thoughts and questions that will help you ponder what you are reading.

An understanding of the history of the Church will help you appreciate the sacrifices and the faith of the early Saints. Understanding their sacrifices and their faith will help strengthen your own testimony of the truth of the gospel and give you the courage to be faithful in the trials that you must face.

A WORD TO PARENTS

The purpose of *Church History for Latter-day Saint Families* is not to rewrite the history of the Church in simpler language but to help the young reader understand and appreciate the great stories of Church history as told by those close to the events and as outlined in the Doctrine and Covenants. The stories included in this book are from trusted and familiar primary sources or from the writings of apostles and prophets. Some of the sources used are generally no longer available and many of these stories have never been available in one volume.

In addition to the helpful features mentioned under the heading "To the Young Reader" above, this volume provides several other kinds of help for your family:

- A **glossary** at the back of the book explains difficult terms and concepts, such as *Consecration* and *Keys of the Priesthood*. Words found in the glossary are colored pink in the text.

- The history of the Church is divided into easily understood **units** or **time periods** (for example, "The Church in Illinois, 1839–1846"). A unit **introduction** provides an overview for each time period.

- Each unit is divided into **chapters** with a central topic or theme (for example, "The Mission of the Twelve to England"). A chapter **introduction** provides a brief overview of the chapter with a suggestion of important things to look for to give purpose to family members' reading.

- Every chapter is divided by **subheadings** that introduce each part of the story told in that chapter. These subheadings help the young reader follow the flow of the chapter through different storytellers without getting lost.

Helping our young people gain an understanding of, and love for, the history of this great Church is of profound importance. It will better prepare them to participate in Primary, Sunday School, priesthood, Young Women, seminary, missions, and every other aspect of Church service.

President Gordon B. Hinckley said, "Every member of the Church ought to have some understanding of, and familiarity with, the history of this tremendous movement. Without such understanding, it is difficult to sink the roots of faith deep enough that the tree will not topple when false winds of doctrine blow. No man can really appreciate Joseph Smith without reading his history. No one can really understand the tremendous heritage we have, which has been made possible by the sacrifices of the generations who have gone before. Without such understanding, it is not likely that there will be much of gratitude or appreciation" (*Teachings of Gordon B. Hinckley*, 104).

KINDS OF HELPS FOUND IN
CHURCH HISTORY FOR LATTER-DAY SAINT FAMILIES

When you see a footnote number, it means you will find additional help at the bottom of the page.

If a word is **blue,** the word is explained at the bottom of the page.

Chapter introductions give a brief overview of each chapter.

Topic headings help you see when the subject changes.

If a word is **pink,** you will find an explanation of that word in the glossary at the back of the book.

The **question mark** means you will find some thoughts and questions that will help you ponder what you are reading.

The **sun picture** means you will find more light from modern scriptures or modern prophets.

The **magnifying glass** means you will find information about the meaning of a verse or about the history, the people, or the customs that make the verse interesting.

47

The Lost Manuscript

"And the vision of all is become unto you as the words of a book that is sealed, which men deliver to one that is learned, saying, Read this, I pray thee: and he saith, I cannot; for it is sealed:[116]

"And the book is delivered to him that is not learned, saying, Read this, I pray thee: and he saith, I am not learned"[117] (Isaiah 29:11–12).

Martin returned to Pennsylvania and explained to Joseph what had happened. He was delighted that scholars had agreed with his translations. Joseph Fielding Smith wrote that "if Martin went to them with some *misgivings*[118] in his mind, these were evidently quieted by the report which he received. From that time forth he became enthusiastic over the work the Prophet was doing"[119] (*Church History and Modern Revelation*, 1:20n).

CHAPTER 10:
THE LOST MANUSCRIPT

Joseph Smith and Martin Harris worked many long hours together to translate the Book of Mormon. And while Martin believed in and was excited about the work, Martin's wife, Lucy, doubted the work of the translation. She felt that her husband

was being deceived by Joseph Smith. Martin wanted to show his wife the important work he was doing. He asked Joseph if he could take the 116 pages they had translated from the gold plates to show his wife. These precious pages were taken by Martin and eventually lost. As you read, think about what you would have done in Martin's situation.

MARTIN HARRIS ASKS FOR PERMISSION TO SHOW 116 TRANSLATED PAGES TO HIS FAMILY AND FRIENDS

Joseph and Martin continued to work through the spring and early summer of 1828. By June 14, 1828, Martin had written 116 pages of manuscript,[120] recording everything that Joseph translated from the gold plates. In his history of the Church, Joseph wrote that "some time after Mr. Harris had begun to write for me, he began to *importune*[121] me to give him *liberty*[122] to carry the writings home and show them; and desired of me that I would inquire of the Lord, through the **Urim and Thummim,** if he might not do so. I did inquire, and the answer was that he must not. However, he was not satisfied with this answer, and desired that I should inquire again.

---

116. Joseph Fielding Smith explained: "Unwittingly both Martin Harris and Professor Anthon fulfilled the words of Isaiah. Martin by taking the copies of the hieroglyphics to the professor and the professor in saying, 'I cannot read a sealed book.' In the prophetic words of Isaiah the learned man was to say, when the words of

A portion of the gold plates was sealed

the book were presented to him, and he was asked to read them, 'I cannot, for it is sealed'" (The Restoration of All Things, 97).

117. Joseph Fielding Smith verified that "Joseph Smith [was] the unlearned man unto whom the book was delivered" (Church History and Modern Revelation, 1:20).

118. **misgivings**—unbelief about the work

119. How does knowing that ancient prophets, such as Isaiah, prophesied about the Book of Mormon strengthen your testimony?

NOTES FOR CHAPTER 10

120. The 116 pages were a translation from the writings of Lehi. The writings of Lehi were a part of what were called the large plates of Nephi. The large plates of Nephi also included the books of Mosiah, Alma, Helaman, Third Nephi, Fourth Nephi, and Mormon.

121. **importune**—ask

122. **liberty**—permission

PRELUDE TO THE RESTORATION

Since the world began, Heavenly Father has called prophets to teach his children his eternal plan of happiness. Heavenly Father has given his children the freedom to choose to follow his plan or to reject it. This freedom is called agency. Whenever the people have chosen to reject the plan and the prophets, it is called apostasy.

"When Jesus lived on the earth, he established his Church, the only true Church. He organized his Church so the truths of the gospel could be taught to all people and the ordinances of the gospel could be administered correctly with authority. . . .

"After the Savior ascended into heaven, men changed the ordinances and doctrines that he and his Apostles had established. Because of apostasy, there was no direct revelation from God. The true Church was no longer on the earth. Men organized different churches that claimed to be true but taught conflicting doctrines. There was much confusion and contention over religion. . . .

"For many years people lived in spiritual darkness. About 1700 years after Christ, people were becoming more and more interested in knowing the truth about God and religion. Some of them could see that the gospel Jesus taught was no longer on the earth. Some recognized that there was no revelation and no true authority and that the Church that Christ organized did not exist on the earth. The time had arrived for the Church of Jesus Christ to be restored to the earth" (Gospel Principles, *109–10*).

CHAPTER 1:
APOSTASY, REFORMATION, AND THE NEED FOR A RESTORATION

The Great Apostasy occurred after Jesus Christ was crucified and Peter and other apostles were killed. Without living prophets or apostles, revelation ceased. False teachings crept into the Church and some true teachings were lost. The true Church, as well as the authority to act in God's name, was taken from the earth.

After centuries of spiritual darkness and confusion, some people—who we call reformers—tried to bring the teachings of Jesus Christ back into their churches. They could see from the Bible that errors and false teachings were being presented in their churches, but they did not have the proper power and authority from Jesus Christ to truly act in his name. Many of these reformers were persecuted and even put to death because of their beliefs. Their courage and teachings helped prepare the way for the restoration of all things by helping the world to become more religiously tolerant. As you read this chapter, look for what events helped prepare the way for the restoration of the Church of Jesus Christ.

THE SAVIOR ORGANIZES HIS CHURCH DURING HIS MORTAL MINISTRY

During his mortal ministry, the Savior performed many significant acts, none more essential or compassionate[1] than the Atonement. His ministry was brief, lasting only three years. But, as Elder M. Russell Ballard of the Quorum of the Twelve explained, "in those three years He taught the human family everything that is necessary to receive all of the blessings our Father in Heaven has in store for His children. . . . One of the most important

---

NOTES FOR CHAPTER 1

1. 📖 **compassionate**—kind

📖 = Word Help	🔍 = A Closer Look
🌟 = More Light	📖 = Ponder This

Words in pink are explained in the Glossary.

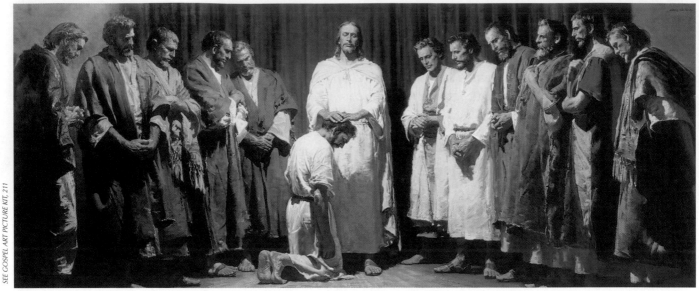

SEE GOSPEL ART PICTURE KIT, 211

Jesus Christ called and ordained Peter to be His chief apostle

accomplishments of the Savior was the establishment of His church upon the earth. Paul taught that Christ 'gave some, apostles; and some, prophets;[2] and some, evangelists;[3] and some, pastors[4] and teachers; for the perfecting of the saints, for the work of the ministry, for the edifying of the body of Christ'[5] (Eph. 4:11–12)" ("Restored Truth," *Ensign,* November 1994, 65).

The apostles who were called in Jesus' day were called of God, just as they are today. Jesus ordained them and set them apart with his own hands. He gave them the authority to act in his name as they led his church. After Jesus' death, resurrection, and ascension, Peter became the chief apostle and leader of the Church.

THE DEATH OF THE APOSTLES AND THE LOSS OF PRIESTHOOD AUTHORITY

In a 1994 general conference address, Elder M. Russell Ballard spoke about the early apostles and their struggles to teach the gospel to the Christian people, who began to suffer persecutions from those around them: "Early Christians endured the challenges of persecution and hardship. Peter and his brethren had a difficult time holding the Church together and keeping the doctrine pure. They traveled extensively and wrote to one another about the problems they were facing, but information moved so slowly and the Church and its teachings were so new that heading off false teachings before they became firmly entrenched[6] was difficult.

---

2. Bruce R. McConkie taught that "apostles and prophets have been set in the Church for the purpose of teaching and identifying true doctrine. . . . If a church has no prophets and apostles, then it has no way of knowing whether its doctrines are true or false" (*Mormon Doctrine,* 205).

3. "Evangelists are patriarchs and they hold the right to bless and pronounce by the spirit of revelation the lineage of members of the Church. . . .There is in the Church the office of patriarch to, or of, the Church, sometimes called the 'presiding' patriarch. This ofice

was first conferred upon Joseph Smith, Sen., in this dispensation, and was given to him by revelation and right of lineage" (Joseph Fielding Smith, *Church History and Modern Revelation,* 2:20–21).

4. ***pastors**—bishops*

5. ***the edifying of the body of Christ**—to teach and inspire the members of the Church*

6. ***firmly entrenched**—widely believed*

The New Testament indicates that the early apostles worked hard to preserve the church that Jesus Christ left to their care and keeping, but they knew their efforts would ultimately be in vain.[7] Paul wrote to the Thessalonian Saints,[8] who were anxiously anticipating[9] the second coming of Christ, that 'that day shall not come, except there come a falling away first' (2 Thessalonians 2:3). He also warned Timothy that 'the time will come when they will not endure[10] sound doctrine; . . . And they shall turn away their ears from the truth, and shall be turned unto fables'[11] (2 Timothy 4:3–4).

"And Peter presupposed[12] the falling away, or the Apostasy, when he spoke of 'the times of refreshing'[13] that would come before God would again send Jesus Christ, who 'before was preached unto you: Whom the heaven must receive until the times of restitution of all things, which God hath spoken by the mouth of all his holy prophets since the world began' (Acts 3:19–21).[14]

"Eventually, with the known exception of John the Beloved,[15] Peter and his fellow Apostles were martyred.[16] The Apostle John and members of the Church struggled for survival in the face of horrifying oppression. To their everlasting credit, Christianity did survive and was truly a prominent force by the end of the second century A.D. Many valiant Saints were instrumental in helping Christianity to endure.

"Despite the significance of the ministries of these Saints, they did not hold the same apostolic authority that Peter and the other Apostles had received through ordination under the hands of the Lord Jesus Christ Himself. When that authority was lost, men began looking to other sources for doctrinal understanding. As a result, many plain and precious truths were lost"[17] ("Restored Truth," 65–66).

THE SAVIOR'S DOCTRINE IS CHANGED BY UNINSPIRED LEADERS

By A.D. 325, Christianity had become the official religion of the Roman Empire. However, the Christian people were still unable to agree on basic doctrines and principles of the church. The Roman Emperor Constantine[18] wanted to resolve these differences and called a group of Christian bishops to Nicaea,[19] where a great meeting was held to define the doctrines of the church.

---

7. *ultimately be in vain*—in the end, without hope

8. The Thessalonian Saints were members of the Church living in Thessalonica, the capital city of Macedonia in Paul's day (see Bible Dictionary, s.v. "Thessalonica," 785). Modern Thessalonica is in Greece.

9. *anxiously anticipating*—greatly looking forward to

10. *endure*—live according to

11. Paul explained that a "falling away" or apostasy would happen because the people would turn the truth into "fables" or would not listen to the true doctrine or teachings of Jesus Christ.

12. *presupposed*—thought of

13. *refreshing*—restoration

14. The Apostle Peter's prophecies about "times of refreshing" and the "restitution of all things" both refer to the restoration of the gospel in our day. President Harold B. Lee said: "You and I have been privileged to be born in a dispensation [period of time] known in the scriptures as the fulness of times, which is to precede the second coming of Jesus Christ" (*Stand Ye in Holy Places*, 71).

15. John the Beloved was the only one of the Twelve Apostles called by Jesus to not taste of death. John had asked the Savior for "power over death" so he could "bring souls unto [Jesus]" (D&C 7:2). The Lord granted his request and John is as a "flaming fire and a ministering angel" unto this day (D&C 7:6).

16. *martyred*—killed

17. From whom did your father or bishop receive his priesthood authority? Why do you think it is important for men to receive their priesthood from someone who has the authority from God?

18. Constantine made Christianity the state religion, even though he didn't accept baptism until just before his own death. He called the council at Nicaea because the disagreements over doctrine "threatened to rend [tear down] the Church to its foundation" (see James E. Talmage, *The Great Apostasy*, 75–76, 102).

19. Nicaea is a city on the southeastern coast of France.

But, as Elder Ballard explained, "Consensus[20] did not come easily. Opinions on such basic subjects as the nature of God were diverse and deeply felt, and debate was spirited. Decisions were not made by inspiration or revelation but by majority vote, and some disagreeing factions[21] split off and formed new churches. Similar doctrinal councils were held later in A.D. 451, 787, and 1545 with similarly divisive results.

"The beautiful simplicity of Christ's gospel was under attack from an enemy that was even more destructive than the scourges and the crosses of early Rome: the philosophical meanderings[22] of uninspired men. The doctrine became based more on popular opinion than on revelation. This period of time was called the Dark Ages.[23] They were dark largely because the light of the gospel of Jesus Christ had been lost" ("Restored Truth," 66).

THE DARKNESS OF THE GREAT APOSTASY

Centuries passed by, and in the words of President Gordon B. Hinckley, "A cloud of darkness settled over the earth. Isaiah described it: 'For, behold, the darkness shall cover the earth, and gross darkness the people' (Isa. 60:2).

"It was a season of plunder and suffering, marked by long and bloody conflict. . . .

"It was an age of hopelessness, a time of masters and serfs.[24]

"The first thousand years passed, and the second millennium dawned. . . . It was a time fraught[25] with fear and suffering. The great and deadly plague[26] of the 14th century began in Asia. It spread to Europe and on up to England. Everywhere it went there was sudden death. . . . In five years it took the lives of 25 million, one-third the population of Europe" ("At the Summit of the Ages," *Ensign,* November 1999, 73).

THE REFORMATION AND FIGHT FOR RELIGIOUS FREEDOM

Elder Ballard explained that "in 1517 the Spirit moved Martin Luther, a German priest who was disturbed at how far the church had strayed from the

---

20. *consensus*—agreement

21. *factions*—groups

22. "Greek philosophy was a potent influence throughout the Roman world" and eventually its ideas seeped deeply into the Christian Church, replacing Christ's simple truths with the ideas of men (see Mark E. Petersen, *The Great Prologue,* 11).

23. What blessings do you enjoy today that you would not have had if you had lived during the Dark Ages, without the gospel of Jesus Christ? How do some people today live in a similar condition as those who lived in the Dark Ages? What can you do to help them?

24. *serfs*—enslaved servants

25. *fraught*—filled

26. This plague, known as the Black Death, killed hundreds of thousands throughout the Middle Ages, sometimes destroying entire villages and cities.

SUPERSTOCK

Martin Luther and other Protestant reformers helped open the door to religious freedom and eventually the restoration of the gospel

gospel as taught by Christ. His work led to a reformation,[27] a movement that was taken up by such other visionaries as John Calvin, Huldrych Zwingli, John Wesley, and John Smith.

"I believe these reformers were inspired to create a religious climate in which God could restore lost truths, and priesthood authority" ("Restored Truth," 66).

President Hinckley called the Reformers "men of great courage, some of whom suffered cruel deaths because of their beliefs." These reformers broke away from the Catholic Church and began organizing their own churches. "They did so without priesthood authority," President Hinckley explained. "Their one desire was to find a niche[28] in which they might worship God as they felt He should be worshiped.

"While this great ferment[29] was stirring across the Christian world, political forces were also at work. Then came the American Revolutionary War, resulting in the birth of a nation whose constitution declared that government should not reach its grasping hand into matters of religion. A new day had dawned, a glorious day. Here there was no longer a state church. No one faith was favored above another" ("At the Summit of the Ages," 73).

ANCIENT PROPHECIES OF A RESTORATION

The reformations and excitement of the times were ideal for the restoration of the gospel,[30] a restoration which prophets throughout the ages had spoken and written about. President Hinckley explained, "All of the history of the past had pointed to this season. The centuries with all of their

suffering and all their hope had come and gone. The Almighty Judge of the nations, the Living God, determined that the times of which the prophets had spoken had arrived. Daniel had foreseen a stone which was cut out of the mountain without hands and which became a great mountain and filled the whole earth (see Daniel 2:34–35).

"'And in the days of these kings shall the God of heaven set up a kingdom, which shall never be destroyed: and the kingdom shall not be left to other people, but it shall break in pieces and consume[31] all these kingdoms, and it shall stand for ever' (Daniel 2:44)" ("At the Summit of the Ages," 73).

The story of the coming forth of this great latter-day kingdom is an inspiring one. To some it is too simple or fantastic to be true. But to the millions who have come to know of its truth, it is a story to love and to remember forever.[32]

CHAPTER 2: JOSEPH SMITH'S ANCESTORS

Brigham Young said of the Prophet Joseph Smith: "It was decreed in the counsels of eternity, long before the foundations of the earth were laid, that he, Joseph Smith, should be the man, in the last dispensation of this world, to bring forth the word of God to the people, and receive the fulness of the keys and power of the Priesthood of the Son of God. The Lord had his eye upon him, and upon his father, and upon his father's father, and upon their [ancestors] clear back to Abraham, and from Abraham to the flood, from the flood to Enoch, and from Enoch to Adam" (Discourses of Brigham Young, 108).

27. Bruce R. McConkie wrote: "Beginning in the 14th century, the Lord began to prepare those social, educational, religious, economic, and governmental conditions under which he could more easily restore the gospel for the last time among men. The spirit of inspiration rested upon Wycliffe, Huss, Luther, Zwingli, Calvin, Knox, and others, causing them to rebel against the religious evils of the day and seek to make the Bible and other truth available to all who would receive such. The age of Renaissance and Reformation were part of the Lord's program preparatory to ushering in his great latter-day work" (*Mormon Doctrine*, 717).

28. *niche*—place

29. *ferment*—uproar

30. Ezra Taft Benson testified: "The Church and kingdom of God was restored in these latter days, even The Church of Jesus Christ of Latter-day Saints, with all the gifts, rights, powers, doctrines, officers, and blessings of the former-day Church" ("I Testify," *Ensign*, November 1988, 86).

31. *consume*—devour

32. Have you ever wondered what the world would be like today if the gospel of Jesus Christ had never been restored through the Prophet Joseph Smith? How would your life be different?

The Prophet Joseph Smith remembered: "Love of liberty was diffused into my soul by my grandfathers while they [held] me on their knees" (History of the Church, *5:498)*

By any measure the Prophet Joseph Smith was an extraordinary man. In addition, he also had some remarkable ancestors. As you read this chapter, look for how their experiences and influence helped prepare young Joseph for the calling he would receive.

JOSEPH'S ANCESTORS ON HIS FATHER'S SIDE OF THE FAMILY

While he was a member of the Quorum of the Twelve Apostles, Joseph Fielding Smith compiled the history of the Church into one volume. As part of this history he detailed the ancestry of the Prophet Joseph Smith: "Joseph Smith had descended on his paternal side[33] from Robert Smith, who emigrated from England in the year 1638. . . . He landed in Boston, Massachusetts, and moved to . . . Essex County. . . . Here, later, he purchased two hundred eight acres of land, a portion of which was in Topsfield township.[34] He married Miss Mary French. They were the parents of ten children. Robert was known among his neighbors as a quiet, unassuming[35] man, devoted to the welfare of the settlement. Through his industry he was able to provide some comforts for his family, who were reared in the prevailing[36] religious teachings of that day, but strictly in the knowledge of the scriptures.

"Samuel, son of Robert and Mary, was born January 26, 1666. He married Rebecca, daughter of John Curtis, a prominent citizen of the town of Topsfield. After his father's death, Samuel moved to Topsfield, where he became an influential member of that community and was honored by the citizens with several offices of trust. He was the father of nine children. His son Samuel, born January 26, 1714, was one of the most prominent citizens of Topsfield. The greater part of his life was spent in the service of the people. He passed through the stormy days of the American Revolution and bore arms in defense of the liberties of the people. . . .

"He was known as Captain Samuel Smith, receiving his military title during service in the militia[37] of Massachusetts. He married Priscilla, daughter of Zacheus Gould of Topsfield. They had five children, two sons and three daughters. . . . He died November 14, 1785, leaving an estate valued at more than 544 pounds sterling.[38] . . .

Joseph Smith Jr. was part of a wonderful, loving family

NOTES FOR CHAPTER 2

33. *paternal side*—father's side of the family

34. According to Noah Webster's *An American Dictionary of the English Language* (1828), a township is the "district or territory of a town. In *New England*, the states are divided into townships of five, six, seven, or perhaps ten miles square, and the inhabitants of such townships are invested with certain powers for regulating their own affairs, such as repairing roads, providing for the poor, &c" (s.v. "township").

35. *unassuming*—humble

36. *prevailing*—common

37. *militia*—armed force made up of citizens

38. A pound sterling is similar to an American dollar and is the basic monetary unit of England.

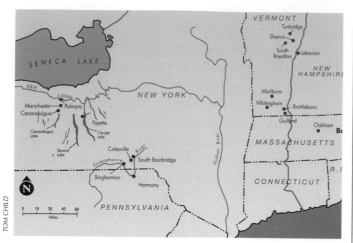

Joseph Smith's family lived in New England

"Asael Smith was the second son and youngest child of Samuel. He was born in Topsfield, March 7, 1744. . . . February 12, 1767, he took to wife, Mary Duty, of Windham, New Hampshire, and later moved to that place. . . . During the Revolution[39] he followed the example of his illustrious father and served with the Colonial forces.[40] After the death of his father in 1785, he returned to Topsfield and made his home on the family estate. He lived in the old home, about one mile north of the town, where a number of his children were born, notably Joseph, father of the Prophet Joseph Smith.

"Asael was a man of very liberal[41] views, far in advance of his time. Some of his children were members of the Congregational Church, but in his religious views he leaned toward the teachings of the Universalists. However, he held aloof from all sects,[42] because he could not reconcile his understanding of the scriptures with their many conflicting creeds.[43] He advocated[44] the truth very strongly, that all men should have free and equal religious liberty. In his opinions he was frank and explicit, expressing himself without fear of the prevailing opinions of his neighbors.[45] . . .

"At times the spirit of inspiration rested upon him. On one occasion he said: 'It has been borne in upon my soul that one of my descendants will promulgate[46] a work to revolutionize the world of religious faith.' Perhaps he did not expect to live to see that day, but such proved to be the case. The first summer after the organization of the Church [1830], his son Joseph [Sr.] and grandson, Don Carlos Smith, paid him a visit and presented him with a copy of the Book of Mormon. At the time he was in feeble health, but he diligently read the book, or most of it, and said he was convinced that the work of his grandson, Joseph Smith, was of divine origin. He was not baptized, due to his weakened physical

39. The "Revolution" refers to the Revolutionary War, in which Asael Smith served. "Asael enlisted as a soldier and saw military action in New York. In an address written on 10 April 1799, Asael Smith urged his family to be loyal to the United States and impressed upon them his own sense of patriotism and conviction that the Constitution was inspired. Clearly, the ancestors of the Prophet Joseph Smith were as patriotic as any of the founding fathers" (Donald Q. Cannon, "Topsfield, Massachusetts: Ancestral Home of the Prophet Joseph Smith," *BYU Studies* 14, no. 1, [1973], 71).

40. Do you know anyone who has served in the military? Why should we be thankful for those who have served to protect our freedom? What does that teach you about their love of country?

41. *liberal*—open-minded

42. *held aloof from all sects*—refused to join any church

43. *creeds*—beliefs or doctrines

44. *advocated*—supported

45. What characteristics did Joseph's grandfather Asael Smith have that would have made him a good missionary for the Church? What can you learn from him about how to stand up for your own beliefs?

46. *promulgate*—spread

Joseph Smith Sr. was born on July 12, 1771

condition, and died shortly after this visit.[47] His wife, Mary Duty Smith, later moved to Kirtland, where she died in 1836, firm in the faith of the restored gospel" (*Essentials in Church History,* 2nd ed., 22–25).

JOSEPH'S ANCESTORS ON HIS MOTHER'S SIDE OF THE FAMILY

Joseph Fielding Smith wrote this about the Prophet's mother's family: "On his maternal side,[48] Joseph Smith was descended from John Mack, who was born in Inverness, Scotland, March 6, 1653. John Mack came to America about 1669, and resided, first in Salisbury, Massachusetts. He married Sarah, daughter of Orlando and Sarah Bagley, and moved to Lyme, Connecticut, where eight or more of their twelve children were born. . . . He died Feb. 24, 1721.

"Ebenezer, son of John Mack, was born in Lyme, Conn., Dec. 8, 1697. He was a man of thrift[49] and was well respected by the people of Lyme, where he served for many years as minister of the Second Congregational Church. He married Hannah, daughter of Aaron Huntly, an honored citizen of Lyme. At one time, Ebenezer Mack possessed considerable property and 'lived in good style, commanding all the attention and respect which are ever shown to those who live in fine circumstances and habits of

strict morality' [*History of Joseph Smith by his Mother,* 1]. Reverses came, however, and he was reduced, in his declining years, to poverty. He was the father of nine children.

"Solomon, son of Ebenezer Mack, was born in Lyme, Conn., Sept. 26, 1735. At the age of twenty-one years he enlisted in the services of his country.[50] . . . He was engaged in the king's service with two teams carrying supplies to Fort Edwards. In 1748 he . . . was engaged in several bloody engagements in which his life was spared miraculously. He served until the spring of 1759, when he received his honorable discharge.[51] . . . That same year he met a young school teacher, Lydia Gates, daughter of Nathan Gates, a wealthy citizen of East Haddam, Connecticut. The friendship of these young people ripened and they were married after a short acquaintance. In 1761 Solomon and his young wife moved to Marlow where they took up their residence in a wilderness. Only four other families [lived] within forty miles of them. It was while here he learned to fully appreciate the excellent virtues of his wife, 'For,' he writes, 'as our children were deprived of schools she assumed charge of their education, and performed the duties of instructress as none, save a mother, is capable of. Precepts,[52] accompanied with examples such as theirs, were calculated[53] to make impressions on the minds of the young, never to be

---

47. Fortunately, as a message of hope to Asael Smith and others who have lived without a knowledge of the gospel, it was revealed to the Prophet that all "who would have received [the gospel] if they had been permitted to tarry, shall be heirs of the celestial kingdom of God" (D&C 137:7).

48. **maternal side**—mother's side of the family

49. **of thrift**—who was careful with his money

50. The country to which Solomon Mack gave service was England. Though he lived in America, the United States did not exist as a country until after the Revolutionary War and the establishment of its constitution and government in 1789 (see W. Cleon Skousen, *The Making of America,* 229).

51. **discharge**—release from service

52. **precepts**—teachings

53. **calculated**—intended

Lucy Mack Smith, mother of the Prophet Joseph, was born July 8, 1771, as the youngest child of Solomon Mack and Lydia Gates

forgotten. She, besides instructing them in the various branches of an ordinary education,[54] was in the habit of calling them together both morning and evening, and teaching them to pray,[55] meanwhile urging upon them the necessity of love towards each other as well as devotional feelings towards Him who made them.'

"In this manner their children became confirmed in the virtues[56] and were established in faith in their Redeemer.

"In 1776, Solomon Mack enlisted in the American army. For some time he served in the land forces and later was transferred to the navy. . . . In this service they passed through some thrilling experiences, but escaped without great harm. His service in the [Revolutionary] war covered a period of about four years. After his discharge he went to Gilsum, New Hampshire, to make his home. Owing to the rigorous campaigns[57] through two wars, he became broken in health and suffered considerably in his declining years.[58] . . .

"Such is the character of the forbears of Joseph Smith" (*Essentials in Church History,* 26–27).

JOSEPH SMITH SR. MARRIES LUCY MACK

In B. H. Robert's *Comprehensive History of the Church,* the author wrote about the Prophet's father, Joseph Smith Sr.: "Joseph Smith, son of . . . Asael Smith, and father of the Prophet, was born at Topsfield, Massachusetts, July 12, 1771. He accompanied his father . . . to Tunbridge, Vermont, where he assisted in clearing a farm of which, four years after it was first cleared, he took possession . . . while his father and four other sons went on clearing other lands. Here he married Lucy Mack, daughter of Solomon Mack of Gilsum, Cheshire county, New Hampshire. The young people met during the repeated visits of Lucy to her brother, Stephen Mack, who was engaged in the mercantile and tinning business[59] . . . at Tunbridge. The marriage took place on the 24th of January, 1796. . . .

"Six years Joseph Smith cultivated his farm at Tunbridge—Lucy calls it a 'handsome farm;' and then the ambitious pair determined upon a business career in merchandising.[60] The Tunbridge farm was rented and the family removed to Randolph, where

---

54. In those days an "ordinary education" included reading, writing, and arithmetic (see B. H. Roberts, *Comprehensive History of the Church,* 1:25).

55. Consider how closely Lydia Gates, Joseph Smith's grandmother, followed the counsel of the Book of

The foundation of the restoration of the gospel was laid in part by the events of the American Revolution

Mormon. "Counsel with the Lord in all thy doings, and he will direct thee for good; yea, when thou liest down at night lie down unto the Lord, that he may watch over you in your sleep; and when thou risest in the morning let thy heart be full of thanks unto God; and if ye do these things, ye shall be lifted up at the last day" (Alma 37:37).

56. **confirmed in the virtues**—deep-rooted in values that build character

57. **rigorous campaigns**—very difficult suffering

58. Solomon passed his love of country to his children. During the war of 1812, his son Stephen "entered the service of his country. He held the commission of a captain at the time of the siege of Detroit and was ordered by his superior officer to surrender, which he boldly refused to do. Breaking his sword across his knee he threw the parts into the lake and said he would not submit to such a disgraceful compromise while the blood of an American ran in his veins" (Joseph Fielding Smith, *Essentials in Church History,* 27).

59. **mercantile and tinning business**—selling of tin products

60. **merchandising**—selling goods

Joseph Smith was born in Sharon, Vermont

in a short time Joseph Smith learned of the large profits in raising ginseng root, the medicinal properties[61] of his wife's father, Solomon Mack, which he cultivated in the summer, and taught school in the winter. By dint[62] of the father following the two occupations, the affairs of the family began to improve and take on an air of comfort. And here, on the old Mack farm, among the hills of Sharon township, in the beautiful White River Valley, Joseph, the future Prophet of the New Dispensation, was born."

CHAPTER 3:
JOSEPH SMITH'S EARLY BOYHOOD

Elder L. Tom Perry of the Quorum of the Twelve Apostles explained what type of man the Lord needed to bring forth the restoration of the gospel in the latter days. "The Lord needed a strong, vigorous young man who would be teachable," he said. "He needed someone he could mold into the leader who could bring forth the restoration of the gospel. The one

foreordained for this great assignment was Joseph Smith. . . . Few prophets have come from more humble beginnings than those of the Prophet Joseph Smith. He was the fifth child in a family of 11 children. The rugged, rocky soil of New England had not been good to his family. During Joseph Smith's earliest years, the family moved frequently, trying to find fertile soil or a suitable livelihood. . . . Out of this hard, difficult, early beginning, Joseph Smith developed a great reliance on the Lord, trusting in him and gaining exceptional spiritual strength so he could use the gifts the Lord would give to him to organize the Church" ("By the Hands of His Prophets," Ensign, *August 1998, 50–51).*

JOSEPH SMITH IS BORN TO
JOSEPH SMITH SR. AND LUCY MACK

"I was born in the year of our Lord one thousand eight hundred and five, on the twenty-third day of December, in the town of Sharon, Windsor

---

61. *medicinal properties*—medical benefits

62. *dint*—the effort

county, State of Vermont," the Prophet Joseph recorded in Joseph Smith—History. "My father, Joseph Smith, Sen., left the State of Vermont, and moved to Palmyra, Ontario (now Wayne) county, in the State of New York, when I was in my tenth year, or thereabouts. In about four years after my father's arrival in Palmyra, he moved with his family into Manchester in the same county of Ontario[63]—

"His family consisting of eleven souls, namely, my father, Joseph Smith; my mother, Lucy Smith (whose name, previous to her marriage, was Mack, daughter of Solomon Mack); my brothers, Alvin (who died November 19th, 1823, in the 26th year of his age), Hyrum, myself, Samuel Harrison, William, Don Carlos; and my sisters, Sophronia, Catherine, and Lucy" (vv. 3–4).

JOSEPH SUFFERS WITH TYPHUS FEVER AND A DIFFICULT LEG OPERATION

Lucy Mack Smith, the Prophet's mother, knew more about his childhood than anyone else. In her history, she wrote very little about Joseph's early years. She simply said, "Except what has already been said, I shall say nothing respecting him until he arrived at the age of fourteen. However, in this I am aware that some of my readers will be disappointed, for I suppose, from questions which are frequently asked me, that it is thought by some that I shall be likely to tell many very remarkable incidents which attended his childhood; but, as nothing occurred during his early life except those trivial circumstances[64] which are common to that state of human existence, I pass them in silence" (*History of Joseph Smith by His Mother*, 67).

The Prophet's mother did tell of one event in Joseph's childhood that shows his great courage and determination, even at a young age.

"We moved . . . to the town of Lebanon, New Hampshire. . . . As our children had, in a great measure, been debarred[65] from the privilege of schools, we began, to make every arrangement to attend to this important duty. We established our second son Hyrum in an academy at Hanover; and the rest, that were of sufficient age, we were sending to a common school that was quite convenient.[66]

"The typhus fever[67] came into Lebanon and raged tremendously. . . . One after another was taken down, till all the family, with the exception of myself and husband, were prostrated upon beds of sickness. . . .

" . . . Joseph, our third son, having recovered from the typhus fever, after something like two weeks' sickness, one day screamed out while sitting in a chair, with a pain in his shoulder, and, in a very short time he appeared to be in such agony that we feared the consequence would prove to be something very serious. We immediately sent for a doctor. When he arrived and had examined the patient, he said that it was his opinion that this pain was occasioned[68] by a sprain. But the child declared this could not be the case as he had received no injury in any way whatever, but that a severe pain had seized him all at once, of the cause of which he was entirely ignorant.

NOTES FOR CHAPTER 3

63. Joseph Smith's mother wrote about his birth and given name: "In the meantime we had a son whom we called Joseph after the name of his father" (Lucy Mack Smith, *History of Joseph Smith by His Mother*, 46). It was an inspired decision to name this boy Joseph. Later, while translating the Book of Mormon, Joseph learned about his mission through the ancient prophet Joseph who was sold into Egypt. Joseph in Egypt prophesied that in the last days the person who would bring forth the Book of Mormon would be named Joseph after his father (see 2 Nephi 3:15).

64. *trivial circumstances*—little things

65. *debarred*—denied

66. Lucy Mack Smith observed that Joseph "seemed much less inclined to the [reading] of books than any of the rest of our children, but far more given to meditation [thinking] and deep study" (Lucy Mack Smith, *History of Joseph Smith by His Mother*, 82).

67. Typhus is a severe human disease "marked by a high fever, . . . intense headache, and a dark red rash" (*Merriam-Webster's Collegiate Dictionary*, 10th ed., s.v. "typhus," 1279).

68. *occasioned*—caused

Joseph Smith displayed great courage during his leg operation

"Notwithstanding the child's protestations,[69] still the physician insisted that it must be a sprain, and consequently he anointed his shoulder with some bone linament,[70] but this was of no advantage to him, for the pain continued the same after the anointing as before.

"When two weeks of extreme suffering had elapsed, the attendant physician concluded to make closer examination, whereupon he found that a large fever sore had gathered between his breast and shoulder. He immediately lanced[71] it, upon which it discharged fully a quart of matter.

"As soon as the sore had discharged itself the pain left it, and shot like lightning (using his own terms) down his side into the marrow of the bone of his leg[72] and soon became very severe. My poor boy, at this, was almost in despair, and he cried out 'Oh, father! the pain is so severe, how can I bear it!'

"His leg soon began to swell and he continued to suffer the greatest agony for the space of two weeks longer. During this period I carried him much of the time in my arms in order to mitigate[73] his suffering as much as possible; in consequence of which I was taken very ill myself.

"Hyrum, who was rather remarkable for his tenderness and sympathy, now desired that he might take my place. As he was a good, trusty boy, we let him do so, and, in order to make the task as easy for him as possible, we laid Joseph upon a low bed and Hyrum sat beside him, almost day and night for some considerable length of time, holding the affected part of his leg in his hands and pressing it between them, so that his afflicted brother might be enabled to endure the pain which was so excruciating[74] that he was scarcely able to bear it.[75]

"At the end of three weeks, we thought it advisable to send again for the surgeon. When he came he made an incision of eight inches, on the front side of the leg, between the knee and ankle. This relieved the pain in a great measure, and the patient was quite comfortable until the wound began to heal, when the pain became as violent as ever.

"The surgeon was called again, and he this time enlarged the wound, cutting the leg even to the bone. It commenced[76] healing the second time, and as soon as it began to heal it also began to swell again, which swelling continued to rise till we deemed it wisdom to call a council of surgeons; and when they met in consultation they decided that amputation[77] was the only remedy.

"Soon after coming to this conclusion, they rode up to the door and were invited into a room apart from the one in which Joseph lay. They being seated, I addressed them thus: 'Gentlemen, what can you do to save my boy's leg?' They answered, 'We can do nothing; we have cut it open to the bone and find it so affected that we consider his leg incurable and that amputation is absolutely necessary in order to save his life.'

"This was like a thunderbolt to me. I appealed to the principal surgeon, saying, 'Dr. Stone, can you not make another trial? Can you not, by cutting around the bone, take out the diseased part, and perhaps that which is sound will heal over, and by

---

69. *protestations*—objections or arguments

70. *linament*—cream or ointment

71. *lanced*—cut

72. Although seven-year-old Joseph recovered from the typhus fever, he suffered several complications in the following weeks, the most serious being the swelling and infection in his tibia (the inner bone of the leg between the knee and the ankle). The infection, which caused severe pain, would today be called osteomyelitis. Joseph underwent four surgeries as a result of complications from typhus.

73. *mitigate*—relieve

74. *excruciating*—horrible

75. Just as Hyrum Smith stayed by his brother Joseph's side during this ordeal, so was he with Joseph in Carthage Jail before their martyrdom. Elder John Taylor wrote, "In life they were not divided, and in death they were not separated!" (D&C 135:3).

76. *commenced*—began

77. The 1828 edition of Noah Webster's *An American Dictionary of the English Language* called amputation "the act or operation of cutting off a limb or some part of the body" (s.v. "Amputation"). Amputation was often used as a way to cut off the spread of disease that might cause the death of the person.

this means you will save his leg? You will not, you must not, take off his leg, until you try once more. I will not consent to let you enter his room until you make me this promise.'[78]

"After consulting a short time with each other, they agreed to do as I had requested, then went to see my suffering son. One of the doctors, on approaching his bed, said, 'My poor boy, we have come again.' 'Yes,' said Joseph, 'I see you have; but you have not come to take off my leg, have you, sir?' 'No,' replied the surgeon, 'it is your mother's request that we make one more effort, and that is what we have now come for.'[79]

"The principal surgeon, after a moment's conversation, ordered cords to be brought to bind Joseph fast to a bedstead; but to this Joseph objected. The doctor, however, insisted that he must be confined,[80] upon which Joseph said very decidedly, 'No, doctor, I will not be bound, for I can bear the operation much better if I have my liberty.' "'Then,' said Dr. Stone, 'will you drink some brandy?'

"'No,' said Joseph, 'not one drop.'

"'Will you take some wine?' rejoined the doctor. 'You must take something, or you can never endure the severe operation to which you must be subjected.'

"'No,' exclaimed Joseph, 'I will not touch one particle of liquor, neither will I be tied down; but I will tell you what I will do—I will have my father sit on the bed and hold me in his arms, and then I will

do whatever is necessary in order to have the bone taken out.'[81] Looking at me, he said, 'Mother, I want you to leave the room, for I know you cannot bear to see me suffer so; father can stand it, but you have carried me so much, and watched over me so long, you are almost worn out.' Then looking up into my face, his eyes swimming in tears, he continued. 'Now, mother, promise me that you will not stay, will you? The Lord will help me, and I shall get through with it.'[82]

"To this request I consented, and getting a number of folded sheets, and laying them under his leg, I retired, going several hundred yards from the house in order to be out of hearing.

"The surgeons commenced operating by boring into the bone of his leg, first on one side of the bone where it was affected, then on the other side, after which they broke it off with a pair of forceps or pincers. They thus took away large pieces of the bone. When they broke off the first piece, Joseph screamed out so loudly, that I could not forbear running to him. On my entering the room, he cried out, 'Oh, mother, go back, go back; I do not want you to come in—I will try to tough it out, if you will go away.'

"When the third piece was taken away, I burst into the room again—and oh, my God! what a spectacle for a mother's eye! The wound torn open, the blood still gushing from it, and the bed literally covered with blood. Joseph was pale as a corpse, and

---

78. President David O. McKay said, "If I were asked to name the world's greatest need, I should say unhesitatingly wise mothers; and the second, exemplary fathers" (in Jeanette McKay Morrell, *Highlights in the Life of President David O. McKay*, 34).

79. Elder Neal A. Maxwell provided this insight about Joseph's surgery: "The medical doctor in final attendance, it turns out, was Dr. Nathan Smith, founder of the Dartmouth Medical School. He brought two doctors and several medical students with him to attend to young Joseph, who resisted amputation and pain-deadening alcohol. It turns out that Dr. Nathan Smith was highly qualified, and he was using a very advanced technique. Thus 'the only man in America who could save [Joseph's] leg was just five miles away.' Happily, for young Joseph, Dr. Smith's plans to leave the area had been delayed by a typhoid epidemic. Joseph Smith could scarcely have led the long

march of Zion's Camp years later without this dramatic medical help" ("Discipleship and Scholarship," *BYU Studies* 32, no. 3 [1992]: 5).

80. *confined*—tied with ropes

81. Elder Neal A. Maxwell spoke about Joseph Smith's courage during this event: "Courage is one of Joseph Smith's special qualities. Without it, he would have shrunk from carrying out his remarkable role. At about age seven, he had a gravely infected leg. Amputation seemed inevitable. He refused alcoholic anesthetics when his leg bones were surgically and painfully treated in a new technique" ("My Servant Joseph," *Ensign*, May 1992, 37).

82. How do these statements by young Joseph show his maturity and respect for his mother? In what ways can Joseph's example give you courage to do difficult things?

large drops of sweat were rolling down his face, whilst upon every feature was depicted[83] the utmost agony![84]

"I was immediately forced from the room, and detained until the operation was completed; but when the act was accomplished, Joseph put upon a clean bed, the room cleared of every appearance of blood, and the instruments which were used in the operation removed, I was permitted again to enter.

"Joseph immediately commenced getting better, and from this onward, continued to mend until he became strong and healthy. When he had so far recovered as to be able to travel, he went with his uncle, Jesse Smith, to Salem, for the benefit of his health, hoping the sea-breezes would be of service to him, and in this he was not disappointed.

"Having passed through about a year of sickness and distress, health again returned to our family, and we most assuredly realized the blessing; and indeed, we felt to acknowledge the hand of God, more in preserving our lives through such a tremendous scene of affliction, than if we had, during this time, seen nothing but health and prosperity" (*History of Joseph Smith by His Mother,* 51–52, 54–58).[85]

CHAPTER 4:
MOVE TO PALMYRA

Joseph Smith Sr. worked hard as a farmer to provide for the physical needs of his family. In Norwich, Vermont, the Smiths experienced three consecutive years of crop failure. The Prophet's father decided,

after the third disappointing year, to move his family to the state of New York. The Lord's hand directed this move, as Joseph Smith Jr. was needed in Palmyra for the beginning of the restoration of the gospel. In this chapter, consider the great contribution and sacrifice of Joseph Smith and his parents in making this move and why the Lord wanted his family in New York

JOSEPH SMITH SR. AND LUCY MACK SMITH PREPARE TO MOVE TO PALMYRA, NEW YORK

Lucy Mack Smith wrote this about the Smith family's move to New York: "When health returned to us, as one would naturally suppose, it found us in quite low circumstances. We were compelled to strain every energy to provide for our present necessities, instead of making arrangements for the future, as we had previously contemplated.[86]

"Shortly after sickness left our family, we moved to Norwich, in the state of Vermont. In this place we established ourselves on a farm belonging to one Esquire Moredock. The first year our crops failed; yet, by selling fruit which grew on the place, we succeeded in obtaining bread for the family, and, by making considerable exertion[87] we were enabled to sustain ourselves.[88]

"The crops the second year were as the year before—a perfect failure. Mr. Smith now determined to plant once more, and if he should meet with no better success than he had the two preceding years,

---

83. 📖 **depicted**—seen

84. 🌅 Beginning with this experience, Joseph Smith's life seemed to be filled with physical suffering and hardship. The Lord later told the Prophet, "Be patient in afflictions, for thou shalt have many; but endure them, for, lo, I am with thee, even unto the end of thy days" (D&C 24:8).

85. 🤔 What trials have you had in your life? In what ways have they made you feel grateful for your blessings?

NOTES FOR CHAPTER 4

86. 📖 **contemplated**—thought

87. 📖 **exertion**—effort

88. 🌅 Each move and job change made by Joseph Smith Sr. and his wife, Lucy, was necessary to provide for their family. Our own Church leaders have taught that "husband and wife have a solemn responsibility to love and care for each other and for their children. . . . Parents have a sacred duty . . . to provide for their physical and spiritual needs" ("The Family: A Proclamation to the World," *Ensign,* November 1995, 102).

he would then go to the state of New York, where wheat was raised in abundance.[89]

"The next year an untimely frost destroyed the crops, and being the third year in succession in which the crops had failed, it almost caused a famine. This was enough; my husband was now altogether decided upon going to New York. He came in, one day, in quite a thoughtful mood, and sat down; after meditating some time, he observed that, could he so arrange his affairs, he would be glad to start soon for New York with a Mr. Howard, who was going to Palmyra. He further remarked, that he could not leave consistently,[90] as the situation of the family would not admit of[91] his absence; besides, he was owing some money that must first be paid.

"I told him it was my opinion he might get both his creditors and debtors together, and arrange matters between them in such a way as to give satisfaction to all parties concerned; and, in relation to the family, I thought I could make every necessary preparation to follow as soon as he would be ready for us. He accordingly called upon all with whom he had any dealings, and settled up his accounts with them.[92] . . .

"Having thus arranged his business, Mr. Smith set out for Palmyra, in company with Mr. Howard. After his departure, I and those of the family who were of much size, toiled[93] faithfully, until we considered ourselves fully prepared to leave at a moment's warning. We shortly received a communication from Mr. Smith, requesting us to make ourselves ready to take up a journey for Palmyra.[94] In a short time after this, a team came for us. . . .

"My aged mother, who had lived with us some time, assisted in preparing for the journey. She came with us to Royalton, where she resided until she died, which was two years afterwards, in consequence of an injury which she received by getting upset in a wagon while traveling with us"[95] (*History of Joseph Smith by His Mother*, 59–61).

---

89. Joseph Smith Sr. most likely heard about such success in New York from other family members. Richard L. Bushman wrote: "The Smith clan in Tunbridge were uprooting themselves. By 1815 all of Joseph's brothers had migrated to St. Lawrence County in northern New York, except Jesse, and he and Asael followed before 1820" (*Joseph Smith and the Beginnings of Mormonism*, 40).

90. ***could not leave consistently***—did not feel good about leaving

91. ***admit of***—allow for

92. Like Joseph Smith Sr. and Lucy, we need to be honest in all our dealings with others. President Gordon B. Hinckley has taught: "I think the Lord expects of His people that they will be absolutely honest in all of their dealings. In all that they do, they will be honest with others and honest with themselves" ("Excerpts from Recent Addresses of President Gordon B. Hinckley," *Ensign*, Apr. 1999, 71).

93. ***toiled***—worked

94. Elder L. Tom Perry, of the Quorum of the Twelve Apostles, explained that "during Joseph Smith's earliest years, the family moved frequently, trying to find fertile soil or a suitable livelihood, in Vermont, New Hampshire, Vermont again, then Palmyra, Ontario County, New York. Again, we see the hand of the Lord guiding them to the proper destination. It was in this place where the family settled that the miraculous events of the Restoration occurred" ("By the Hand of His Prophets," *Ensign*, August 1998, 51).

95. This would be a long tough journey during the winter months. "Snow covered the ground when Lucy and the eight children left Norwich. They went by sleigh to Royalton where they left Lucy's mother with Daniel Mack. . . . Transferring their goods to a wagon, the little party turned their backs on family and familiar places and headed for Palmyra, 300 miles distant" (Bushman, *Joseph Smith and the Beginnings of Mormonism*, 41-42).

Wagons could either be covered or uncovered.

THE PROPHET'S MOTHER MOVES HER FAMILY TO PALMYRA, NEW YORK

Lucy Mack Smith continued her record of the family's move to Palmyra: "Having traveled a short distance, I discovered that Mr. Howard,[96] our teamster, was an unprincipled[97] and unfeeling wretch,[98] by the way in which he handled both our goods and money, as well as by his treatment of my children, especially Joseph. He would compel him to travel miles at a time on foot, notwithstanding he was still lame.[99] We bore patiently with his abuse, until we got about twenty miles west of Utica, when one morning, as we were getting ready to continue our journey, my oldest son came to me and said, 'Mother, Mr. Howard has thrown the goods out of the wagon, and is about starting off with the team.' Upon hearing this, I told him to call the man in. I met him in the bar-room, in the presence of a large company of travelers, both male and female, and I demanded his reason for the course which he was taking. He told me the money which I had given him was all expended, and he could go no further.

"I then turned to those present and said, 'Gentlemen and ladies, please give your attention for a moment. Now, as sure as there is a God in heaven, that team, as well as the goods, belong to my husband, and this man intends to take them from me, or at least the team, leaving me with eight children, without the means of proceeding on my journey.' Then turning to Mr. Howard, I said, 'Sir, I now forbid you touching the team, or driving it one step further. You can go about your own business; I have no use for you. I shall take charge of the team myself, and hereafter attend to my own affairs.'[100] I accordingly did so, and proceeding on our journey, we in a short time arrived at Palmyra, with a small portion of our affects, and barely two cents in cash" (*History of Joseph Smith by His Mother*, 62–63).

EARLY DAYS IN PALMYRA, NEW YORK

The Prophet's mother, upon arriving in Palmyra, expressed her happiness despite the trials her family had experienced during the journey and in the preceding years. "When I again met my husband at Palmyra, we were much reduced—not from indolence,[101] but on account of many reverses of fortune, with which our lives had been rather singularly marked. Notwithstanding our misfortunes, and the embarrassments with which we were surrounded, I was quite happy in once more having the society of my husband, and in throwing myself and children upon the care and affection of a tender companion and father.[102]

"We all now sat down, and counselled together relative to the course which was best for us to adopt in our destitute circumstances,[103] and we came to the conclusion to unite our energies in endeavoring to obtain a piece of land. Having done considerable at

---

96. Joseph Smith Sr. had already left for Palmyra with a different Mr. Howard. The teamster he sent to help Lucy was Caleb Howard, a cousin of Mr. Howard (see Bushman, *Joseph Smith and the Beginnings of Mormonism*, 41).

97. *unprincipled*—wicked, having no values

98. *wretch*—rascal

99. One scholar explained that "the driver, Caleb Howard, proved troublesome from the start. The Smiths fell in with a Gates family traveling west in sleighs, and Howard wanted the Gates daughters to ride beside him. To make room, he drove Joseph from his place. For days at a time Joseph, who had just discarded his crutches and was still lame, limped along in the snow" (Bushman, *Joseph Smith and the Beginnings of Mormonism*, 42).

100. During this experience, the Prophet's mother showed great courage and faith in God. What does this teach you about trusting in the Lord during difficult situations in your life?

101. *indolence*—laziness

102. Elder M. Russell Ballard has written: "I marvel at the courage and commitment of these Saints who gave everything they had to establish the Church in this, the dispensation of the fulness of times. My thoughts today are drawn to the family of Joseph Smith, Sr., and Lucy Mack. I am amazed when I consider the overwhelming leadership responsibility the Lord placed upon this one family" ("The Legacy of Hyrum," *Ensign*, September 1994, 56–57).

103. *adopt in our destitute circumstances*—take in our poor conditions

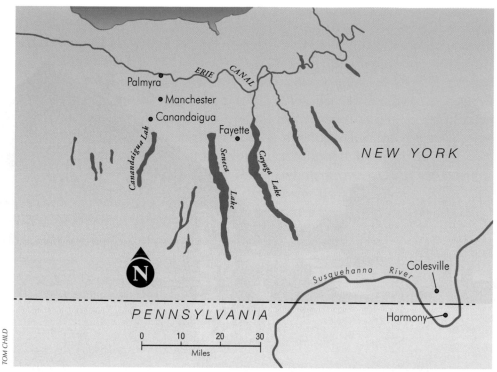

TOM CHILD

The Smiths moved from Vermont to this area of northern New York

painting oil-cloth coverings for tables, stands, etc., I set up the business, and did extremely well. I furnished all the provisions for the family, and besides this, began to replenish our household furniture, in a very short time, by my own exertions.[104]

"My husband and his sons, Alvin and Hyrum, set themselves to work to pay for one hundred acres of land for which Mr. Smith contracted with a land agent. In a year, we made nearly all of the first payment, erected a log house, and commenced clearing. I believe something like thirty acres of land were made ready for cultivation[105] the first year. . . .

"When the time for making the second payment [on the farm] drew nigh, Alvin went from home to get work, in order to raise the money, and after much hardship and fatigue, returned with the required amount. This payment being made, we felt relieved, as this was the only thing that troubled us; for we had a snug log-house, neatly furnished, and the means of living comfortably. It was now only two years since we entered Palmyra, almost destitute of money, property, or acquaintance.[106] The hand of friendship was extended on every side, and we blessed God, with our whole heart, for his 'mercy, which endureth for ever.' And not only temporal blessings were bestowed upon us, but also spiritual were administered.[107]. . .

"The following spring, we commenced making preparations for building another house, one that would be more comfortable for persons in advanced life.

"I now come to the history of Joseph. . . .

---

104. *exertions*—efforts

105. *cultivation*—planting

106. *acquaintance*—friend

107. The Smith family may not have had physical wealth, but they had each other and faith in God.

They "blessed God with [their] whole heart," fully knowing that "in nothing does man offend God, or against none is his wrath kindled, save those who confess not his hand in all things and obey not his commandments" (D&C 59:21).

Great religious excitement swept the land

mentioned above. There were cries of 'lo, here! here is Christ;' to which the response—'nay, but lo, here! here is Christ!'[121] Fierce debates followed, and great divisions in judgment obtained as to what even constituted the essentials of christianity. Grave doubts perplexed[122] the minds of many people, and hindered the progress of religion"[123] (*Comprehensive History of the Church*, 1:50–51).

JOSEPH IS CONFUSED BY THE CONTENTIONS AND DIVISIONS BETWEEN THE CHURCHES

During this period of time, Joseph's mother, his brothers Hyrum and Samuel Harrison, and his sister Sophronia became members of the Presbyterian church. Joseph's father was "unmoved amid the universal excitement."

---

121. The Savior himself prophesied that "there shall arise false Christs, and false prophets, and shall shew great signs and wonders; insomuch that, if it were possible, they shall deceive the very elect" (Matthew 24:24). These religious meetings partially fulfilled this scripture.

122. ***Grave doubts perplexed***—serious doubts confused

123. New Testament leaders prophesied of the latter days. They described the religious turmoil in Joseph Smith's day in passages such as 1 Timothy 4:1–3; 2 Timothy 3:5; Titus 1:16.

B. H. Roberts wrote that "Joseph Smith, Jun., was much wrought up[124] in his spirit, and became 'somewhat partial' to the Methodist sect, and he 'felt some desire to be united with them,' he admits. But the divisions that existed between these several churches perplexed[125] him. Why the divisions? 'Surely God cannot be the author of this confusion,' he reasoned. 'If God has a church in the earth it will not be split up into factions.[126] He will not teach one society to worship in one way and administer in one set of ordinances and teach another principles which are diametrically opposed.'[127] Reason taught him that *unity* must be a characteristic of the church of Christ. Paul's question . . . seemed to reach him— 'Is Christ Divided?'[128] And his reason answered, 'no.' 'Then what is to be done in the midst of all this confusion?' 'Who of all these parties are right? If any one of them be right, which is it, and how shall I know it?' He felt inadequate of himself to answer these questions. 'It was impossible for a person young as I was,' he remarks, 'and so unacquainted with men and things to come to any certain conclusion as to who was right and who was wrong'" (*Comprehensive History of the Church,* 51–52; emphasis in original).

JOSEPH FINDS HOPE IN THE EPISTLE OF JAMES

Joseph Smith recorded his feelings about the religious revival in Palmyra: "During this time of great excitement, my mind was called up to serious reflection and great uneasiness; but, though my feelings were deep and often poignant,[129] still I kept myself aloof[130] from all these parties, though I attended their several meetings as often as occasion would permit. In process of time my mind became somewhat partial to the Methodist sect, and I felt some desire to be united with them; but so great were the confusion and strife among the different denominations, that it was impossible for a person young as I was, and so unacquainted with men and things, to come to any certain conclusion who was right and who was wrong. My mind at times was greatly excited, the cry and tumult[131] were so great and incessant.[132] The Presbyterians were most decided against the Baptists and Methodists, and used all the powers of both reason and sophistry[133] to prove their errors, or, at least, to make the people think they were in error. On the other hand, the Baptists and Methodists in their turn were equally zealous in endeavoring to establish their own tenets[134] and disprove all others.

"In the midst of this war of words and tumult of opinions, I often said to myself, what is to be done? Who of all these parties are right; or, are they all wrong together? If any one of them be right, which is it, and how shall I know it?[135] While I was laboring under the extreme difficulties caused by the contests of these parties of religionists, I was one day reading the Epistle of James, first chapter and fifth verse, which reads:

"If any of you lack wisdom, let him ask of God, that giveth to all men liberally, and upbraideth[136] not, and it shall be given him.[137]

---

124. 📖 ***wrought up***—disturbed

125. 📖 ***perplexed***—confused

126. 📖 ***factions***—different religious groups

127. 📖 ***diametrically opposed***—opposite

128. 🔍 This reference is to 1 Corinthians 1:13, which reads: "Is Christ divided? was Paul crucified for you? or were ye baptized in the name of Paul?"

129. 📖 ***poignant***—deeply emotional

130. 📖 ***aloof***—distant

131. 📖 ***tumult***—excitement

132. 📖 ***incessant***—constant

133. 📖 ***sophistry***—deceptive arguments

134. 📖 ***zealous in endeavoring to establish their own tenets***—strong in trying to prove their own beliefs

135. 🔍 Those who seek after religious truth must make a decision about which church is true. Have you thought about that question yet? Do you know which church is true? How could you find out?

136. 📖 ***upbraideth***—criticizes or scolds

137. 🗣 Elder Bruce R. McConkie testified of the importance of these words from James: "This single verse of scripture has had a greater impact and a more far reaching effect upon mankind than any other single sentence ever recorded by any prophet in any age" (*Doctrinal New Testament Commentary,* 3:247).

These words in James 1:5—"If any of you lack wisdom, let him ask of God"—led Joseph to the grove to kneel in prayer

"Never did any passage of Scripture come with more power to the heart of man than this did at this time to mine. It seemed to enter with great force into every feeling of my heart. I reflected on it again and again, knowing that if any person needed wisdom from God, I did; for how to act I did not know and unless I could get more wisdom than I then had, I would never know; for the teachers of religion of the different sects understood the same passage of Scripture so differently as to destroy all confidence in settling the question by an appeal[138] to the Bible. At length I came to the conclusion that I must either remain in darkness and confusion, or else I must do as James directs, that is, ask of God. I at length came to the determination to 'ask of God,' concluding that if He gave wisdom to them that lacked wisdom, and would give liberally,[139] and not upbraid, I might venture"[140] (*History of the Church*, 1:3–4).[141]

---

138. *an appeal*—going

139. *liberally*—freely

140. *venture*—try

141. In addition to James 1:5, latter-day scripture teaches us that God answers prayers (for example, see Moroni 10:4; D&C 112:10).

A NEW DISPENSATION BEGINS

When Jesus Christ taught his gospel to the Jews during his mortal ministry, he faced great opposition from Jewish leaders. They preferred their own ideas to the truths that Jesus taught. The Lord knew the same thing would happen in our day: much of the opposition the true gospel would face would be from the other religious leaders of the day. When the Lord called Joseph Smith to be his prophet, he prepared him well to face such opposition. The appearance of God the Father and his Son Jesus Christ to the boy Joseph gave him a better understanding of God than any other mortal on earth. Joseph was also given a sacred record, which became the Book of Mormon. This new scripture is a second witness of Jesus Christ and his gospel. It is proof to the world that the true gospel of Jesus Christ has again been restored to the earth.

CHAPTER 6:
THE FIRST VISION

Prophets throughout history spoke of the restoration initiated by the Prophet Joseph Smith. When this young boy knelt in a sacred grove of trees in upstate New York, he was witness to one of the greatest events to occur on the earth. He was visited by God the Father and his Son Jesus Christ. He received answer to his prayers. He learned that he should not join any of the churches on the earth. And, more important, he learned that he would become an instrument in the Lord's hand to establish the gospel of Jesus Christ on the earth once again. As you read this chapter, look for why and how the Lord prepared such a young boy for such great events.

JOSEPH FOLLOWS THE COUNSEL OF THE EPISTLE OF JAMES

Because of the confusion and excitement over religion in Joseph's home area, he read and pondered[1] the teaching in James 1:5. Of his experience with this scripture, Joseph wrote: "So, in accordance with this, my determination to ask God, I retired to the woods to make the attempt.[2] It was on the morning of a beautiful, clear day, early in the spring of eighteen hundred and twenty. It was the first time in my life that I had made such an attempt, for amidst all my anxieties I had never as yet made the attempt to pray vocally" (*History of the Church*, 1:4–5).

"After much reflection of this nature, [Joseph] at last took his resolution.[3] He would put the doctrine[4] of James to the test. He would ask God for wisdom," wrote historian B. H. Roberts. "Reasoning that if God gave wisdom to them that lacked it, and would give liberally and not upbraid,[5] he might venture. Situated directly west of the Smith home, a few hundred yards distant, yet on their own farm, was a beautiful grove sufficiently dense[6] and removed from the road to give the necessary seclusion[7] the youth desired; and here on the morning of a beautiful, clear day in that early spring time, he knelt for the

---

NOTES FOR CHAPTER 6

1. To ponder is to prayerfully and carefully think about an idea, thought, or event. The scriptures command us to ponder the words of the Lord (for example, see 3 Nephi 17:3; Moroni 10:3; D&C 30:3).

2. Jesus also sought a secluded place to pray (see Matthew 14:23). We are commanded to do the same (see Matthew 6:5–6).

3. *resolution*—decision

4. *doctrine*—teaching

5. *give liberally and not upbraid*—give freely and not criticize or scold

6. *sufficiently dense*—thick enough

7. *seclusion*—privacy

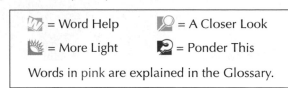

📖 = Word Help	🔍 = A Closer Look
🔆 = More Light	📖 = Ponder This

Words in pink are explained in the Glossary.

The exact location of the First Vision is unknown. This grove of trees, referred to as "the Sacred Grove,"
is directly west of the Smith family home

first time in all his life to make a personal, direct, verbal appeal to God in prayer"[8] (*Comprehensive History of the Church*, 1:53–54).

JOSEPH DESCRIBES THE FIRST VISION

Joseph later described his experience in the grove, saying: "After I had retired into the place where I had previously designed[9] to go, having looked around me, and finding myself alone, I kneeled down and began to offer up the desires of my heart to God. I had scarcely done so, when immediately I was seized upon by some power which entirely overcame me, and had such an astonishing influence[10] over me as to bind my tongue so that I could not speak. Thick darkness gathered around me, and it seemed to me for a time as if I were doomed to sudden destruction.[11]

"But, exerting[12] all my powers to call upon God to deliver me out of the power of this enemy which had seized upon me, and at the very moment when I was ready to sink into despair and abandon myself to destruction—not to an imaginary ruin, but to the power of some actual being from the unseen world, who had such a marvelous power as I had never before felt in any being[13]—just at this moment of great alarm, I saw a pillar of light exactly over my head, above the brightness of the sun, which descended gradually until it fell upon me.

"It no sooner appeared than I found myself delivered from the enemy which held me bound. When the light rested upon me I saw two Personages,[14] whose brightness and glory defy all description,[15] standing above me in the air. One of them spake unto me, calling me by name[16] and said, pointing to the other—'This is My Beloved Son. Hear Him!'

"My object in going to inquire of the Lord was to know which of all the sects[17] was right, that I might know which to join. No sooner, therefore, did I get possession of myself, so as to be able to speak, than I asked the Personages who stood above me in the light, which of all the sects was right . . . and which I should join.

"I was answered that I must join none of them, for they were all wrong; and the Personage who addressed me said that all their creeds[18] were an abomination[19] in his sight; that those professors[20]

---

8. 🔎 Perhaps young Joseph's thought of going to the grove of trees to pray was influenced by an experience of his mother, Lucy Mack Smith. At one time in her marriage she was concerned that she and her husband find the truth. She wrote about what she did to seek the Lord's help: "I retired to a grove not far distant, where I prayed to the Lord" (*History of Joseph Smith by His Mother*, 43).

9. 📖 **designed**—planned

10. 📖 **astonishing influence**—amazing and fearful power

11. 🔎 Satan is real. He opposes the work of God (see 2 Nephi 2:17, 27). Why do you think Joseph Smith felt Satan's influence at this time? What does that teach you about the First Vision? What does Joseph's experience teach you about God's power compared to Satan's power?

12. 📖 **exerting**—using

13. 🔎 One reason the Apostle Paul told the Saints to "put on the whole armour of God" was because we often,

like young Joseph, "wrestle not against flesh and blood, but against principalities [governments], against powers, against the rulers of the darkness of this world" (Ephesians 6:11–12).

14. 📰 In the First Vision Joseph learned truths about God unknown by men for almost 2,000 years. He discovered that God the Father and his Son Jesus Christ are two separate and distinct individuals and that "the Father has a body of flesh and bones as tangible as man's; the Son also" (D&C 130:22).

15. 📖 **defy all description**—cannot be described

16. 🔎 Calling Joseph by name shows that Heavenly Father knows his children personally. How does it make you feel to know of God's personal love for you?

17. 📖 **sects**—churches

18. 📖 **creeds**—basic beliefs

19. 📖 **abomination**—evil thing

20. 📖 **professors**—religious teachers

"I saw a pillar of light exactly over my head, above the brightness of the sun"
(Joseph Smith—History 1:16)

were all corrupt; that 'they draw near to me with their lips, but their hearts are far from me,[21] they teach for doctrines the commandments of men, having a form of godliness, but they deny the power thereof.'

"He again forbade me to join with any of them; and many other things did he say unto me which I cannot write at this time.[22] When I came to myself again, I found myself lying on my back, looking up into heaven. When the light had departed, I had no strength;[23] but soon recovering in some degree, I went home. And as I leaned up to the fireplace, mother inquired what the matter was. I replied, 'Never mind, all is well—I am well enough off.' . . . It seems as though the adversary[24] was aware, at a very early period of my life, that I was destined to prove a disturber and an annoyer[25] of his kingdom; else why should the powers of darkness combine against me? Why the opposition and persecution that arose against me, almost in my infancy?" (Joseph Smith—History 1:15–20).

JOSEPH TELLS HOW OTHERS TREATED HIS SACRED EXPERIENCE

Because of the remarkable nature of Joseph's experience, he naturally wanted to go to a religious leader and share the details of his vision. "A few days after the vision occurred," wrote B. H. Roberts, "young Joseph was in conversation with one of the Methodist preachers who was very active in the before mentioned revival, and gave him an account of the vision. The reception of the story by the minister was most surprising to the youth. Said the Prophet:

"'He treated my communication not only lightly, but with great contempt,[26] saying, it was all of the devil, that there were no such things as visions or revelations in these days; that all such things had ceased with the apostles, and that there would never be any more of them.'

"In fact Joseph Smith soon found that by telling the story he had excited a great deal of prejudice[27]

---

21. Elder Dallin H. Oaks taught this of the First Vision: "We affirm that this divine declaration was a condemnation [criticism] of the creeds, not of the faithful seekers who believed in them. Joseph Smith's first vision showed that the prevailing [popular] concepts of the nature of God and the Godhead were untrue and could not lead their adherents [believers] to the destiny God desired for them" ("Apostasy and Restoration," *Ensign,* May 1995, 84). President Gordon B. Hinckley added: "I believe with all my heart all churches do good. We say to those [of other faiths], you bring all the good you have and let us see if we can add to it" ("South Pacific Visit: Pres. Hinckley Completes 8-Day Tour," *LDS Church News,* May 24, 1997).

22. President Gordon B. Hinckley observed: "To me it is a significant and marvelous thing that in establishing and opening this dispensation our Father did so with a revelation of himself and of his Son Jesus Christ, as if to say to all the world that he was weary of the attempts of men, earnest though these attempts might have been, to define and describe him. . . . The experience of Joseph Smith in a few moments in the grove on a spring day in 1820, brought more light and knowledge and understanding of the personality and reality and substance of God and his Beloved Son than men had arrived at during centuries of speculation" (*Teachings of Gordon B. Hinckley,* 236).

23. Moses had a similar experience after a glorious vision. He "fell to the earth. . . . It was . . . many hours before Moses did again receive his natural strength" (Moses 1:9–10).

24. *adversary*—devil

25. *an annoyer*—a troubler

26. *contempt*—hatred

27. *prejudice*—intolerance; unfairness

GEORGE LANE PORTRAIT. ARTIST UNKNOWN © INTELLECTUAL RESERVE, INC.

The Reverend George Lane (1784–1859) was one Methodist minister who lived at the time of Joseph Smith

against himself among many professors of religion. . . . as he puts it in his own narrative—

"'Yet, men of high standing would take notice sufficient to excite the public mind against me, and create a bitter persecution. It caused me serious reflection then, and often has since, how very strange it was that an obscure[28] boy, of a little over fourteen years of age, . . . should be thought a character of sufficient importance to attract the attention of the great ones of the most popular sects of the day, and in a manner to create in them a spirit of the most bitter persecution and reviling.[29] But strange or not, so it was, and it was often the cause of great sorrow to myself. However, it was nevertheless a fact that I had beheld a vision. . . . I had actually seen a light, and in the midst of that light I saw two personages and they did in reality speak to me; and though I was hated and persecuted for saying that I had seen a vision, yet it was true; and while they were persecuting me, reviling me, and speaking all manner of evil against me falsely for so saying, I was led to say in my heart, why persecute me for telling the truth? I have actually seen a vision, and who am I that I can withstand God? or why does the world think to make me deny what I have actually seen? For I had seen a vision; I knew it, and I knew that God knew it, and I could not deny it, neither dared I do it; at least I knew that by so doing I would offend God, and come under condemnation.'[30] [31]

"But come what might now, [Joseph's] mind was satisfied as to the sectarian world.[32] He knew they were wrong; that he was to join none of them. He had proved the testimony of James to be true. One who lacked wisdom could ask it of God, receive it, and not be upbraided. He knew now that God lived, and that man could hold visible and personal communion with him. With this knowledge he would rest until further directed" (*Comprehensive History of the Church,* 1:56–57).

A NEW PROPHET FOR THE WORLD

"What a change had come to this youth in one brief hour!" wrote B. H. Roberts. "How little that fair-haired lad . . . realized the burden placed upon his shoulders that early spring morning, by reason of the visitation he received in answer to prayer!

"He has found the source of spiritual knowledge, and his life and his life's work have been broadened; but his knowledge will not bring him peace in this world. . . . Everywhere his name will be held up as evil"[33] (*Comprehensive History of the Church,* 1:57–58).

CHAPTER 7:
THE LORD PREPARES A PROPHET— MORONI VISITS

The boy Joseph learned from a glorious vision of the Father and the Son that the true Church was not at that time on the earth. Joseph Smith Jr. was to become the prophet through whom the Lord would again restore his church to the earth. But much preparation was needed. How did the Lord take an uneducated farm boy of fourteen and make him the prophet of the Restoration? The process of preparing a prophet is neither simple nor painless. Look for the different experiences the Lord provided for young Joseph and the lessons he learned from them.

THE FIRST VISIT OF THE ANGEL MORONI

After the First Vision, Joseph Smith continued to work and play the way most fourteen-year-old boys do. He also continued to declare that he had seen a vision, despite the persecutions that came from those around him. Then, on September 21, 1823, Joseph experienced another spectacular event.

The Prophet later wrote about the events that took place beginning that September night. He said:

---

28. 📖 *obscure*—unknown

29. 📖 *reviling*—verbal abuse

30. 📖 *condemnation*—punishment

31. 🔁 Why would it be important to know this vision actually took place? How could a person know if Joseph's story is true?

32. 📖 *sectarian world*—other churches

33. 🔖 Examples of Joseph's persecution and suffering can be found in D&C 122:1–7; 135:7.

"During the space of time which intervened[34] between the time I had the vision and the year eighteen hundred and twenty-three—having been forbidden to join any of the religious sects of the day, and being of very tender years, and persecuted by those who ought to have been my friends and to have treated me kindly, . . . I frequently fell into many foolish errors, and displayed the weakness of youth, and the foibles[35] of human nature; which, I am sorry to say, led me into divers[36] temptations, offensive in the sight of God. In making this confession, no one need suppose me guilty of any great or malignant[37] sins. A disposition to commit such was never in my nature. But I was guilty of levity,[38] and sometimes associated with jovial company,[39] etc., not consistent with that character which ought to be maintained by one who was called of God as I had been. But this will not seem very strange to any one who recollects my youth, and is acquainted with my native cheery temperament. . . . [40] [41]

". . . On the evening of the above-mentioned twenty-first of September, after I had retired to my bed for the night, I betook myself to prayer and supplication to Almighty God for forgiveness of all my sins and follies, and also for a manifestation[42] to me, that I might know of my state and standing before Him; for I had full confidence in obtaining a divine manifestation, as I previously had one.

"While I was thus in the act of calling upon God, I discovered a light appearing in my room, which continued to increase until the room was lighter than at noonday, when immediately a personage appeared at my bedside, standing in the air, for his feet did not touch the floor.

"He had on a loose robe of most exquisite[43] whiteness. It was a whiteness beyond anything earthly I had ever seen; nor do I believe that any earthly thing could be made to appear so exceedingly white and brilliant. His hands were naked and his arms also, a little above the wrist; so, also were his feet naked, as were his legs, a little above the ankles. His head and neck were also bare. I could discover that he had no other clothing on but this robe, as it was open, so that I could see into his bosom.

"Not only was his robe exceedingly white, but his whole person was glorious beyond description, and his countenance[44] truly like lightning. The room was exceedingly light, but not so very bright as immediately around his person.[45] When first I looked upon him, I was afraid; but the fear soon left me.

"He called me by name, and said unto me that he was a messenger sent from the presence of God to me, and that his name was Moroni;[46] that God had a work for me to do; and that my name should be had for good and evil among all nations, kindreds, and tongues, or that it should be both good and evil spoken of among all people.

NOTES FOR CHAPTER 7

34. *intervened*—took place

35. *foibles*—shortcomings or weaknesses

36. *divers*—various; different

37. *malignant*—very serious

38. *levity*—casual cheerfulness

39. *jovial company*—pleasure-loving friends

40. In a letter to Oliver Cowdery, the Prophet Joseph declared that the sins for which he was guilty of were mainly that of being light minded and not serious enough (see *History of the Church*, 1:10).

41. All people make mistakes (see Romans 3:23). Why was it important for Joseph to recognize his mistakes? Why would it be important for you to admit when your actions are not consistent with God's teachings?

42. *manifestation*—sign; message

43. *exquisite*—beautiful

44. *countenance*—face

45. The angel Moroni was a resurrected person. What do we learn here about the nature of glorified resurrected beings? Is there anything Satan could offer you in this life that would be more important or more valuable than being worthy of such a glorious resurrection?

46. Moroni was the last of the Nephite prophets and the son of Mormon. He was the last person to write on the gold plates before burying them in the Hill Cumorah (see Mormon 8:14). He was also directed by God to care for the gold plates (see Ether 4:5). Moroni taught us all how we could know whether or not the Book of Mormon record is true (see Moroni 10:3–5). To find out more about Moroni, see Book of Mormon Index, s.v. "Moroni," 231–32.

The angel Moroni appears to Joseph Smith

"He said there was a book deposited, written upon gold plates, giving an account of the former inhabitants of this continent, and the sources from whence they sprang.[47] He also said that the fulness of the everlasting Gospel was contained in it, as delivered by the Savior to the ancient inhabitants;

"Also that there were two stones in silver bows—and these stones, fastened to a breastplate, constituted what is called the Urim and Thummim—deposited with the plates; and the possession and use of these stones were what constituted[48] 'seers' in ancient or former times; and that God had prepared them for the purpose of translating the book.

"After telling me these things, he commenced quoting the prophecies of the Old Testament. . . .

"In addition to these, he quoted . . . [from] the third chapter of Acts. . . .

"He also quoted the second chapter of Joel, from the twenty-eighth verse to the last. He also said that this was not yet fulfilled, but was soon to be.[49] And he further stated that the fulness of the Gentiles was soon to come in.[50] He quoted many other passages of scripture, and offered many explanations which cannot be mentioned here.

"Again, he told me, that when I got those plates of which he had spoken—for the time that they should be obtained was not yet fulfilled—I should not show them to any person; neither the breastplate with the Urim and Thummim; only to those to whom I should be commanded to show them; if I did I should be destroyed. While he was conversing with me about the plates, the vision was opened to my mind that I could see the place where the plates were deposited, and that so clearly and distinctly that I knew the place again when I visited it" (Joseph Smith—History 1:27–36, 40–42).

THE SECOND AND THIRD VISITS OF MORONI

Joseph wrote that, "After this communication, I saw the light in the room began to gather immediately around the person of him who had been speaking to me, and it continued to do so, until the room was again left dark, except just around him; when instantly I saw, as it were, a conduit[51] open right up into heaven, and he ascended till he entirely disappeared, and the room was left as it had been before this heavenly light had made its appearance.

"I lay musing[52] on the singularity[53] of the scene, and marveling greatly at what had been told to me by this extraordinary messenger; when, in the midst of my meditation, I suddenly discovered that my

---

47. *the sources from whence they sprang*—where they came from

48. *constituted*—made

49. President Gordon B. Hinckley, quoting this prophecy of Joel, taught, "The era in which we live is the fulness of times spoken of in the scriptures, when God has brought together all of the elements of previous dispensations. From the day that He and His Beloved Son manifested themselves to the boy Joseph, there has been a tremendous . . . enlightenment poured out upon the world. The hearts of men have turned to their fathers in fulfillment of the words of Malachi. The vision of Joel has been fulfilled" ("Living in the Fulness of Times," *Ensign*, November 2001, 4).

50. The times of the Gentiles began just after the death of the Savior, when the Jews of the time did not accept the gospel and the apostles began taking it to the Gentiles. The times of the Gentiles continues to this day.

Author Hoyt W. Brewster explained, "The gospel was first taken to the Jews and only later to the Gentiles, that is, those not of the house of Israel, particularly of Judah. In fact, it took a dramatic vision to Peter to convince him that the 'times of the Gentiles' had arrived (Acts 10).

"The gospel is not presently being preached in an organized fashion to the Jews, for they who were 'first' to hear it in the days of the Savior, shall be 'last' to hear it in our day (Matt. 20:16; D&C 90:9). We are still in the 'times of the Gentiles.' When this time has been fulfilled, then Judah will again receive the gospel" (*Doctrine and Covenants Encyclopedia*, 597).

51. *conduit*—channel or passageway

52. *musing*—thinking

53. *singularity*—unusualness

Moroni buried the gold plates in the Hill Cumorah, where they remained until Joseph Smith was commanded to retrieve them

room was again beginning to get lighted, and in an instant, as it were, the same heavenly messenger was again by my bedside.

"He commenced,[54] and again related the very same things which he had done at his first visit, without the least variation;[55] which having done, he informed me of great judgments which were coming upon the earth, with great desolations by famine, sword, and pestilence; and that these grievous judgments would come on the earth in this generation. Having related these things, he again ascended as he had done before.

"By this time, so deep were the impressions made on my mind, that sleep had fled from my eyes, and I lay overwhelmed in astonishment at what I had both seen and heard. But what was my surprise when again I beheld the same messenger at my bedside, and heard him rehearse or repeat over again to me the same things as before; and added a caution to me, telling me that Satan would try to tempt me (in consequence of the indigent circumstances[56] of my father's family), to get the plates for the purpose of getting rich. This he forbade me, saying that I must have no other object in view in getting the plates but to glorify God, and must not be influenced by any other motive than that of building his kingdom; otherwise I could not get them.[57]

"After this third visit, he again ascended into heaven as before, and I was again left to ponder on the strangeness of what I had just experienced; when almost immediately after the heavenly messenger had ascended from me the third time, the cock crowed, and I found that day was approaching, so that our interviews must have occupied the whole of that night" (Joseph Smith—History 1:43–47).

JOSEPH UNCOVERS THE PLATES—THE FOURTH VISIT OF MORONI

Joseph continues: "I shortly after arose from my bed, and, as usual, to the necessary labors of the day; but in attempting to work as at other times, I found my strength so exhausted as to render me entirely unable. My father, who was laboring along with me, discovered something to be wrong with me, and told me to go home. I started with the intention of going to the house; but, in attempting to cross the fence out of the field where we were, my strength entirely failed me, and I fell helpless on the ground, and for a time was quite unconscious of anything.

"The first thing that I can recollect was a voice speaking unto me, calling me by name. I looked up, and beheld the same messenger standing over my head, surrounded by light as before. He then again related unto me all that he had related to me the previous night, and commanded me to go to my father and tell him of the vision and commandments which I had received.

"I obeyed; I returned to my father in the field, and rehearsed the whole matter to him. He replied to me that it was of God, and told me to go and do as commanded by the messenger. I left the field, and went to the place where the messenger had told me the plates were deposited; and owing to the distinctness[58] of the vision which I had had concerning it, I knew the place the instant that I arrived there.

"Convenient[59] to the village of Manchester, Ontario county, New York, stands a hill of considerable size, and the most elevated of any in the neighborhood. On the west side of this hill, not far from the top, under a stone of considerable size, lay the plates, deposited in a stone box. This stone was thick and rounding in the middle on the upper side, and thinner towards the edges, so that the middle

---

54. *commenced*—began

55. *the least variation*—any change

56. *indigent circumstances*—poverty

57. Why do you think it was important that young Joseph's desires were centered on using the plates to

do God's will and not thinking about how much money the plates were worth?

58. *distinctness*—clearness

59. *convenient*—close

The Hill Cumorah near Palmyra, New York

part of it was visible above the ground, but the edge all around was covered with earth.

"Having removed the earth, I obtained a lever, which I got fixed under the edge of the stone, and with a little exertion raised it up. I looked in, and there indeed did I behold the plates, the Urim and Thummim, and the breastplate, as stated by the messenger. The box in which they lay was formed by laying stones together in some kind of cement. In the bottom of the box were laid two stones cross-wise of the box, and on these stones lay the plates and the other things with them" (Joseph Smith—History 1:48–52).

JOSEPH IS SHOWN THE POWERS OF GOOD AND EVIL

"As Joseph Smith journeyed to the Hill Cumorah on that memorable first visit, he was beset[60] by many conflicting emotions," one writer explained. "His father's family were poor and in financial distress. Creditors[61] had been bearing down heavily upon them. The adversary of all righteousness took advantage of these conditions to sorely tempt the youth with all his power. The plates of the book were made of gold and were of great intrinsic[62] value. Could they not be used to relieve the financial embarrassment of the family? Or was there not something else deposited with the plates that might be used for such purpose? Such were the thoughts Satan put into his heart as he approached the hill, and the admonition[63] of the angel was temporarily forgotten.

" . . . Putting forth his hand he attempted to remove the plates, but received a shock, which in a measure deprived him of[64] his strength. After a moment's hesitation he made a second attempt, but received a greater shock than at first. The cause of this was unknown to him, for he supposed that physical strength and exertion were all that were necessary for him to obtain the record. The third time he stretched forth his hand to take the plates and again received a shock with considerable violence, which sapped his strength and made him powerless. In his great excitement and without meditation[65] he exclaimed: 'Why cannot I obtain the book?' 'Because you have not kept the commandments of the Lord,' answered a voice near by him. Looking up he was astonished to behold the heavenly messenger of his former visits.

"In humble repentance he sought the Lord in prayer. His vision was opened and the glory of the Lord shone around about him, and he was made to feel the sweet influence of the power of righteousness. While he was beholding this vision the angel said, 'Look!' Joseph beheld the prince of darkness surrounded by his innumerable train of associates[66] in all their diabolical fury.[67] As the visions of evil passed before him, the angel said: 'All this is shown, the good and the evil, the holy and impure, the glory of God and the power of darkness, that you may know, hereafter, the two powers and never be influenced or overcome by that wicked one.

60. *beset*—weighed down

61. *Creditors*—People to whom Joseph's father owed money

62. *intrinsic*—real or genuine

63. *admonition*—warning

64. *deprived him of*—took away

65. *meditation*—careful thought

66. *prince of darkness surrounded by his innumerable train of associates*—Satan with his many followers

67. *diabolical fury*—evil power and anger

Behold, whatever entices and leads to good and to do good is of God, and whatever does not is of that wicked one. It is he who fills the hearts of men with evil, to walk in darkness and blaspheme God;[68] and you may learn from henceforth, that his ways are to destruction; but the way of holiness is peace and rest'"[69] (Joseph Fielding Smith, *Essentials in Church History,* 48–50).

FOUR YEARS OF PREPARATION

After this experience, Joseph Smith said he "made the attempt to take [the plates] out, but was forbidden by the messenger, and was again informed that the time for bringing them forth had not yet arrived, neither would it, until four years from that time; but he told me that I should come to that place precisely in one year from that time, and that he would there meet with me, and that I should continue to do so until the time should come for obtaining the plates.

"Accordingly, as I had been commanded, I went at the end of each year, and at each time I found the same messenger there, and received instruction and intelligence from him at each of our interviews, respecting what the Lord was going to do, and how and in what manner his kingdom was to be conducted in the last days" (Joseph Smith—History 1:53–54).

CHAPTER 8:
THE YOUNG PROPHET
RETRIEVES THE PLATES

During the four years of preparation the Prophet Joseph Smith learned much from the angel Moroni.

One might think it was a joyous time for Joseph and his family. And indeed there was much to rejoice over; but the Smith family also had much sorrow and trial to deal with. As you read this chapter, take note of the events you think brought Joseph Smith the most joy. Notice also the experiences that were the most difficult to deal with.

JOSEPH TEACHES HIS FAMILY

Lucy Mack Smith, the Prophet Joseph's mother, relates what happened on the evening of September 22, 1823, when Joseph returned from his first visit to the Hill Cumorah. "When the family were altogether, Joseph made known to them all that he had communicated to his father in the field, and also of his finding the record, as well as what passed between him and the angel while he was at the place where the plates were deposited.

"Sitting up late that evening, in order to converse upon[70] these things, together with over-exertion of mind,[71] had much fatigued[72] Joseph; and when Alvin[73] observed it, he said, 'Now, brother, let us go to bed, and rise early in the morning, in order to finish our day's work at an hour before sunset, then, if mother will get our suppers early, we will have a fine long evening, and we will all sit down for the purpose of listening to you while you tell us the great things which God has revealed to you.'

"Accordingly, by sunset the next day, we were all seated, and Joseph commenced[74] telling us the great and glorious things which God had manifested[75] to him; but, before proceeding, he charged[76] us not to mention out of the family that which he was about to say to us, as the world was so wicked

---

68. *blaspheme God*—speak evil of God

69. Think about times when you have felt the sweet peace and joy that comes from doing good. Contrast those feelings with times when you have lost those feelings because of something you said or did. What do these experiences teach you about the truth of Moroni's words to Joseph Smith?

NOTES FOR CHAPTER 8

70. *converse upon*—talk about

71. *over-exertion of mind*—deep thinking

72. *much fatigued*—tired

73. Alvin Smith was born to Joseph Smith Sr. and Lucy Mack Smith on February 11, 1798, at Tunbridge, Vermont. He was their second child. Lucy's first child, born in 1797, did not live.

74. *commenced*—began

75. *manifested*—revealed or told

76. *charged*—instructed

that when they came to a knowledge of these things they would try to take our lives. . . . [77]

"After giving us this charge, he proceeded to relate further particulars concerning the work which he was appointed to do, and we received them joyfully, never mentioning them except among ourselves, agreeable to the instructions which we had received from him.

"From this time forth, Joseph continued to receive instructions from the Lord, and we continued to get the children together every evening for the purpose of listening while he gave us a relation of the same.[78] I presume our family presented an aspect as singular[79] as any that ever lived upon the face of the earth—all seated in a circle, father, mother, sons and daughters, and giving the most profound attention to a boy, eighteen years of age, who had never read the Bible through in his life. . . .

"During our evening conversations, Joseph would occasionally give us some of the most amusing recitals[80] that could be imagined. He would describe the ancient inhabitants of this continent,[81] their dress, mode[82] of traveling, and the animals upon which they rode; their cities, their buildings, with every particular; their mode of warfare; and

also their religious worship. This he would do with as much ease, seemingly, as if he had spent his whole life among them" (*History of Joseph Smith by His Mother,* 81–83).

THE DEATH OF ALVIN, JOSEPH'S OLDEST BROTHER

Joseph's family shared many happy times discussing the things Joseph learned from the angel Moroni. But the family also experienced much sadness during these years. Joseph's mother remembers one of their greatest trials: "On the 15th of November, 1823, about 10 o'clock in the morning, Alvin[83] was taken very sick with the bilious colic.[84] He came to the house in much distress, and requested his father to go immediately for a physician. He accordingly went, obtaining one by the name of Greenwood, who, on arriving, immediately administered to the patient a heavy dose of calomel.[85] I will here notice, that this Dr. Greenwood was not the physician commonly employed by the family; he was brought in consequence[86] of the family physician's absence. And on this account, as I suppose, Alvin at first refused to take the medicine,

---

77. The young Prophet's instruction not to talk to others about his experiences was correct. His conversations with the angel Moroni were sacred. The Lord cautions us to speak reverently about spiritual things: "Remember that that which cometh from above is sacred, and must be spoken with care, and by constraint of the Spirit" (D&C 63:64).

78. *gave us a relation of the same*—told us about his experiences

79. *an aspect as singular*—as unique a picture

80. *amusing recitals*—entertaining telling of events

81. *ancient inhabitants of this continent*—people who lived in the Americas long ago

82. *mode*—type or kind

83. Joseph loved and admired his brother Alvin. Nearly twenty years after Alvin's death, Joseph said: "I remember well the pangs of sorrow that swelled my youthful bosom and almost burst my tender heart when [Alvin] died. He was the oldest and noblest of my father's family. He was one of the noblest of the

sons of men" (in *History of Joseph Smith by His Mother,* 333).

On January 21, 1836, Joseph had a vision of the celestial kingdom. He saw his brother Alvin in that kingdom and asked the Lord how Alvin had been able to enter the Lord's presence even though he had not been baptized or received any of the blessings of the restored gospel while on earth. The Lord taught Joseph that those who die without the opportunity to accept the gospel but who would have accepted it given the chance "shall be heirs of the celestial kingdom of God" (D&C 137:5–7).

84. *bilious colic*—severe stomach pain

85. Dr. Greenwood prescribed a large dose of calomel, a preparation of mercury used frequently in medicine in the nineteenth century (see Noah Webster, *An American Dictionary of the English Language,* 1828, s.v. "calomel"). Mercury is considered a dangerous substance today and is used very rarely in medicine.

86. *in consequence*—because

but by much persuasion, he was prevailed on[87] to do so. . . .

"On the third day of his sickness, Dr. McIntyre, whose services were usually employed by the family, as he was considered very skillful, was brought, and with him four other eminent[88] physicians. But it was all in vain, their exertions proved unavailing,[89] just as Alvin said would be the case—he told them the calomel was still lodged in [his intestines], after some exertion had been made to carry it off, and that it must take his life.

"On coming to this conclusion, he called Hyrum to him, and said, "Hyrum, I must die. Now I want to say a few things, which I wish to have you remember. I have done all I could to make our dear parents comfortable. I want you to go on and finish the house and take care of them in their old age, and do not any more let them work hard, as they are now in old age. . . .

"In the latter part of the fourth night he called for all the children, and exhorted them separately in the same strain as above. But when he came to Joseph, he said, 'I am now going to die, the distress which I suffer, and the feelings that I have, tell me my time is very short. I want you to be a good boy, and do everything that lies in your power to obtain the Record. Be faithful in receiving instruction, and in keeping every commandment that is given you.'" (Lucy Mack Smith, *History of Joseph Smith by His Mother*, 86–87). Alvin died November 19, 1823.

Joseph Obtains the Sacred Record

Joseph listened to Alvin's advice and was faithful in receiving instruction from the angel Moroni. It is certain that Joseph must have kept busy during the four years between Moroni's first visit and the time he received the plates. Little is recorded about that time. We do know that the January before returning to the Hill Cumorah, he married Emma Hale. Later that year, according the Prophet's record in Joseph Smith—History, "the time arrived for obtaining the plates, the Urim and Thummim, and the breastplate. On the twenty-second day of September, one thousand eight hundred and twenty-seven, having gone as usual at the end of another year to the place where they were deposited,[90] the same heavenly messenger delivered them up to me with this charge: that I should be responsible for them; that if I should let them go carelessly, or through any neglect of mine, I should be cut off; but that if I would use all my endeavors to preserve them, until he, the messenger, should call for them, they should be protected."[91]

---

87. *prevailed on*—convinced or persuaded

88. *eminent*—skilled; well-known

89. *exertions proved unavailing* efforts were unsuccessful

90. Prior to the time the Prophet received the gold plates, he met and fell in love with Miss Emma Hale. They were married on January 18, 1827. Emma was with Joseph the night he went to the Hill Cumorah. She stayed in a wagon, while Joseph climbed the hill and retrieved the gold plates (see *Church History in the Fulness of Times*, 44).

91. Joseph's mother explained that "Joseph kept the Urim and Thummim constantly about his person, by the use of which he could in a moment tell whether the plates were in any danger" (Lucy Mack Smith, *History of Joseph Smith by His Mother*, 107).

PHOTOGRAPH BY ALEXANDER BAUGH

Joseph Smith's oldest brother, Alvin, died November 19, 1823, and was buried in the general memorial cemetery in Palmyra, New York

Joseph receives the gold plates from the angel Moroni

"I soon found out the reason why I had received such strict charges to keep them safe, and why it was that the messenger had said that when I had done what was required at my hand, he would call for them. For no sooner was it known that I had them, than the most strenuous exertions[92] were used to get them from me. Every stratagem[93] that could be invented was resorted to for that purpose.[94] The persecution became more bitter and severe than before, and multitudes were on the alert continually to get them from me if possible. But by the wisdom of God, they remained safe in my hands, until I had accomplished by them what was required at my hand" (1:59–60).

THE ARRIVAL OF MARTIN HARRIS, FRIEND AND RESCUER

Joseph explained that "the persecution . . . became so intolerable[95] that I was under the necessity of leaving Manchester, and going with my wife to Susquehanna county, in the state of Pennsylvania. While preparing to start—being very poor, and the persecution so heavy upon us that there was no probability that we would ever be otherwise—in the midst[96] of our afflictions we found a friend in a gentleman by the name of Martin Harris,[97] who came to us and gave me fifty dollars to assist us on our journey. Mr. Harris was a resident of Palmyra

---

92. 📖 **most strenuous exertions**—greatest efforts

93. 📖 **stratagem**—plan

94. 🔍 Joseph did not bring the plates home immediately after receiving them in the early morning hours of September 22, 1827. Lucy Mack Smith explained: "The plates were [hidden] about three miles from home, in the following manner: Finding an old birch log much decayed, excepting the bark, which was in a measure sound, he took his pocket knife and cut the bark with some care, then turned it back and made a hole of sufficient size to receive the plates, and, laying them in the cavity thus formed, he replaced the bark; after which he laid across the log, in several places, some old stuff that happened to lay near, in order to conceal as much as possible the place in which they were deposited.

The gold plates were kept safe in this box

"Joseph, on coming to them, took them from their secret place, and, wrapping them in his linen frock, placed them under his arm and started for home.

"After proceeding a short distance, he thought it would be more safe to leave the road and go through the woods. Traveling some distance after he left the road, he came to a large windfall, and as he was jumping over a log, a man sprang up from behind it and gave him a heavy blow with a gun. Joseph turned around and knocked him down, then ran at the top of his speed. About half a mile farther he was attacked again in the same manner as before; he knocked this man down in like manner as the former and ran on again; and before he reached home he was assaulted the third time. In striking the last one, he dislocated his thumb, which, however, he did not notice until he came within sight of the house, when he threw himself down in the corner of the fence in order to recover his breath. As soon as he was able, he arose and came to the house. He was still altogether speechless from fright and the fatigue of running" (*History of Joseph Smith by His Mother*, 107–8).

95. 📖 **intolerable**—difficult

96. 📖 **midst**—middle

97. 🔍 Martin Harris was born May 18, 1783, at Easttown, New York. He was the son of Nathan Harris and Rhoda Lapham. He was a prosperous farmer in the Palmyra, New York, area when he became acquainted with the family of Joseph Smith. He became a great supporter and friend to the Prophet Joseph.

Martin Harris

MARTIN AND JOSEPH, BY CLARK KELLY PRICE

Martin Harris lost the 116 pages of Book of Mormon manuscript

disobedience"[146] (*History of Joseph Smith by His Mother*, 125–29).

JOSEPH LOSES THE POWER TO TRANSLATE

Joseph knew that he had made a mistake in giving the 116 pages to Martin and was very troubled. Because Heavenly Father loves his children, he taught Joseph what he had done wrong:

"For although a man may have many revelations, and have power to do many mighty works, yet if he boasts in his own strength, and sets at naught[147] the counsels of God, and follows after the dictates[148] of his own will and carnal[149] desires, he must fall and incur the vengeance of a just God upon him.

"And behold, how oft you have . . . gone on in the persuasions of men.

"For, behold, you should not have feared man more than God. Although men set at naught the counsels of God, and despise his words" (D&C 3:4, 6–7).

For some time Joseph lost the ability to translate. The angel Moroni took away the Urim and Thummim and the gold plates. Eventually, the Lord, in his mercy, taught Joseph what to do to be worthy to translate again.

"But remember, God is merciful; therefore, repent of that which thou hast done which is contrary to the commandment which I gave you, and thou art still chosen, and art again called to the work" (D&C 3:10).

JOSEPH CAN TRANSLATE AGAIN BUT CANNOT RETRANSLATE THE LOST PAGES

Some days later, after Joseph had returned to Pennsylvania, he was "walking out a little distance, when, behold, [Moroni] appeared and handed to me the Urim and Thummim again—for it had been

---

146. Sin always causes sorrow (see Alma 41:10–11).

147. **sets at naught**—considers to be of no value

148. **dictates**—instructions

149. **carnal**—worldly

JOSEPH SMITH TRANSLATING, BY ROBERT BARRETT

Though the Lord had forbidden Joseph to retranslate the missing 116 pages, Joseph was able to continue translating

the things which mostly concerned him. And the next morning they commenced the work of translation, in which they were soon deeply engaged" (Lucy Mack Smith, *History of Joseph Smith by His Mother*, 141–42).

OLIVER LEARNS THE LORD WANTS HIM TO WORK ON THE TRANSLATION

Before he met the Prophet Joseph Smith, Oliver Cowdery had prayed to the Lord about the gold plates and asked whether or not God had commanded Joseph Smith to translate them. Oliver did not tell anyone about his prayer. Soon after Oliver began helping Joseph translate the Book of Mormon, the Lord gave the Prophet a revelation for Oliver. In it the Lord referred to Oliver's prayer.

"Verily, verily, I say unto thee, blessed art thou for what thou hast done; for thou hast inquired[160] of me, and behold, as often as thou hast inquired thou hast received instruction of my Spirit. If it had not been so, thou wouldst not have come to the place where thou art at this time.[161]

"Behold, thou knowest that thou hast inquired of me and I did enlighten[162] thy mind; and now I tell thee these things that thou mayest know that thou hast been enlightened by the Spirit of truth;

"Yea, I tell thee, that thou mayest know that there is none else save God that knowest thy thoughts and the intents of thy heart. . . .

"Verily, verily, I say unto you, if you desire a further witness, cast your mind upon the night that you cried unto me in your heart, that you might know concerning the truth of these things.

"Did I not speak peace to your mind concerning the matter? What greater witness can you have than from God?[163]

"And now, behold, you have received a witness; for if I have told you things which no man knoweth have you not received a witness?" (D&C 6:14–16, 22–24).

The Prophet recorded, "After we had received this revelation, Oliver Cowdery stated to me that after he had gone to my father's to board and after the family had communicated to him concerning my having obtained the plates, that one night after he had retired to bed he called upon the Lord to know if these things were so, and the Lord manifested to him[164] that they were true, but he had kept the circumstance entirely secret, and had mentioned it to no one; so that after this revelation was given, he knew that the work was true, because no being living knew of the thing alluded to in the revelation, but God and himself" (Joseph Smith, *History of the Church,* 1:35).

OLIVER WRITES TO DAVID WHITMER ABOUT HIS EXPERIENCE WITH THE YOUNG PROPHET

As promised, Oliver had been writing to his friend David Whitmer. In his letters, Oliver told David that he knew Joseph had the gold plates, which recorded the history of the ancient inhabitants of the Americas. He also included a few lines of the translation and told David that he had "revealed knowledge" of importance of this work and its truth (see B. H. Roberts, *Comprehensive History of the Church,* 1:123).

---

160. *inquired*—asked

161. Oliver was told that the Lord has always answered his prayers. In what ways have your prayers been answered by the Lord? How has the Lord guided your life?

162. *enlighten*—give understanding or knowledge to

163. President Brigham Young explained that the Prophet Joseph Smith taught how members of the Church can know when the Spirit of the Lord is with them. Joseph said, "They can tell the Spirit of the Lord from all other spirits—it will whisper peace and joy to their souls" (*Manuscript History of Brigham Young,* February 23, 1847).

164. *manifested to him*—let him know

Oliver Cowdery served as scribe for the Prophet Joseph Smith

Oliver Cowdery

CHAPTER 12:
OLIVER COWDERY'S DESIRE TO TRANSLATE

The Lord revealed to the Prophet Joseph Smith that Oliver Cowdery had been given the gift of revelation (see D&C 6:10–12). Oliver was also promised that he could receive the gift to translate like the Prophet Joseph (see D&C 6:25). Soon after the Prophet and Oliver started working together, the Lord granted Oliver the opportunity to translate. But Oliver soon lost this privilege. As you study this chapter, look for Oliver's strengths and weaknesses.

OLIVER WORKS AS JOSEPH'S SCRIBE

Oliver Cowdery described the experience of serving as scribe[165] for the Prophet Joseph Smith, saying, "These were days never to be forgotten—to sit under the sound of a voice dictated by the inspiration of heaven, awakened the utmost gratitude of this bosom![166] Day after day I continued, uninterrupted, to write from his mouth, as he translated with the Urim and Thummim . . . the history or record called 'The Book of Mormon'" (Joseph Smith—History, 1:71n).

OLIVER DESIRES TO TRANSLATE

"While the Prophet and Oliver were working on the translation during the month of April, 1829," Joseph Fielding Smith wrote, "Oliver Cowdery became exceedingly anxious to have the power to translate and made that request of the Prophet. Inquiry was made by Urim and Thummim and the Lord gave consent[167] in the revelation known as

section 8. At this time the Lord seemed perfectly willing that Oliver Cowdery as well as Joseph Smith should engage[168] in this labor of translating the plates. . . . Oliver was informed that this power [to translate] could not be received except by the exercise of faith with an honest heart, and by this faith, knowledge of the ancient records[169] and their engravings[170] should be made known" (*Church History and Modern Revelation,* 1:46–47n).

In the revelation to Oliver and Joseph, the Lord said:

"Oliver Cowdery, verily, verily, I say unto you, that assuredly[171] as the Lord liveth, who is your God and your Redeemer, even so surely shall you receive a knowledge of whatsoever things you shall ask in faith, with an honest heart, believing that you shall receive a knowledge concerning the engravings of old records, which are ancient, which contain those parts of my scripture of which has been spoken by the manifestation of my Spirit.[172]

"Yea, behold, I will tell you in your mind and in your heart, by the Holy Ghost, which shall come upon you and which shall dwell in your heart.[173]

"Now, behold, this is the spirit of revelation" (D&C 8:1–3).

Following the revelation in Doctrine and Covenants section 8, Oliver began the work of translating and the Prophet Joseph Smith was the scribe.

OLIVER IS NOT ABLE TO TRANSLATE

Oliver's attempt to translate, however, was a failure. "It seems," Joseph Fielding Smith recorded, "that Oliver Cowdery thought that it would be an easy matter with the aid of the Urim and Thummim to understand the engravings and give their

---

NOTES FOR CHAPTER 12

165. *scribe*—someone who writes down what another person is reading or speaking

166. *awakened the utmost gratitude of this bosom*—made me feel very thankful

167. *consent*—permission

168. *engage*—work

169. *ancient records*—gold plates

170. Engravings are writings made on metal. The Book of Mormon writers engraved their words on metal plates (see 1 Nephi 1:17).

171. *assuredly*—as sure

172. *manifestation of my Spirit*—power of the Holy Ghost

173. The Lord can communicate to us through thoughts in our minds and feelings in our hearts. What has the Lord helped you to know? How do you feel when the Holy Ghost is near? Why do you think it is important to listen as well as speak when we pray?

equivalent[174] meaning in the English language, without taking thought or studying it out in his mind. He therefore failed to comprehend[175] the instructions the Lord had given him, notwithstanding the Lord told him he should have the gift of revelation.

"It seems probable that Oliver Cowdery desired to translate out of curiosity, and the Lord taught him his place by showing him that translating was not the easy thing he had thought it to be. In [Doctrine and Covenants 9], the explanation was made that Oliver's failure came because he did not continue as he commenced,[176] and the task being a difficult one his faith deserted[177] him. The lesson he learned was very necessary for he was shown that his place was to act as scribe for Joseph Smith . . . who was called and appointed by command of the Lord to do the translating. There must have been some desire on the part of Oliver Cowdery to be equal with the Prophet and some impatience in having to sit and act as scribe, but when he failed to master the gift of translating he was then willing to accept the will of the Lord" (*Church History and Modern Revelation*, 1:47–48n).

In Doctrine and Covenants section 9, the Lord said to Oliver:

"Be patient, my son, for it is wisdom in me, and it is not expedient[178] that you should translate at this present time.

"Behold, the work which you are called to do is to write for my servant Joseph.

"And, behold, it is because that you did not continue as you commenced, when you began to translate, that I have taken away this privilege from you.[179]

"Do not murmur,[180] my son, for it is wisdom in me that I have dealt with you after this manner.

"Behold, you have not understood; you have supposed that I would give it unto you, when you took no thought save it was to ask me.

"But, behold, I say unto you, that you must study it out in your mind; then you must ask me if it be right, and if it is right I will cause that your bosom shall burn within you;[181] therefore, you shall feel that it is right.[182]

"But if it be not right you shall have no such feelings, but you shall have a stupor of thought[183] that shall cause you to forget the thing which is wrong; therefore, you cannot write that which is sacred save it be given you from me.

"Now, if you had known this you could have translated; nevertheless, it is not expedient that you should translate now.

---

174. *equivalent*—same

175. *comprehend*—understand

176. *commenced*—began

177. *deserted*—left

178. *expedient*—desirable or good

179. Oliver Cowdery's experience in losing the power to translate may be compared to Peter the apostle who was able to walk on water until his faith failed (see Matthew 14:29–31).

180. *murmur*—complain

181. Elder Dallin H. Oaks of the Quorum of the Twelve Apostles said, "Surely, the word 'burning' in this scripture signifies a feeling of comfort and serenity [calmness, peacefulness]" ("Teaching and Learning by the Spirit," *Ensign*, March 1997, 13). President Boyd K. Packer, also of the Twelve, said, "This burning in the bosom is not purely a physical sensation. It is more like a warm light shining within your being" ("Personal Revelation: The Gift, the Test, and the Promise," *Ensign*, November 1994, 60).

182. President Ezra Taft Benson, thirteenth president of the Church, taught, "We hear the words of the Lord most often by a feeling. If we are humble and sensitive, the Lord will prompt us through our feelings" ("Seek the Spirit of the Lord," *Ensign*, April 1988, 4).

183. *stupor of thought*—a period of time where you stop thinking about something

"Behold, it was expedient when you commenced; but you feared, and the time is past, and it is not expedient now" (vv. 3–11).[184]

OLIVER COWDERY IS COMMANDED TO CONTINUE AS JOSEPH'S SCRIBE

"After his failure to translate," Joseph Fielding Smith recorded, "Oliver Cowdery was instructed to continue as scribe for Joseph Smith. . . .[185]

"The Lord told him that he was to continue as scribe until the translation of the Book of Mormon was completed, and that there were other ancient records to come forth, and that he might have the privilege of translating these at some future day if he would remain faithful. We learn from the Book of Mormon that there are many records and that at some time when the people are prepared by faith to receive them that they shall also be translated and published for the knowledge and salvation of the faithful" (*Church History and Modern Revelation,* 1:48).

PHOTOGRAPH BY ROBERT CASEY

"You must study it out in your own mind; then you must ask me if it be right" (D&C 9:8)

184. Have you ever missed an opportunity to use one of your talents to help someone else because you were afraid of failure? How can you get the Lord's help when you wish to serve him more effectively?

185. Oliver Cowdery continued to write for the Prophet until the Book of Mormon was completed. Years later he said, "I wrote with my own pen the entire Book of Mormon (save a few pages) as it fell from the lips of the Prophet" (cited in Richard Lloyd Anderson, "Reuben Miller, Recorder of Oliver Cowdery's Reaffirmations," *BYU Studies* 8, no. 3 [1968], 278).

GRAIN FIELDS, BY EDWIN EVANS © INTELLECTUAL RESERVE, INC.

The Lord compares doing missionary work to harvesting a field

JOSEPH RECEIVES A REVELATION FOR HIS FATHER

During Joseph Smith Sr. and Lucy Mack Smith's visit in February 1829, Joseph received this vision for his father, which outlines how Joseph Smith Sr.—and each of us—can serve the Lord:[5]

"Now behold, a marvelous work is about to come forth among the children of men.

"Therefore, O ye that embark[6] in the service of God, see that ye serve him with all your heart, might, mind and strength, that ye may stand blameless[7] before God at the last day.[8]

---

5. Joseph Smith Sr. spent his life valiantly fulfilling the words of this revelation. He was "filled with the testimony of the truth, and was always anxious to share it with others. He was almost sixty when he made the tedious journey . . . to carry the gospel to his father and mother, his sisters and brothers. Soon after his return [home,] he was imprisoned for a small debt of fourteen dollars, rather than deny the divinity of the Book of Mormon and be forgiven the debt! He was cast into a cell with a condemned murderer and left for four days without food. Later he was transferred to the prison workyard where he preached the gospel and converted two persons whom he later baptized. He was in prison a full month before his family was able to obtain his release" (E. Cecil McGavin, *The Family of Joseph Smith*, 68; see also Lucy Mack Smith, *History of Joseph Smith by His Mother*, 172–73, 179–86).

6. **embark**—begin

7. **blameless**—without sin

8. Elder Henry B. Eyring of the Quorum of the Twelve Apostles taught that part of serving with all our "heart, might, mind, and strength," is to serve now and not wait for the "right time." To illustrate, he told this story: "Years ago I worked for a man in California. He hired me, he was kind to me, he seemed to regard me highly. I may have been the only Latter-day Saint he ever knew well. I don't know all the reasons I found to wait for a better moment to talk with him about the gospel. I just remember my feeling of sorrow when I learned, after he had retired and I lived far away, that he and his wife had been killed in a late night drive to their home in Carmel, California. He loved his wife. He loved his children. He had loved his parents. He loved his grandchildren, and he will love their children and will want to be with them forever.

"Now, I don't know how the crowds will be handled in the world to come. But I suppose that I will meet him, that he will look into my eyes, and that I will see in them the question: 'Hal, you knew. Why didn't you tell me?'" ("A Voice of Warning," *Ensign*, November 1998, 33).

"Therefore, if ye have desires to serve God ye are called to the work;[9]

"For behold the field is white already to harvest; and lo, he that thrusteth in his sickle[10] with his might,[11] the same layeth up in store[12] that he perisheth not, but bringeth salvation to his soul" (D&C 4:1–4).

SAMUEL SMITH IS BAPTIZED

Others in Joseph's family received revelation about the importance of the work Joseph was doing for the Lord. In May of the same year, a few days after Joseph and Oliver received the Aaronic Priesthood from John the Baptist,[13] Joseph explained that his "brother Samuel H. Smith came to visit us. We informed him of what the Lord was about to do for the children of men, and began to reason with him out of the Bible. We also showed him that part of the work which we had translated, and labored to persuade him concerning the Gospel of Jesus Christ, which was now about to be revealed in its fulness. He was not, however, very easily persuaded of these things, but after much inquiry[14] and explanation he retired to the woods, in order that by secret and fervent prayer he might obtain of a merciful God, wisdom to enable him to judge for

himself. The result was that he obtained revelation for himself sufficient[15] to convince him of the truth of our assertions[16] to him; and on the twenty-fifth day of that same month in which we had been baptized and ordained, Oliver Cowdery baptized him; and he returned to his father's house, greatly glorifying and praising God, being filled with the Holy Spirit" (*History of the Church*, 1:44).

HYRUM SMITH DESIRES TO SERVE THE LORD

Another brother was also blessed with answers from the Lord. "Not many days afterwards," Joseph recorded, "my brother Hyrum Smith came to us to inquire concerning these things, when at his earnest[17] request, I inquired of the Lord through the Urim and Thummim, and received for him [a revelation]" (*History of the Church*, 1:44–45).

The Lord told Hyrum, "If you desire, you shall be the means of doing much good in this generation" (D&C 11:8). The Lord also explained how the Holy Ghost would help him be a good missionary:

"And now, verily, verily, I say unto thee, put your trust in that Spirit which leadeth to do good—yea, to do justly, to walk humbly, to judge righteously; and this is my Spirit.

---

9. President David O. McKay said, "[A] significant feature of this revelation, and others given about the same period, is the naming of essential qualifications of those who were to participate in the bringing about of this marvelous work. These qualifications were not the possession of wealth, not social distinction, not political preferment, not military achievement, not nobility of birth; but a desire to serve God with all your 'heart, mind, and strength'—spiritual qualities that contribute to nobility of soul" (in Conference Report, April 1954, 22–23).

10. **sickle**—long curved knife for cutting grain

11. Why do you think the Lord compares missionary work to harvesting a field?

12. **layeth up in store**—will receive blessings

13. To learn more about John the Baptist and the restoration of the Aaronic Priesthood, see chapter 14, "Restoration of the Priesthood and Baptism."

14. **much inquiry**—many questions

15. **sufficient**—enough

16. **assertions**—words

17. **earnest**—serious

HYRUM SMITH, ARTIST UNKNOWN © INTELLECTUAL RESERVE, INC.

Hyrum Smith, older brother of the Prophet Joseph

"Verily, verily, I say unto you, I will impart[18] unto you of my Spirit, which shall enlighten[19] your mind, which shall fill your soul with joy;[20]

"And then shall ye know, or by this shall you know, all things whatsoever you desire of me, which are pertaining unto things of righteousness, in faith believing in me that you shall receive" (D&C 11:12–14).

Even though Hyrum had great desires to begin serving the Lord, his time to serve would not come until he further prepared himself. The Lord explained: "Seek not to declare my word, but first seek to obtain my word, and then shall your tongue be loosed; then, if you desire, you shall have my Spirit and my word, yea, the power of God unto the convincing of men" (D&C 11:21).

The Lord also explained that what he had told Hyrum was true for all people who wish to serve the Lord (see D&C 11:27).[21]

JOSEPH KNIGHT ALSO DESIRES TO SERVE

"About the same time," Joseph Smith recorded, "an old gentleman came to visit us of whose name I wish to make honorable mention—Mr. Joseph Knight, Sen., of Colesville, Broome county, New York, who, having heard of the manner in which we were occupying our time, very kindly and considerately brought us a quantity of provisions,[22] in order

that we might not be interrupted in the work of translation by the want of such necessaries of life; and I would just mention here, as in duty bound, that he several times brought us supplies, a distance of at least thirty miles, which enabled us to continue the work when otherwise we must have relinquished it[23] for a season. . . .

"Being very anxious to know his duty as to this work, I inquired of the Lord for him, and obtained [a revelation]" (*History of the Church*, 1:47–48).

Brother Knight's revelation is recorded in Doctrine and Covenants section 12.[24] In this revelation, Joseph Knight and all who wish to serve the Lord are told, "And no one can assist in this work except he shall be humble and full of love,[25] having faith, hope, and charity, being temperate in all things, whatsoever shall be entrusted to his care" (v. 12).[26]

CHAPTER 14:
RESTORATION OF THE PRIESTHOOD
AND BAPTISM

In the spring of 1829 Joseph Smith and Oliver Cowdery were translating the Book of Mormon. They translated passages that spoke of baptism for the forgiveness of sins and had many questions about such a baptism. They went to the banks of the nearby Susquehanna River to ask the Lord what they should

---

18. *impart*—give

19. *enlighten*—give light or understanding to

20. In these verses are found blessings of the Spirit that the Holy Ghost brings to all people who receive it. Another list of blessings of the Spirit is found in Galatians 5:22–23.

21. The Lord later said wonderful things about Hyrum Smith. "Blessed is my servant Hyrum Smith; for I, the Lord, love him because of the integrity of his heart, and because he loveth that which is right before me, saith the Lord" (D&C 124:15).

22. *quantity of provisions*—many supplies

23. *relinquished it*—given it up

24. This revelation was given to Joseph Knight Sr. through the Prophet Joseph Smith. Brother Knight, of Colesville, New York, was one of the first people to believe in Joseph Smith's account of the First Vision.

He helped the Prophet during the translation of the Book of Mormon. Joseph Knight remained faithful to the Church until he died at Mount Pisgah, Iowa, in 1847 while traveling to the Salt Lake Valley (see Lyndon W. Cook, *The Revelations of the Prophet Joseph Smith*, 20–22).

25. President Ezra Taft Benson taught: "The Lord has said that no one can assist with this work unless he is humble and full of love. . . . But humility does not mean weakness. It does not mean timidity; it does not mean fear. A man can be humble and also fearless. A man can be humble and also courageous. Humility is the recognition of our dependence upon a higher power, a constant need for the Lord's support in His work" (*Come unto Christ*, 94).

26. How would having these qualities help you be a better missionary? What can you do to develop these qualities?

HARMONY, PENNSYLVANIA, BY AL ROUNDS

The Susquehanna River near Harmony, Pennsylvania

do. As you read this chapter, look for the ways in the which the Lord answered their prayer.

JOSEPH SMITH'S ACCOUNT OF THE RESTORATION OF THE AARONIC PRIESTHOOD

Joseph and Oliver were working on translation of the plates when, as Joseph Smith later described, "we on a certain day went into the woods to pray and inquire of the Lord respecting baptism for the remission[27] of sins, that we found mentioned in the translation of the plates. While we were . . . praying and calling upon the Lord, a messenger from heaven descended in a cloud of light, and having laid his hands upon us, he ordained us, saying:

"Upon you my fellow servants, in the name of Messiah, I confer the Priesthood of Aaron, which holds the keys of the ministering of angels,[28] and of the gospel of repentance,[29] and of baptism by immersion[30] for the remission of sins; and this shall

---

NOTES FOR CHAPTER 14

27. *remission*—forgiveness

28. Elder Robert L. Backman said that the key of the ministering of angels "means that you are entitled to have inspiration and guidance in all phases of your life—at home, school, work, play, as well as in Church. . . . It provides protection to you from evil and danger" ("They Were Awesome," *New Era*, May 1983, 7).

29. Speaking of the gospel of repentance, President Gordon B. Hinckley said, "Many of you are teachers and priests and have home teaching assignments. You have authority in this service to be teachers of repen-tance—that is, to encourage those Latter-day Saints for whom you have some responsibility to live the gospel principles more faithfully" (in Conference Report, October 1982, 64).

30. President Gordon B. Hinckley said, "It is no small or unimportant thing to baptize an individual. [A] young priest, acting in the name of the Lord and under divine authority, wipes out, as it were, by the mar-velous process of baptism, the sins of the past and bring about a birth into a new and better life. What a tremendous responsibility . . . to live worthy of the exercise of this sacred power!" (in Conference Report, October 1982, 65).

John the Baptist restored the Aaronic Priesthood on May 15, 1829

never be taken again from the earth until the sons of Levi[31] do offer again an offering[32] unto the Lord in righteousness" (Joseph Smith—History 1:68–69).

JOSEPH AND OLIVER ARE COMMANDED TO BAPTIZE EACH OTHER

"[John the Baptist] said this Aaronic Priesthood had not the power of laying on hands for the gift of the Holy Ghost," Joseph explained, "but that this should be conferred on[33] us hereafter; and he commanded us to go and be baptized, and gave us directions that I should baptize Oliver Cowdery, and that afterwards he should baptize me.

"Accordingly we went and were baptized. I baptized him first, and afterwards he baptized me—after which I laid my hands upon his head and ordained him to the Aaronic Priesthood, and afterwards he laid his hands on me and ordained me to the same Priesthood—for so we were commanded.

"The messenger who visited us on this occasion and conferred this Priesthood upon us, said that his name was John, the same that is called John the Baptist in the New Testament, and that he acted under the direction of Peter, James and John, who held the keys of the Priesthood of Melchizedek, which Priesthood, he said, would in due time[34] be conferred on us" (Joseph Smith—History 1:70–72).[35]

THE SPIRIT OF PROPHECY RESTED UPON JOSEPH AND OLIVER FOLLOWING BAPTISM

"Immediately on our coming up out of the water after we had been baptized," Joseph wrote, "we experienced great and glorious blessings from our Heavenly Father. No sooner had I baptized Oliver Cowdery, than the Holy Ghost fell upon him, and he stood up and prophesied many things which should shortly come to pass. And again, so soon as I had been baptized by him, I also had the spirit of prophecy, when, standing up, I prophesied concerning the rise of this Church, and many other things connected with the Church, and this generation of the children of men. We were filled with the

---

31. ☀ Anciently, the "sons of Levi" (called Levites) were one of the twelve tribes of Israel, whose duty was to perform the sacrifices of the law of Moses in Old Testament times (see LDS Bible Dictionary, s.v. "Levites," 724). In our day, the sons of Levi are "by virtue of the blessings of the Almighty, those who are ordained by those who hold the authority to officiate in the offices of the priesthood" (Joseph Fielding Smith, *Doctrines of Salvation,* 3:93).

Joseph and Oliver were commanded to be baptized

32. ☀ What sort of offering will the sons of Levi make? President Joseph Fielding Smith said, "We are living in the dispensation of the fulness of times . . . and all things are to be restored since the beginning. . . . Sacrifice by the shedding of blood was instituted in the days of Adam and of necessity will have to be restored. The sacrifice of animals will be done to complete the restoration when the temple spoken of is built; at the beginning of the millennium, or in the restoration, blood sacrifices will be performed long enough to complete the fulness of the restoration in this dispensation. Afterwards sacrifice will be of some other character" (*Doctrines of Salvation,* 3:94).

33. ✍ **conferred on**—given to

34. 🔍 Some days later the Apostles Peter, James, and John, who were called by Jesus Christ when he lived on earth, appeared to Joseph Smith and Oliver Cowdery and gave them the higher, or Melchizedek, priesthood (see D&C 128:20).

35. 💬 What difference would it make to you and your family if the power to baptize had not been restored to the Prophet Joseph Smith?

Peter, James, and John conferred the Melchizedek Priesthood upon Joseph Smith in 1829

Holy Ghost, and rejoiced in the God of our salvation.

"Our minds being now enlightened,[36] we began to have the scriptures laid open to our understandings, and the true meaning and intention of their more mysterious passages revealed unto us in a manner which we never could attain to previously, nor ever before had thought of. In the meantime we were forced to keep secret the circumstances of having received the Priesthood and our having been baptized, owing to a spirit of persecution which had already manifested itself in the neighborhood" (Joseph Smith—History 1:73–74).

OLIVER COWDERY'S TESTIMONY OF RECEIVING THE AARONIC PRIESTHOOD

"I shall not attempt to paint to you the feelings of this heart, nor the majestic beauty and glory which surrounded us on this occasion," Oliver Cowdery recalled of the event, "but you will believe me when I say, that earth, nor men, with the eloquence of time, cannot begin to clothe language[37] in as interesting and sublime a manner as this holy personage. No; nor has this earth power to give the joy, to bestow the peace, or comprehend the wisdom which was contained in each sentence as they were delivered by the power of the Holy Spirit![38] . . . The assurance that we were in the presence of an angel,

the certainty that we heard the voice of Jesus, and the truth unsullied[39] as it flowed from a pure personage, dictated by the will of God, is to me past description" (Joseph Smith—History, 1:71n).

CHAPTER 15: RESTORATION OF THE MELCHIZEDEK PRIESTHOOD

On the fifteenth of May 1829, John the Baptist conferred the Aaronic Priesthood upon the Prophet Joseph Smith and his scribe Oliver Cowdery. On that occasion, John the Baptist said he was acting "under the direction of Peter, James and John, who held the keys of the Priesthood of Melchizedek, which Priesthood, he said, would . . . be conferred" upon Joseph and Oliver (JS—H 1:72). Within a short time that day arrived. As you read this chapter, try to imagine the excitement young Joseph Smith and Oliver Cowdery felt as they awaited and then received the power, authority, and keys of the Melchizedek Priesthood.

PETER, JAMES, AND JOHN RESTORE THE MELCHIZEDEK PRIESTHOOD

Although Joseph Smith never recorded the date or actual events of the restoration of the Melchizedek Priesthood,[40] he spoke to the Church

---

36. *enlightened*—given truth

37. *clothe language*—use words

38. Nephi taught that "angels speak by the power of the Holy Ghost; wherefore, they speak the words of Christ" (2 Nephi 32:3), which explains why Oliver Cowdery was so deeply moved by this experience.

39. *unsullied*—without error; pure

NOTES FOR CHAPTER 15

40. "The Melchizedek Priesthood is the higher or greater priesthood; the Aaronic Priesthood is the lesser priesthood. The Melchizedek Priesthood includes the keys of the spiritual blessings of the Church. Through the ordinances of the higher priesthood, the power of godliness is made manifest to men (D&C 84:18–25; 107:18–21).

"God first revealed this higher priesthood to Adam. The patriarchs and prophets in every dispensation had

this authority (D&C 84:6–17). It was first called the Holy Priesthood, after the Order of the Son of God. It later became known as the Melchizedek Priesthood (D&C 107:2–4).

"When the children of Israel failed to live up to the privileges and covenants of the Melchizedek Priesthood, the Lord took away the higher law and gave them a lesser priesthood and a lesser law (D&C 84:23–26). These were called the Aaronic Priesthood and the law of Moses. When Jesus came to the earth, he restored the Melchizedek Priesthood to the Jews and began to build up the Church among them. However, the priesthood and the Church were lost again through apostasy. They were later restored through Joseph Smith, Jr. (D&C 27:12–13; 128:20; JS—H 1:73)" (See *Guide to the Scriptures*, s.v. "Melchizedek Priesthood," 161).

"For, behold, the Lord your Redeemer suffered death in the flesh; wherefore he suffered the pain of all men,[71] that all men might repent and come unto him.

"And he hath risen again from the dead, that he might bring all men unto him, on conditions of repentance.[72]

"And how great is his joy in the soul that repenteth!

"Wherefore, you are called to cry repentance unto this people.

"And if it so be that you should labor all your days in crying repentance unto this people, and bring, save it be one soul unto me, how great shall be your joy with him in the kingdom of my Father!"[73] (vv. 10–15).

CHAPTER 17:
THE THREE AND EIGHT WITNESSES TO THE PLATES

While translating the Book of Mormon plates in June 1829 at Fayette, New York, the Prophet Joseph Smith learned that three people could become witnesses of the gold plates. In addition, the Lord provided eight other witnesses to see and handle the plates. As you read this chapter, ask yourself why the Lord provided testimonies to his marvelous work and wonder. How are the testimonies of the three witnesses different than the testimonies of the eight witnesses?

THE LORD PROVIDES SPECIAL WITNESSES TO THE BOOK OF MORMON

"In the course of the work of translation," Joseph Smith explained, "we ascertained[74] that three special witnesses were to be provided by the Lord, to whom He would grant that they should see the plates from which this work (the Book of Mormon) should be translated; and that these witnesses should bear record of the same, as will be found recorded. . . . Almost immediately after we had made this discovery, it occurred to Oliver Cowdery, David Whitmer and the aforementioned Martin Harris (who had come to inquire after our progress in the work) that they would have me inquire of the Lord to know if they might not obtain of him the privilege to be these three special witnesses; and finally they became so very solicitous,[75] and urged me so much to inquire that at length I complied; and through the Urim and Thummim, I obtained of the Lord for them [a revelation]" (*History of the Church*, 1:52–53). That revelation is recorded in Doctrine and Covenants section 17.

"Behold, I say unto you, that you must rely upon my word, which if you do with full purpose of heart, you shall have a view of the plates, and also of the breastplate, the sword of Laban, the Urim and Thummim, which were given to the brother of Jared upon the mount, when he talked with the Lord face to face, and the miraculous directors which were given to Lehi while in the wilderness, on the borders of the Red Sea.[76]

---

71.   Concerning the suffering of Jesus Christ during the Atonement, Elder Bruce R. McConkie taught, "It was on the cross that he 'suffered death in the flesh,' even as many have suffered agonizing deaths, but it was in Gethsemane that 'he suffered the pain of all men, that all men might repent and come unto him.' (D&C 18:11.)" (*The Mortal Messiah*, 4:127).

72.   How does the Savior's suffering for our sins and death show how much we are worth to our Heavenly Father?

73.   How do you think doing missionary work would help prepare for the organization of the Church?

NOTES FOR CHAPTER 17

74.   *ascertained*—learned

75.   *solicitous*—concerned; anxious

76.   Along with the gold plates, the Three Witnesses would see the breastplate and the Urim and Thummim, which were both used to help in the translation (see Joseph Smith—History 1:35). In addition, they were to view the sword of Laban, carried from Jerusalem by Nephi (see 1 Nephi 4:9; 2 Nephi 5:14), and the "miraculous directors," or Liahona, which guided Lehi's family in the wilderness (see Alma 37:38–42).

"And it is by your faith that you shall obtain a view of them, even by that faith which was had by the prophets of old.[77]

"And after that you have obtained faith, and have seen them with your eyes, you shall testify of them, by the power of God" (vv. 1–3).

SEEKING TO FULFILL THE PROMISE GIVEN BY THE LORD

Joseph recalled that several days after the revelation in Doctrine and Covenants section 17 was given, "Martin Harris, David Whitmer, Oliver Cowdery and myself agreed to retire into the woods, and try to obtain, by fervent and humble prayer, the fulfilment of the promises given in the above revelation—that they should have a view of the plates. We accordingly made choice of a piece of woods convenient to Mr. Whitmer's house to which we retired, and having knelt down, we began to pray in much faith to Almighty God to bestow upon us a realization of these promises.

"According to previous arrangement, I commenced prayer to our Heavenly Father, and was followed by each of the others in succession.[78] We did not at the first trial, however, obtain any answer or manifestation of divine favor in our behalf. We again observed the same order of prayer, each calling on and praying fervently to God in rotation, but with the same result as before" (*History of the Church*, 1:54).

THE ANGEL MORONI SHOWS THE PLATES TO JOSEPH, DAVID, AND OLIVER

"Upon this, our second failure," Joseph recalled, "Martin Harris proposed that he should withdraw himself from us, believing, as he expressed himself, that his presence was the cause of our not obtaining what we wished for. He accordingly withdrew from us, and we knelt down again, and had not been many minutes engaged in prayer, when presently we beheld a light above us in the air, of exceeding brightness; and behold, an angel stood before us. In his hands he held the plates which we had been praying for these to have a view of. He turned over the leaves one by one, so that we could see them, and discern the engravings thereon distinctly. He then addressed himself to David Whitmer, and said, 'David, blessed is the Lord, and he that keeps His commandments;' when, immediately afterwards, we heard a voice from out of the bright light above us, saying, 'These plates have been revealed by the power of God, and they have been translated by the power of God. The translation of them which you have seen is correct, and I command you to bear record of what you now see and hear'" (*History of the Church,* 1:54–55).

MARTIN HARRIS SEES THE PLATES

Joseph remembers that he then "left David and Oliver, and went in pursuit of Martin Harris, whom I found at a considerable distance, fervently engaged in prayer. He soon told me, however, that he had not yet prevailed[79] with the Lord, and earnestly requested me to join him in prayer, that he also might realize the same blessings which we had just received. We accordingly joined in prayer, and ultimately obtained our desires, for before we had yet finished, the same vision was opened to our view, at least it was again opened to me, and I once more beheld and heard the same things; whilst[80] at the same moment, Martin Harris cried out, apparently in an ecstasy of joy, ''Tis enough; 'tis enough; mine eyes have beheld; mine eyes have beheld;' and jumping up, he shouted, 'Hosanna,' blessing God,

---

77. "The true Church of Jesus Christ is not man-made. Thus, God provides and gives his own witness by His power. The strength of the testimony of these three men did not come from any mortal man, including Joseph Smith" (Leaun G. Otten and C. Max Caldwell, *Sacred Truths of the Doctrine and Covenants,* 1:39).

78. *succession*—one after another

79. *prevailed*—succeeded

80. *whilst*—while

Oliver Cowdery, David Whitmer, and Martin Harris were the Three Witnesses

and otherwise rejoiced exceedingly"[81] (*History of the Church,* 1:55).

THE TESTIMONY OF THE THREE WITNESSES

"Having thus, through the mercy of God, obtained these glorious manifestations," Joseph wrote, "it now remained for these three individuals to fulfil the commandment which they had received, viz.,[82] to bear record of these things; in order to accomplish which, they drew up and subscribed the following document:[83]

"Be it known unto all nations, kindreds,[84] tongues,[85] and people, unto whom this work shall come; That we, through the grace of God the Father, and our Lord Jesus Christ, have seen the plates which contain this record, which is a record of the people of Nephi, and also of the Lamanites, their brethren, and also of the people of Jared, who came from the tower of which hath been spoken. And we also know that they have been translated by the gift and power of God, for his voice hath declared it unto us; wherefore we know of a surety that the work is true. And we also testify that we have seen the engravings[86] which are upon the plates; and they have been shown unto us by the power of God, and not of man. And we declare with words of soberness,[87] that an angel of God came down from heaven, and he brought and laid before our eyes, that we beheld and saw the plates, and the engravings thereon; and we know that it is by the grace of God the Father, and our Lord Jesus Christ, that we beheld and bear record that these things are true. And it is marvelous in our eyes. Nevertheless, the voice of the Lord commanded us that we should bear record of it; wherefore, to be obedient unto the commandments of God, we bear testimony of these things. And we know that if we are faithful in Christ, we shall rid our garments of the blood of all men,[88] and be found spotless[89] before the judgment seat of Christ, and shall dwell with him eternally in the heavens. And the honor be to the Father, and to the Son and to the Holy Ghost, which is one God. Amen."

Oliver Cowdery
David Whitmer
Martin Harris
(*History of the Church,* 1:56–57.)

---

81. Joseph Smith's mother wrote, "When they returned to the house it was between three and four o'clock p.m. Mrs. Whitmer, Mr. Smith and myself, were sitting in a bedroom at the time. On coming in, Joseph threw himself down beside me, and exclaimed, "Father, Mother, you do not know how happy I am: the Lord has now caused the plates to be shown to three more besides myself. They have seen an angel, who has testified to them, and they will have to bear witness to the truth of what I have said, for now they know for themselves, that I do not go about to deceive the people, and I feel as if I was relieved of a burden which was almost too heavy for me to bear, and it rejoices my soul, that I am not any longer to be entirely alone in the world'" (Lucy Mack Smith, *History of Joseph Smith by His Mother,* 152).

82. *viz.*—namely

83. Elder Dallin H. Oaks, of the Quorum of the Twelve Apostles, said, "The testimony of the Three Witnesses to the Book of Mormon stands forth in great strength. Each of the three had ample reason and opportunity to renounce his testimony if it had been false, or to equivocate on details if any had been inaccurate. As is well known, because of disagreements or jealousies involving other leaders of the Church, each one of these three witnesses was excommunicated from The Church of Jesus Christ of Latter-day Saints by about eight years after the publication of their testimony. All three went their separate ways, with no common interest to support a collusive effort. Yet to the end of their lives—periods ranging from 12 to 50 years after their excommunications—not one of these witnesses deviated from his published testimony or said anything that cast any shadow on its truthfulness" ("The Witness: Martin Harris," *Ensign,* May 1999, 36).

84. *kindreds*—family groups

85. *tongues*—languages

86. *engravings*—carved or etched words

87. *soberness*—seriousness

88. "Rid our garments of the blood of all men" is a phrase that means we will not be responsible for other people's sins.

89. *found spotless*—judged to be without sin

JOSEPH SMITH AND THE EIGHT WITNESSES VIEW THE PLATES, BY DALE KILBOURN © INTELLECTUAL RESERVE, INC.

These eight men were shown the plates by Joseph Smith and handled them

THE TESTIMONY OF THE EIGHT WITNESSES

Soon after the Three Witnesses saw the angel Moroni and the plates, the Lord selected eight other witnesses to see and handle the plates.

This is their testimony:

"Be it known unto all nations, kindreds, tongues, and people, unto whom this work shall come: that Joseph Smith, Jun., the translator of this work, has shown unto us the plates of which hath been spoken, which have the appearance of gold; and as many of the leaves as the said Smith has translated we did handle with our hands; and we also saw the engravings thereon, all of which has the appearance of ancient work, and of curious workmanship.[90] And this we bear record with words of soberness, that the said Smith has shown unto us, for we have seen and hefted,[91] and know of a surety that the said Smith has got the plates of which we have spoken. And we give our names unto the world to witness

90. *curious workmanship*—skillful work

91. *hefted*—lifted

unto the world that which we have seen. And we lie not, God bearing witness of it.[92]

Christian Whitmer

Jacob Whitmer

Peter Whitmer, Jun.

John Whitmer

Hiram Page

Joseph Smith, Sen.

Hyrum Smith

Samuel H. Smith"

(*History of the Church,* 1:57–58.)

CHAPTER 18:
PUBLICATION OF THE BOOK OF MORMON

The Prophet Joseph Smith and Oliver Cowdery were able to translate the majority of the Book of Mormon in less than three months. It took nine months to publish the book. During this time, the Prophet had a tremendous responsibility to take care of the sacred record. Evil men tried to destroy the work of the Lord and prevent the Book of Mormon from being published. As you read this chapter, watch how the Lord helped the Prophet during this challenging time.

THE MIRACLE OF THE TRANSLATION OF THE BOOK OF MORMON

Elder Joseph Fielding Smith described the miracle of the translation of the Book of Mormon when he said, "Between April seventh [1829] and some time near the middle of June [1829], the translation continued and was practically finished. In other words in less than three months time the work was done. Those who have endeavored[93] to translate any work of considerable size will realize the miraculous nature of this translation. It is physically impossible for a mortal man, unaided by the inspiration of the Lord, to accomplish such a task in such a short space of time. Those who have read the Book of Mormon, and have obtained a testimony of its truth, will likewise marvel at this wonderful work accomplished in so brief a time. Without the help of the Lord it could not have been done" (*Church History and Modern Revelation,* 1:70–71).

JOSEPH SMITH AND OTHERS ARRANGE FOR THE PUBLICATION OF THE BOOK OF MORMON

As translation came to an end, Joseph looked for someone who would print the book. "We went to Palmyra, Wayne county, New York," he said, "secured[94] the copyright,[95] and agreed with Mr. Egbert B. Grandin[96] to print five thousand copies for

---

92.   These witnesses had a miraculous experience when they saw the plates. Why would the Lord provide two types of witnesses? The Three Witnesses' experience was spiritual with the seeing of the angel Moroni. The Eight Witnesses' experience was quite different because they did not see the angel. They were simply shown the plates and were privileged to handle them. How do these different testimonies make the Book of Mormon more convincing and powerful?

NOTES FOR CHAPTER 18

93.   *endeavored*—tried

94.   *secured*—received

95.   *copyright*—a court order saying no one else can publish the book

96.   "Born 30 March 1806, [Egbert B.] Grandin was about three months younger than the twenty-three-year old Prophet-translator when Joseph Smith and Martin Harris asked him to bid on the job in June

1829. . . . He accepted after the Prophet and Martin Harris got a bid from a Rochester printer and assured him that if he didn't publish it, someone else would" ("Historic Discoveries at the Grandin Building," *Ensign,* July 1980, 48).

Egbert B. Grandin was the Palmyra printer who published the first edition of the Book of Mormon

THE BOOK OF MORMON PUBLISHED BY E. B. GRANDIN, BY GARY SMITH © INTELLECTUAL RESERVE, INC.

This press was used by E. B. Grandin to print the Book of Mormon

the sum of three thousand dollars"[97] (*History of the Church,* 1:71). The agreement was made on August 17, 1829.

According to an *Ensign* article, "Printing 5,000 copies of the Book of Mormon was a gigantic job, ahead of the book industry by nearly twenty years. . . . Grandin, principally a newspaper and job printer, was brand new to the book publishing business, having begun advertizing himself as a book printer only three months before he was first contacted regarding printing of the Book of Mormon. He had purchased Palmyra's newspaper, the *Wayne* [County] *Sentinel* and a bookstore on 13 April 1827 from John Henry Gilbert, the printer who, as Grandin's employee, would actually set type for the Book of Mormon.[98] . . . [The printing press] was apparently acquired just three months before, in March 1829" ("Historic Discoveries at the Grandin Building," *Ensign,* July 1980, 48).

97. To convince E. B. Grandin that he would get his money if he printed the Book of Mormon, Martin Harris signed "a mortgage agreement guaranteeing payment for the printing through the sale of part of his Palmyra farm if necessary" (*Church History in the Fulness of Times,* 63).

98. "Setting type and printing was a laborious hand job. Each character had to be picked out of the type case, set up by hand, inked form by form, and printed, sixteen pages at a time. One study estimates that it took eleven hours a day, six days a week, excluding Sundays and holidays, for nine months, to print the almost six hundred pages of the Book of Mormon's 5,000 copies" ("Historic Discoveries at the Grandin Building," *Ensign,* July 1980, 48).

SPECIAL PRECAUTIONS ARE TAKEN WHILE THE BOOK OF MORMON IS PRINTED

Joseph was able to receive a copyright for the book and made plans to return to Pennsylvania. Before leaving, he received a commandment from the Lord.

"First," explained Lucy Mack Smith, Joseph was told "that Oliver Cowdery should transcribe[99] the whole manuscript. Second, that he should take but one copy at a time to the [printing] office, so that if one copy should get destroyed, there would still be a copy remaining. Third, that in going to and from the office, he should always have a guard to attend him, for the purpose of protecting the manuscript. Fourth, that a guard should be kept constantly on the watch, both night and day, about the house, to protect the manuscript from malicious[100] persons, who would infest[101] the house for the purpose of destroying the manuscript. All these things were strictly attended to, as the Lord commanded Joseph. After giving these instructions, Joseph returned to Pennsylvania" (*History of Joseph Smith by His Mother,* 157).

MOBS TRY TO STOP THE PRINTING

"Oliver Cowdery commenced the work immediately after Joseph left," Lucy wrote, "and the printing went on very well for a season, but the clouds of persecution again began to gather. The rabble[102] . . . began to counsel together, as to the most efficient means of putting a stop to our proceedings" (*History of Joseph Smith by His Mother,* 158).

The group seeking to stop the printing held a meeting one night and promised with each other that they would not let the printing continue and that they would never let anyone in their families read the book if it were published. They vowed to do whatever they could to stop Joseph from proceeding.

THE RECORD IS PROTECTED BY THE LORD

Oliver learned of the group's plan and was very worried about what would happen. He went to Joseph's mother, Lucy, for advice about what to do.

Lucy reassured Oliver that the manuscript would be safe and told him that she would hide it in a chest under the head of her bed. "I then placed it in a chest," Lucy wrote, "which was so high that when placed under the bed, the whole weight of the bedstead rested upon the lid. Having made this arrangement, we felt quite at rest, and that night, the family retired to rest at the usual hour, all save Peter Whitmer, who spent the night on guard. But as for myself, soon after I went to bed I fell into a train of reflections[103] which occupied my mind, and which caused sleep to forsake my eyelids till the day dawned, for, when I meditated upon the days of

The E. B. Grandin printing offices

99. transcribe—rewrite or make another copy of

100. malicious—hateful

101. infest—come in

102. rabble—mob

103. train of reflections—series of thoughts

toil, and nights of anxiety, through which we had all passed for years previous, in order to obtain the treasure that then lay beneath my head; when I thought upon the hours of fearful apprehensions which we had all suffered on the same account, and that the object was at last accomplished, I could truly say that my soul did magnify the Lord, and my spirit rejoiced in God my Savior. I felt that the heavens were moved in our behalf, and that the angels who had power to put down the mighty from their seats, and to exalt those who were of low degree, were watching over us; that those would be filled who hungered and thirsted after righteousness. . . . Therefore, we could safely put our trust in [God], as he was able to help in every time of need"[104] (*History of Joseph Smith by His Mother,* 159–60).

ABNER COLE TRIES TO PUBLISH THE BOOK OF MORMON IN HIS NEWSPAPER

"The work of printing still continued with little or no interruption," Lucy wrote, "until one Sunday afternoon, when Hyrum became very uneasy as to the security of the work left at the printing office, and requested Oliver to accompany him thither, to see if all was right. . . .

"On arriving at the printing establishment, they found it occupied by an individual by the name of [Abner] Cole, an ex-justice of the peace, who was busily employed in printing a newspaper. . . .

"Upon reading the prospectus[105] of his paper, they found that he had agreed with his subscribers to publish one form[106] of 'Joe Smith's Gold Bible' each week, and thereby furnish them with the principal portion of the book in such a way that they would not be obliged to pay the Smiths for it. His paper was entitled, *Dogberry Paper on Winter Hill.* . . . Hyrum was shocked, as well as indignant[107] at the dishonest course which Mr. Cole had taken, in order to possess himself of the work.

"'Mr. Cole,' said he, 'what right have you to print the Book of Mormon in this manner? Do you not know that we have secured the copyright?'

"'It is none of your business,' answered Cole, 'I have hired the press, and will print what I please.' . . .

"Hyrum endeavored to dissuade him from his purpose,[108] but finding him inexorable,[109] left him to issue his paper, as he had hitherto done; for when they found him at work, he had already issued six or eight numbers, and had managed to keep them out of our sight.

"On returning from the office, they asked my husband [Joseph Smith, Sr.] what course was best for them to pursue, relative to Mr. Cole. He told them that he considered it a matter with which Joseph ought to be made acquainted. Accordingly, he set out himself for Pennsylvania, and returned with Joseph the ensuing Sunday. The weather was so extremely cold, that they came near perishing before

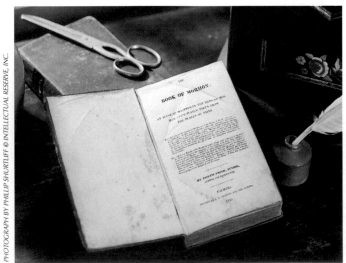

A first edition of the Book of Mormon

104. Think of times when you have been worried or afraid but after you prayed to Heavenly Father felt safe. Why is it that you often feel safer following prayer?

105. *the prospectus*—the proposed plan

106. *one form*—several pages

107. *indignant*—angered

108. *dissuade him from his purpose*—talk him out of printing pages of the Book of Mormon

109. *inexorable*—unwilling to change his mind

MARTIN HARRIS FARM, BY AL ROUNDS

Martin Harris sold some of his farm to pay the printer's debt

they arrived at home, nevertheless, as soon as Joseph made himself partially comfortable, he went to the printing office, where he found Cole employed, as on the Sunday previous. 'How do you do, Mr. Cole,' said Joseph, 'you seem hard at work.'

"'How do you do, Mr. Smith,' answered Cole, dryly.

"Joseph examined his *Dogberry Paper*, and then said firmly, 'Mr. Cole, that book [the Book of Mormon], and the right of publishing it, belongs to me, and I forbid you meddling with it any further.'

"At this Mr. Cole threw off his coat, rolled up his sleeves, and came towards Joseph, smacking his fists together with vengeance, and roaring out, 'Do you want to fight, sir? do you want to fight?' . . .

" . . . 'Now, Mr. Cole,' said [Joseph], 'you had better keep your coat on—it is cold, and I am not going to fight you, nevertheless, I assure you, sir, that you have got to stop printing my book, for I know my rights, and shall maintain them. . . . There

is law, and you will find that out, if you do not understand it. . . . '

"At this, the ex-justice began to cool off a little, and finally concluded to submit to an arbitration,[110] which decided that he should stop his proceedings forthwith, so that he made us no further trouble" (*History of Joseph Smith by His Mother,* 164–66).

JOSEPH CONVINCES MR. GRANDIN TO KEEP PRINTING THE BOOK OF MORMON

"When the inhabitants of the surrounding country perceived that the work still progressed," Lucy wrote, "they became uneasy, and again called a large meeting. At this time, they gathered their forces together, far and near, and organizing themselves into a committee of the whole, they resolved, as before, never to purchase one of our books, when they should be printed. They then appointed a committee to wait upon E. B. Grandin, and inform

110. **submit to an arbitration**—see what a court of law would say

April 6, 1830

"Whilst the Book of Mormon was in the hands of the printer, we still continued to bear testimony and give information, as far as we had opportunity," Joseph Smith wrote, "and also made known to our brethren that we had received a commandment to organize the Church; and accordingly we met together for that purpose, at the house of Mr. Peter Whitmer, Sen., (being six in number,)[3] on Tuesday, the sixth day of April, A. D., one thousand eight hundred and thirty. Having opened the meeting by solemn[4] prayer to our Heavenly Father, we proceeded, according to previous commandment, to call on our brethren to know whether they accepted us as their teachers in the things of the Kingdom of God,[5] and whether they were satisfied that we should proceed and be organized as a Church according to said commandment which we had received. To these several propositions they consented by a unanimous vote.[6] I then laid my hands upon Oliver Cowdery, and ordained him an Elder of the 'Church of Jesus Christ of Latter-day Saints;' after which, he ordained me also to the office of an Elder of said Church. We then took bread, blessed it, and brake it with them; also wine, blessed it, and drank it with them. We then laid our hands on each individual member of the Church present, that they might receive the gift of the Holy Ghost, and be confirmed members of the Church of Christ. The Holy Ghost was poured out upon us to a very great degree—some prophesied, whilst we all praised the Lord, and rejoiced exceedingly" (*History of the Church*, 1:74–78).

The Importance of the Organization of the Church

President Gordon B. Hinckley testified of the importance of this day and the sacred event that took place in the Whitmers' small home. "This day of organization was, in effect, a day of commencement,[7] the graduation for Joseph from ten years of remarkable schooling. It had begun with the incomparable vision in the grove in the spring of 1820, when the Father and the Son appeared to the fourteen-year-old boy. It had continued with the tutoring[8] from Moroni, with both warnings and instructions given on multiple occasions.[9] Then there was the translation of the ancient record,[10] and the inspiration, the knowledge, the revelation that came from that experience. There was the bestowal[11] of divine authority, the ancient priesthood again conferred upon[12] men by those who were its rightful possessors—John the Baptist in the case of the Aaronic Priesthood, and Peter, James, and John in the case of the Melchizedek. There were revelations, a number of them, in which the voice of God was heard again, and the channel of communication opened between man and the Creator. All of these were preliminary to that historic April 6" (*Be Thou an Example*, 109).

A Revelation Given at the Organization of the Church

During the organization of the Church the Lord revealed the following to the Prophet Joseph Smith:

---

3.   🔍 The "six in number" Joseph refers to were Joseph Smith, Oliver Cowdery, Hyrum Smith, Peter Whitmer Jr., Samuel H. Smith, and David Whitmer. Others also attended, including Joseph's parents and Joseph Knight Sr.

4.   📖 *solemn*—serious

5.   🕮 Elder Bruce R. McConkie taught that "The Church of Jesus Christ of Latter-day Saints as it is now constituted is the kingdom of God on earth" (*Mormon Doctrine*, 415).

6.   📖 **propositions they consented by a unanimous vote**—suggestions everyone agreed to

7.   📖 **commencement**—beginning

8.   📖 **tutoring**—training or teaching

9.   🕮 On these occasions, Moroni taught Joseph Smith using the scriptures (see Joseph Smith—History 1:36–46).

10. 🔍 The ancient record spoken of is the Book of Mormon.

11. 📖 **bestowal**—giving

12. 📖 **conferred upon**—given to

"Behold, there shall be a record kept among you; and in it thou shalt be called a seer,[13] a translator,[14] a prophet,[15] an apostle[16] of Jesus Christ, an elder[17] of the church through the will of God the Father, and the grace of your Lord Jesus Christ,[18]

"Being inspired of the Holy Ghost to lay the foundation thereof, and to build it up unto the most holy faith.

"Which church was organized and established in the year of your Lord eighteen hundred and thirty, in the fourth month, and on the sixth day of the month which is called April" (D&C 21:1–3).

PRIESTHOOD OFFICES BEGIN

After taking the sacrament and receiving the commandment to keep of record of their work, Joseph recalled that the group "proceeded to call out and ordain some others of the brethren to different offices of the Priesthood, according as the Spirit manifested unto us: and after a happy time spent in witnessing and feeling for ourselves the powers and blessings of the Holy Ghost, through the grace of God bestowed upon us, we dismissed with the pleasing knowledge that we were now individually members of, and acknowledged of God, 'The Church of Jesus Christ,' organized in accordance with commandments and revelations given by Him to ourselves in these last days, as well as according to the order of the Church as recorded in the New Testament. Several persons who had attended the above meeting, became convinced of the truth and came forward shortly after, and were received into the Church; among the rest, my own father and mother were baptized, to my great joy and consolation;[19] and about the same time,

13. Elder John A. Widtsoe wrote that "a seer is one who sees with spiritual eyes. . . . This he does by the power of the Lord operating through him directly, or indirectly with the aid of divine instruments such as the Urim and Thummim. In short, he is one who sees, who walks in the Lord's light with open eyes (Mosiah 8:15–17)" (*Evidences and Reconciliations,* 258; see also Moses 6:36).

14. "The title 'translator' may refer to one who has received two blessings given a prophet by the spirit of God: 1. The power to convert the written or spoken word into another language (see D&C 20:8). 2. The power to give a clearer meaning to a given language. Through the gift of translation a prophet does not merely convey in the language of the reader the words that were recorded by the writer but by revelation preserves for the reader the thoughts or intent of the original writer" (*Doctrine and Covenants Student Manual: Religion 324–325,* 2d ed., 44).

15. Elder John A. Widtsoe taught: "A prophet is a teacher. That is the essential meaning of the word. He teaches the body of truth, the gospel, revealed by the Lord to man; and under inspiration explains it to the understanding of the people" (*Evidences and Reconciliations,* 257).

16. "An Apostle is a messenger and special witness of Jesus Christ; one who has a divine message to all men" (in Smith and Sjodahl, *Doctrine and Covenants Commentary,* 116).

17. Elder Bruce R. McConkie stated: "What is an elder? An elder is a minister of the Lord Jesus Christ. He holds the holy Melchizedek Priesthood. He is commissioned to stand in the place and stead of his Master—who is the Chief Elder—in ministering to his fellowmen. He is the Lord's agent. His appointment is to preach the gospel and perfect the Saints" (Bruce R. McConkie, "Only an Elder," *Ensign,* June 1975, 66).

18. Who does the Church sustain today as a prophet, seer, and revelator? How can you show the Lord that you sustain his prophet?

19. *consolation*—comfort

COURTESY CHURCH ARCHIVES, THE CHURCH OF JESUS CHRIST OF LATTER-DAY SAINTS

Orrin Porter Rockwell

THE ORGANIZATION OF THE CHURCH, BY ROBERT BARRETT

The Prophet Joseph and Oliver Cowdery in the Peter Whitmer Sr. home on the day of the organization of the Church of Jesus Christ

Martin Harris and Orrin Porter Rockwell"[20] (*History of the Church,* 1:79).

THE LORD EXPLAINS THE DUTIES OF THE FIRST MEMBERS OF THE CHURCH

The first members of the Church were given counsel from the Lord through the Prophet Joseph Smith concerning their duties:

"Behold, I speak unto you, Oliver, a few words. Behold, thou art blessed, and art under no condemnation.[21] But beware of pride,[22] lest thou shouldst enter into temptation.

"Make known thy calling unto the church, and also before the world, and thy heart shall be opened to preach the truth from henceforth and forever. Amen.

---

20. Orrin Porter Rockwell (1813–1878) was born in Belcher, Massachusetts, on June 28, 1813. A close friend of the Prophet Joseph Smith, Porter Rockwell was baptized in 1830, shortly after the organization of the Church. Hated by enemies of the Church, he was charged with many crimes, including trying to kill ex-Governor Lilburn W. Boggs in 1842. Unable to convict him, the state of Missouri finally released him on December 13, 1843. A colorful personality, Porter Rockwell played an important role in the Mormon exodus to the Salt Lake Valley. He died June 9, 1878, in Salt Lake City.

21. *condemnation*—blame or guilt

22. Elder Dallin H. Oaks said, "Preoccupied with self, the pride of self-satisfaction is always accompanied by an aloofness [distance] and a withdrawal from concern for others." Elder Oaks wrote further: "The pride of self-satisfaction is probably the kind of pride that prominent members were warned against in the early revelations of this dispensation" (Dallin H. Oaks, *Pure in Heart,* 92–93).

"Behold, I manifest unto you, Joseph Knight,[23] by these words, that you must take up your cross,[24] in the which you must pray vocally[25] before the world as well as in secret, and in your family, and among your friends, and in all places.[26]

"And, behold, it is your duty to unite with the true church, and give your language to exhortation[27] continually, that you may receive the reward of the laborer. Amen" (D&C 23:1–2, 6–7).

CHAPTER 20:
THE MINISTRY IN COLESVILLE

Joseph Knight Sr.'s family lived in Colesville, New York. Colesville is located thirty miles north of Joseph Smith's home in Harmony, Pennsylvania. Joseph Knight Sr. and his sons Joseph Jr. and Newel were friends to Joseph Smith. As you read this chapter, notice how important the Knight family was to the Prophet and the growth of the young Church.

THE PROPHET TRAVELS TO COLESVILLE

After the organization of the Church, Joseph Smith went to visit Joseph Knight, of Colesville, New York. Joseph Knight Sr. had been particularly kind and helpful to the Prophet during the translation of the Book of Mormon. "Mr. Knight and his family were Universalists,"[28] Joseph wrote, "but were willing to reason with me upon my religious views, and were, as usual, friendly and hospitable.[29] We held several meetings in the neighborhood; we had many friends, and some enemies. Our meetings were well attended, and many began to pray fervently to Almighty God, that He would give them wisdom to understand the truth" (*History of the Church,* 1:81).[30]

REMARKABLE EXPERIENCE OF NEWEL KNIGHT: THE FIRST MIRACLE IN THE CHURCH

"Amongst those who attended our meetings regularly," Joseph recalled, "was Newel Knight, son of Joseph Knight. He and I had many serious conversations on the important subject of man's eternal

---

23. Joseph Knight Sr. of Colesville, New York, was one of the first to believe in Joseph Smith's account of the First Vision. He helped the Prophet with money and food during the translation of the Book of Mormon. He remained faithful to the Church until he died in 1847 while traveling to the Salt Lake Valley (see Susan Easton Black, *Who's Who in the Doctrine and Covenants,* 166–68).

24. The phrase "take up your cross" is defined in the Joseph Smith Translation of the Bible: "And now for a man to take up his cross, is to deny himself all ungodliness, and every worldly lust, and keep my commandments" (JST Matthew 16:26).

25. *vocally*—out loud

26. Why do you think it is important to pray vocally in public as well as in private?

27. *exhortation*—preaching or teaching

NOTES FOR CHAPTER 20

28. Universalism is "the doctrine or belief that all men will be saved or made happy in a future life" (Noah Webster, *An American Dictionary of the English Language,* 1828.)

29. *hospitable*—kind

30. How did the people listening to the Prophet Joseph come to know the truth? What must you do to gain a testimony of the truth today?

PHOTOGRAPH BY KENNETH MAYS

The first branch of the Church met at the Joseph Knight Sr. farm

salvation.[31] We had got into the habit of praying much at our meetings, and Newel had said that he would try and take up his cross, and pray vocally during meeting; but when we again met together, he rather excused himself. I tried to prevail upon him, making use of the figure, supposing that he should get into a mud-hole,[32] would he not try to help himself out? And I further said that we were willing now to help him out of the mud-hole. He replied, that provided he had got into a mud-hole through carelessness, he would rather wait and get out himself, than to have others help him; and so he would wait until he could get into the woods by himself, and there he would pray. Accordingly, he deferred[33] praying until next morning, when he retired[34] into the woods; where, according to his own account afterwards, he made several attempts to pray, but could scarcely do so, feeling that he had not done his duty, in refusing to pray in the presence of others. He began to feel uneasy, and continued to feel worse both in mind and body, until, upon reaching his own house, his appearance was such as to alarm his wife very much. He requested her to go and bring me to him. I went and found him suffering very much in his mind, and his body acted upon in a very strange manner; his visage[35] and limbs distorted and twisted in every shape and appearance possible to imagine; and finally he was caught up off the floor of the apartment, and tossed about most fearfully.[36]

"His situation was soon made known to his neighbors, and relatives and in a short time as many as eight or nine grown persons had got together to witness the scene. After he had thus suffered for a time, I succeeded in getting hold of him by the hand, when almost immediately he spoke to me, and with great earnestness requested me to cast the devil out of him,[37] saying that he knew he was in him, and that he also knew that I could cast him out.

"I replied, 'If you know that I can, it shall be done,' and then almost unconsciously[38] I rebuked the devil, and commanded him in the name of Jesus Christ to depart from him; when immediately Newel spoke out and said that he saw the devil leave him and vanish from his sight. This was the first miracle which was done in the Church, or by any member of it; and it was done, not by man, nor by the power of man, but it was done by God, and by the power of godliness. . . .

---

31. Elder Bruce R. McConkie taught: "True devotion consists in a man loving and worshiping Deity with all his heart, and with all his might, mind, and strength. It presupposes that he will keep the commandments, walk uprightly, serve in the Church with an eye single to the glory of God, and put first in his life the things of God's kingdom. True devotion to the end gives an absolute guarantee of eternal salvation" (*Mormon Doctrine*, 109).

32. The phrase "mud-hole" describes placing one's self in trouble that one may need help getting out of.

33. *deferred*—put off; delayed

34. *retired*—went

35. *visage*—appearance or features

36. We should not fear the power of Satan if we are keeping the commandments. The Prophet Joseph Smith taught, "All beings who have bodies have power over those who have not. The devil has no power over us only as we permit him. The moment we revolt at anything which comes from God, the devil takes power" (*Teachings of the Prophet Joseph Smith*, 181).

37. In 1837 Elder Heber C. Kimball and others were called to Great Britain to preach the gospel. Shortly after arriving there, for an hour and a half, they had an awful demonstration of Satan's power. "President Heber C. Kimball, in writing about it afterward, said: 'I cannot even now look back upon the scene without feelings of horror, yet by it I learned the power of the adversary; his enmity against the servants of God, and got some understanding of the invisible world'" (cited by Elder Harold B. Lee, in Conference Report, April, 1960, 107).

When he returned home, Heber C. Kimball asked the Prophet Joseph what was the matter with them that they had to be subjected to such an experience. The Prophet surprised them when he said: "'When I heard of it [your experience] it gave me joy, for I then knew that the work had taken root in that land [of England.]' Joseph then related some of his own experience . . . he had had with the evil one, and said: 'The nearer a person approaches the Lord, a greater power will be manifested by the adversary to prevent the accomplishment of his purposes'" (*Life of Heber C. Kimball*, 1888 ed., 132).

38. *unconsciously*—without thinking

"This scene was now entirely changed, for as soon as the devil had departed from our friend, his countenance[39] became natural, his distortions of body ceased, and almost immediately the Spirit of the Lord descended upon him, and the visions of eternity were opened to his view. So soon as consciousness returned, his bodily weakness was such that we were obliged[40] to lay him upon his bed, and wait upon him for some time. He afterwards related his experience as follows:

"'I now began to feel a most pleasing sensation resting on me, and immediately the visions of heaven were opened to my view. I felt myself attracted upward, and remained for some time enwrapt in contemplation,[41] insomuch that I knew not what was going on in the room. By and by, I felt some weight pressing upon my shoulder and the side of my head, which served to recall me to a sense of[42] my situation, and I found that the Spirit of the Lord had actually caught me up off the floor, and that my shoulder and head were pressing against the [ceiling] beams.'

"All this was witnessed by many, to their great astonishment and satisfaction, when they saw the devil thus cast out, and the power of God, and His Holy Spirit thus made manifest. As may be expected, such a scene as this contributed much to make believers of those who witnessed it, and finally the greater part of them became members of the Church.[43] . . .

"During the last week in May, the above-mentioned Newel Knight came to visit us at Fayette, and was baptized by David Whitmer" (*History of the Church,* 1:82–84).

EFFORTS TO BAPTIZE IN COLESVILLE ARE DELAYED

A few weeks later the Prophet, his wife, Emma, and others returned to Colesville. Joseph recorded, "We found a number in the neighborhood still believing, and now anxious to be baptized. We appointed a meeting for the Sabbath, and on the afternoon of Saturday we erected[44] a dam across a stream of water, which was convenient, for the purpose of there attending to the ordinance of baptism; but during the night a mob collected and tore down our dam, which hindered[45] us from attending to the baptism on the Sabbath. We afterward found out that this mob had been instigated[46] to this act of molestation[47] by certain sectarian priests[48] of the neighborhood, who began to consider their craft[49] in danger, and took this plan to stop the progress of the truth. . . . The Sabbath arrived, and we held our meeting. Oliver Cowdery preached, and others of us bore testimony to the truth of the Book of Mormon, the doctrine of repentance, baptism for the remission of sins, and laying on of hands for the gift of the Holy Ghost, etc.[50] Amongst our audience were those who had torn down our dam, and who seemed desirous to give us trouble, but did not until after the meeting was dismissed, when they immediately commenced talking to those whom they considered our friends, and tried to turn them against us and our doctrines" (*History of the Church,* 1:86–87).

BAPTISMS AND TRIALS IN COLESVILLE

"Early on Monday morning," Joseph continued, "we were on the alert, and before our enemies were

---

39. *countenance*—appearance

40. *obliged*—required

41. *enwrapt in contemplation*—completely lost in deep thinking

42. *served to recall me to a sense of*—helped me to recognize

43. Though miracles can bring baptisms, they do not always lead to true, long-lasting conversion (see D&C 63:7–9).

44. *erected*—built

45. *hindered*—delayed

46. *instigated*—encouraged

47. *molestation*—disturbance

48. *sectarian priests*—religious leaders

49. *craft*—occupation

50. Joseph Smith listed the first four principles and ordinances of the gospel (Articles of Faith 1:4).

The baptism of Joseph Smith Sr.

aware of our proceedings, we had repaired the dam, and the following thirteen persons baptized, by Oliver Cowdery; viz.,[51] Emma Smith, Hezekiah Peck and wife, Joseph Knight, Sen., and wife, William Stringham and wife, Joseph Knight, Jun., Aaron Culver and wife, Levi Hale, Polly Knight, and Julia Stringham.

"Before the baptizing was entirely finished, the mob began again to collect, and shortly after we had retired, they amounted to about fifty men. They surrounded the house of Mr. Knight—whither we had retired—raging with anger, and apparently determined to commit violence upon us. Some asked us questions, others threatened us, so that we thought it wisdom to leave and go to the house of Newel Knight. There also they followed us, and it was only by the exercise of great prudence[52] on our part, and reliance in our heavenly Father, that they were kept from laying violent hands upon us; and so long as they chose to stay, we were obliged to answer them various unprofitable questions, and bear with insults and threatenings without number. . . .

"I was visited by a constable,[53] and arrested by him on a warrant, on the charge of being a disorderly person, of setting the country in an uproar by preaching the Book of Mormon, etc. The constable informed me, soon after I had been arrested, that the plan of those who had got out the warrant was to get me into the hands of the mob, who were now lying in ambush for me; but that he was determined to save me from them, as he had found me to be a different sort of person from what I had been represented to him. I soon found that he had told me the truth in this matter, for not far from Mr. Knight's house, the wagon in which we had set out was surrounded by a mob, who seemed only to await some signal from the constable; but to their great disappointment, he gave the horse the whip, and drove me out of their reach" (*History of the Church,* 1:88–87).

THE TRIAL AND RELEASE OF THE PROPHET JOSEPH

Although Joseph escaped the mob that night, a trial was still scheduled and Joseph, it seemed, would be tried. He wrote, "At length the trial commenced amidst a multitude of spectators, who in general evinced[54] a belief that I was guilty of all that had been reported concerning me, and of course were very zealous that I should be punished according to my crimes. Among many witnesses called up against me, was Mr. Josiah Stoal—of whom I have made mention as having worked for him some time" (*History of the Church,* 1:89).

Josiah Stoal's daughters were also called to testify against the Prophet. Finding no evidence upon which to convict the Prophet, the court found him innocent. However, no sooner was he set free than another constable arrested the Prophet on a second false charge.

The Prophet stated: "He took me to a tavern,[55] and gathered in a number of men, who used every means to abuse, ridicule and insult me. They spit upon me, pointed their fingers at me, saying, 'Prophesy, prophesy!' and thus did they imitate those who crucified the Savior of mankind, not knowing what they did" (*History of the Church,* 1:91).

A second trial was held, and the Prophet was again set free. Joseph was allowed to return safely to his wife, Emma. Of that experience he said, "But through the instrumentality[56] of my new friend the constable, I was enabled to escape them and make my way in safety to my wife's sister's house, where I found my wife awaiting with much anxiety the issue of those ungodly proceedings, and in company with her I arrived next day in safety at my own house" (*History of the Church,* 1:96).

CHAPTER 21: EARLY CHURCH GROWTH

The Satan-inspired opposition experienced in the first weeks after the young church's organization

---

51.   *viz.*—namely

52.   *prudence*—caution

53.   *constable*—officer of the peace

54.   *evinced*—proved

55.   *tavern*—inn

56.   *instrumentality*—help

made it difficult for members, but did not stop the Church's growth. As the Lord declared to Joseph in an earlier revelation, "The works, and the designs, and the purposes of God cannot be frustrated. . . . Remember, remember that it is not the work of God that is frustrated, but the work of men" (D&C 3:1, 3). As you read the stories of these early days of the Restoration, notice how the Lord guides his Church, with revelations of heavenly truths and with instructions on how to escape their enemies.

JOSEPH IS COMMANDED TO BEGIN REVISING THE BIBLE

While the enemies of the Church continued to try and stop the work, Church members continued to share the gospel and worked to strengthen one another with greater efforts. "It was in the summer of the year 1830," Joseph Fielding Smith explained, "that the Lord called on Joseph Smith to commence[57] his correction of the Bible.[58] In June, the word of the Lord came to him that other scripture, in addition to the Book of Mormon was to be given. This was according to the promise made to Oliver Cowdery and Joseph Smith as given in Section 6:25–27, in April, 1829. In June, 1830, the Prophet commenced to translate the words of Moses which

were given to Moses when he was caught up into a high mountain where he talked with the Lord face to face. This vision of Moses, is one of the most remarkable revelations given in this dispensation. . . . It should be carefully studied because of its great importance and the remarkable information which it reveals" (*Church History and Modern Revelation,* 1:110).

THE VISION OF MOSES, A LOST REVELATION RESTORED

The Prophet Joseph continued to translate other portions of Moses' writings, which can be found in the Pearl of Great Price.[59] Joseph Fielding Smith taught that "some of the important knowledge imparted[60] in this revelation is as follows: The works of the Lord are without end. No man can behold all the works of the Father without partaking of his glory, and that cannot be given in mortal life. Moses was created in the similitude, or likeness, of the Only Begotten Son. The generations of men passed before his view and he saw from the beginning to the end—all through the spiritual eye,[61] for the natural eye cannot behold the glory of the Lord. After this vision had passed, Moses was left unto himself and it was several hours before he gained his

---

NOTES FOR CHAPTER 21

57. 📖 *commence*—begin

58. 🔍 Joseph Smith's revision or correction of the Bible is called the Joseph Smith Translation. It is "a revision or translation of the King James Version of the Bible begun by the Prophet Joseph Smith in June of 1830. He was divinely commissioned to make the translation and regarded it as 'a branch of his calling' as a prophet. Although the major portion of the work was completed by July of 1833, he continued to make modifications while preparing a manuscript for the press until his death in 1844. . . .

"The translation process was a learning experience for the Prophet, and several sections of the Doctrine and Covenants (and also other revelations that are not published in the Doctrine and Covenants) were received in direct consequence of the work (i.e., D&C 76; 77;

91)" (*LDS Bible Dictionary*, s.v. "Joseph Smith Translation," 717).

59. 📜 The Pearl of Great Price is a volume of scripture and is one of the four standard works of the Church. It is a "selection of choice materials touching many significant aspects of the faith and doctrine of The Church of Jesus Christ of Latter-day Saints" (Pearl of Great Price, introductory note). Its contents include portions of the Book of Moses and the Book of Abraham, Joseph Smith—Matthew, Joseph Smith—History, and the Articles of Faith.

60. 📖 *imparted*—given

61. 📜 In this vision Moses was given the power to see as God sees, for with God, "all things . . . are manifest past, present, and future, and are continually before the Lord" (D&C 130:7; see also D&C 38:2 and Moses 1:6).

THE BURNING BUSH, BY JERRY THOMPSON © INTELLECTUAL RESERVE, INC.

The burning bush was "a bush in which the Lord appeared to Moses when he gave him
his commission to bring Israel out of Egypt (Ex. 2:2–4)" (Bible Dictionary, s.v. "Burning Bush")

natural strength.[62] Then Satan came, tempting him and commanding him to worship him, but Moses said: 'Who art thou? For behold, I am a son of God, in the similitude[63] of his Only Begotten Son; and where is thy glory, that I should worship thee? For behold, I could not look upon God, except his glory should come upon me, and I were strengthened[64] before him. But I can look upon thee in the natural man.' Moreover, Moses said: 'I will not cease to call upon God, I have other things to inquire[65] of him; for his glory has been upon me, wherefore I can judge between him and thee. Depart hence, Satan.' When Moses had said this Satan cried with a loud voice saying he was the Only Begotten. Then Moses feared exceedingly but did not cease to call upon the Lord and there was opened to his vision the bitterness of hell, and in the strength of his power [and in the name of the Only Begotten] Moses again

62.   Notice the similarities of Moses' experience to others who have also experienced how physically exhausting it is to receive revelations from God (for example, Lehi in 1 Nephi 1:7 and Joseph Smith in Joseph Smith—History 1:20). What does this teach you about the work involved in being a prophet? What kind of effort and sincerity do you think is needed in order to receive answers to our personal prayers?

63.   *similitude*—likeness or resemblance

64.   The strengthening that must occur for a mortal to see God is called transfiguration. God is so powerful that if a mortal is not changed by the power of the Holy Ghost, he would melt down in God's presence (see Bruce R. McConkie, *Mormon Doctrine*, 803).

65.   *inquire*—ask

"BE PATIENT IN AFFLICTIONS FOR THOU SHALT HAVE MANY"

"The Lord continued to pour out knowledge upon them," wrote Joseph Fielding Smith, "here a little, and there a little, as they were able to receive it. Early in July (1830) another revelation was given to Joseph Smith and Oliver Cowdery, in Harmony, Pennsylvania. They were commanded to return to the Saints in Colesville, Manchester and Fayette, and the members would support them. They should expound[81] the scriptures and devote their time exclusively to the cause of Zion, and if the members should not support them in these labors, then would the Lord withdraw his blessings. 'Be patient in afflictions,'[82] said the Lord, 'for thou shalt have many: but endure them, for lo, I am with thee, even unto the end of thy days.' The afflictions surely came, for Joseph Smith was called on to suffer, as few men have had to suffer. . . .

"Oliver Cowdery was also commanded to continue in the ministry and not suppose that he could say enough in the cause, and if he would be faithful the Lord would open his mouth and he should have strength such as is not known among men. This promise was fulfilled, for the Lord blessed Oliver in preaching to that extent that those who heard him were caused to quake and tremble.[83] Power was given to these men to bless or curse; those who received them they were to bless, and from those who rejected them they were to withhold their blessing and to wash their feet against them as a testimony. Should any lay violent hands upon them, they should command them to be smitten, and the Lord would smite them in his own due time. They were to take neither purse nor scrip,[84] neither two coats, as they went forth to prune the vineyard, with a mighty pruning, 'even for the last time'" (Joseph Fielding Smith, *Essentials in Church History*, 90–91).

AN ANGEL INSTRUCTS JOSEPH ON THE SACRAMENT

In August 1830, Newel Knight and his wife came to Harmony to visit Joseph and Emma. Neither Emma nor Newel Knight's wife had been confirmed members of the Church. Joseph decided they would be confirmed that day. The four of them, along with John Whitmer, held a meeting at the time and wanted to partake of the sacrament in that meeting. As Joseph was leaving to purchase wine for the sacrament, he was met by an angel who gave him the revelation in Doctrine and Covenants section 27.

81.　*expound*—explain

82.　*afflictions*—trials and suffering

83.　President Wilford Woodruff testified of Oliver's receiving great power with these words: "I have seen Oliver Cowdery when it seemed as though the earth trembled under his feet. I never heard a man bear a stronger testimony than he did when under the influence of the Spirit. But the moment he left the kingdom of God, that moment his power fell like lightning from heaven. He was shorn of his strength, like Samson in the lap of Delilah. He lost the power and testimony which he had enjoyed, and he never recovered it again in its fulness while in the flesh, although he died in the church. It does not pay a man to sin or to do wrong" (address given March 3, 1889, in Brian H. Stuy, ed., *Collected Discourses*, 1:220).

84.　*purse nor scrip*—suitcases nor money

A sacrament goblet used in the Nauvoo Temple

PHOTOGRAPH BY KENNETH MAYS

"For, behold, I say unto you, that it mattereth not what ye shall eat or what ye shall drink when ye partake of the sacrament, if it so be that ye do it with an eye single to my glory—remembering unto the Father my body which was laid down for you, and my blood which was shed for the remission of your sins.[85]

"Wherefore, a commandment I give unto you, that you shall not purchase wine neither strong drink of your enemies;

"Wherefore, you shall partake of none except it is made new among you; yea, in this my Father's kingdom which shall be built up on the earth" (vv. 2–4).

Joseph Fielding Smith explained that the knowledge that it matters not what we eat or drink, if we partake of the sacrament in the Spirit of the Lord and by divine authority, is the foundation for the present practice in the Church of using water instead of wine, for so the Lord has commanded.

"In September the Lord added to this revelation stating that the time would come when he would 'drink of the fruit of the vine' on the earth with the ancient prophets and apostles, from Michael, or Adam, the 'ancient of days,' down to our own day, including all the faithful whom the Father has given him out of the world.

"In obedience to the above commandment, they prepared wine of their own making and partook of the sacrament, confirming the two sisters as members of the Church" (*Essentials in Church History*, 93).

JOSEPH IS TAUGHT THE DOCTRINE OF THE GATHERING

Joseph continued to receive many important revelations about the Church and the things the Lord would have him do. One of those was the doctrine of the gathering, which is found in Doctrine and Covenants section 29. Joseph Fielding Smith explained, "Again the heavens were opened and the Lord made known many of his purposes and decrees[86] which were for these latter days. A

revelation . . . was given shortly before the second conference of the Church, containing instruction which was helpful for the guidance of the elders at that conference. They were taught the doctrine of the gathering of the Saints. The decree had gone forth from the mansions of the Father, that the Saints should be gathered into one place, for they were chosen out of the world, and they were to prepare their hearts against the day when tribulation and desolation[87] would be sent forth upon the wicked. The hour is nigh, the Lord declared, when the earth should be ripe for destruction, for wickedness shall cease" (*Essentials in Church History*, 94–95).

CHAPTER 22: THE MISSIONS OF SAMUEL SMITH AND JOSEPH SMITH SR.

Samuel Smith, the Prophet Joseph's younger brother, was called to missionary service shortly after the Church was organized. He made several trips in the summer of 1830 through western New York State to share the gospel by selling copies of the newly published Book of Mormon. Most people rejected him and his message but he planted some seeds that would eventually produce a harvest of some of the most important converts for the young Church, including Brigham Young and Heber C. Kimball. Joseph Smith Sr. also took the message of the Restoration to his parents, Asael Smith and Mary Duty Smith. Notice how the Lord carefully guided these events so the gospel message reached those souls who would become powerful leaders in his kingdom.

SAMUEL SMITH BEGINS HIS MISSION

Shortly after the Church was organized on April 6, 1830, all of Joseph Smith's brothers, even fourteen-year-old Don Carlos, were ordained to be missionaries. Lucy Mack Smith recorded that "Samuel was directed to take a number of the Books

---

85. The Lord reminds us to "always remember him" in the words of the sacrament prayers (see D&C 20:77, 79). How have the emblems of the bread and water helped remind you of the Savior? Why is partaking of

the sacrament an important part of your weekly worship?

86. *decrees*—orders or commandments

87. *tribulation and desolation*—trials and destruction

Samuel Smith was the first official missionary in the latter-days

of Mormon, and go on a mission to Livonia, to preach, and make sale of the books, if possible. . . .

"On the thirtieth of June, Samuel started on the mission to which he had been set apart by Joseph, and in traveling twenty-five miles, which was his first day's journey, he stopped at a number of places in order to sell his books, but was turned out of doors as soon as he declared his principles.[88] When evening came on, he was faint and almost discouraged, but coming to an inn, which was surrounded with every appearance of plenty, he called to see if the landlord would buy one of his books. On going in, Samuel enquired of him, if he did not wish to purchase a history of the origin of the Indians.

"'I do not know,' replied the host; 'how did you get hold of it?'

"'It was translated,' rejoined Samuel, 'by my brother, from some gold plates that he found buried in the earth.'

"'You liar!' cried the landlord, 'get out of my house—you shan't stay one minute with your books.'

"Samuel was sick at heart, for this was the fifth time he had been turned out of doors that day. He left the house, and traveled a short distance, and washed his feet in a small brook, as a testimony against the man.[89] He then proceeded five miles further on his journey, and seeing an apple tree a short distance from the road, he concluded to pass the night under it; and here he lay all night upon the cold, damp ground. In the morning, he arose from his comfortless bed, and observing a small cottage

at no great distance, he drew near, hoping to get a little refreshment. The only inmate[90] was a widow, who seemed very poor. He asked her for food, relating the story of his former treatment. She prepared him victuals,[91] and, after eating, he explained to her the history of the Book of Mormon. She listened attentively, and believed all that he told her, but, in consequence of her poverty, she was unable to purchase one of the books. He presented her with one, and proceeded to Bloomington, which was eight miles further. Here he stopped at the house of John P. Greene,[92] who was a Methodist preacher, and was at that time about starting on a preaching mission. He, like the others, did not wish to make a purchase of what he considered at that time to be a nonsensical fable,[93] however, he said that he would take a subscription paper,[94] and, if he found anyone on his route who was disposed[95] to purchase, he would take his name, and in two weeks, Samuel might call again, and he would let him know what the prospect[96] was of selling. After making this arrangement, Samuel left one of his books with him, and returned home. At the time appointed, Samuel started again for the Rev. John P. Greene's, in order to learn the success which this gentleman had met with in finding sale for the Book of Mormon. This time, Mr. Smith, and myself accompanied him, and it was our intention to have passed near the tavern, where Samuel was so abusively treated a fortnight previous,[97] but just before we came to the house, a sign of small-pox[98] intercepted[99] us. We turned aside,

---

NOTES FOR CHAPTER 22

88. *declared his principles*—explained his purpose

89. The act of cleansing his feet, which Samuel did as a testimony against the innkeeper, is mentioned in scripture (see Matthew 10:11–15 and D&C 24:15–16). Joseph Fielding Smith clarified the appropriateness of this act, saying, "While the Lord has instructed the elders who go forth, just as he instructed Oliver Cowdery, to cleanse their feet, or wash them, as a witness against those who persecute them or in bitterness reject their message, yet the performance of such a responsibility should not be done unless the Spirit of the Lord indicates that it should be done" (*Church History and Modern Revelation*, 1:115).

90. *inmate*—person living there

91. *victuals*—food

92. John P. Greene was born in Herkimer County, New York, in 1793. His wife, Rhoda Young, was Brigham Young's sister.

93. *nonsensical fable*—foolish story

94. A subscription paper is a paper used to write down the names of those John found who would be interested in buying a book.

95. *disposed*—willing

96. *prospect*—chance

97. *abusively treated a fortnight previous*—badly treated 14 days ago

98. Before modern medicine found a cure, smallpox was a disease that spread quickly and was often fatal.

99. *intercepted*—stopped

Emma Smith helped compile the hymns for a hymnal published for the first time in 1835

many insults and threats" (Joseph Fielding Smith, *Church History and Modern Revelation,* 1:107–8).

EMMA HELPS COMPILE THE FIRST HYMN BOOK

Once Emma was baptized and confirmed[148] she, like all who receive the Holy Ghost, was entitled to inspiration and revelation from the Spirit. Emma was blessed with specific and personal revelation that is now found in Doctrine and Covenants section 25. Joseph Fielding Smith wrote that "the Lord gave a revelation to Emma Smith . . . in which she was commanded not to murmur[149] because of the things which she had not seen [see D&C 25:4]. As many other wives have thought, she could not understand why her husband should withhold from her a view of sacred things.[150] The Lord assured her that it was for a wise purpose, in him, that these things were withheld, except from the few who were called to be witnesses to the world. . . . She was also chosen to make a selection of sacred hymns for the Church, 'for,' said the Lord, 'my soul delighteth in the song of the heart, yea, the song of the righteous is a prayer unto me, and it shall be answered with a blessing upon their heads' [D&C 25:12].[151] If she would continue in meekness, and beware of pride, and keep the commandments of the Lord, she should receive a crown of righteousness; except she did this, where the Lord was she should not come, which truth applied to all [see D&C 25:14–16]" (*Essentials in Church History,* 91).

Joseph Fielding Smith also wrote: "Evidently she had talent for this work. That talent is shown in the selection which was made. With the help of Elder William W. Phelps she went to work, and a selection of hymns was made, but it was not published until 1835. Wisdom and discretion are shown in this collection of hymns. The title page of this book is as follows: 'A Collection of Sacred Hymns for the Church of the Latter-day Saints. Selected by Emma Smith, Kirtland, Ohio. Printed by F. G. Williams & Co., 1835.' In this collection are found, because of lack of Latter-day Saint composers many sectarian hymns, but it also contains a goodly number of hymns by William W. Phelps, Parley P. Pratt and Eliza R. Snow"[152] (*Church History and Modern Revelation,* 1:118n).

EMMA SUFFERED MUCH PERSECUTION AND HAD MANY TRIALS

The Lord commanded Emma, "lay aside the things of this world, and seek for the things of a better" (D&C 25:10).[153] Her sacrifice and willingness to give up the pleasures of this world to follow her husband were described by her mother-in-law, Lucy Mack Smith:

"I have never seen a woman in my life, who would endure every species of fatigue[154] and hardship, from month to month, and from year to year, with that unflinching courage, zeal,[155] and patience, which she has ever done; for I know that which she has had to endure—she has been tossed upon the

---

148. To read about the events of Emma's confirmation, see to chapter 21, "Early Church Growth."

149. **murmur**—complain

150. "It was difficult for [Emma] to understand why she could not view the plates, the Urim and Thummim, and other sacred things, which view had been given to special witnesses. At times this human thought caused her to murmur and ask the question of the prophet why she was denied this privilege" (Joseph Fielding Smith, *Church History and Modern Revelation,* 1:117).

151. The First Presidency taught: "Inspirational music is an essential part of our church meetings. The hymns invite the Spirit of the Lord, create a feeling of rever-

ence, unify us as members, and provide a way for us to offer praises to the Lord" ("First Presidency Preface," *Hymns of The Church of Jesus Christ of Latter-day Saints,* 1985, ix).

152. The Church's most recent hymnbook was published in 1985. How does the singing of hymns add to the power of our meetings? What is one of your favorite hymns? Why?

153. The scriptures contain many lists of God's expectations. Another list of God's expectations for women can be found in Proverbs 31:10–31.

154. **species of fatigue**—kind of exhaustion

155. **zeal**—enthusiasm

preachers, and some against, but I observed the Spirit that stimulated[210] those for, and those against. I met Squire[211] Waldo, who was a Campbellite who was bitterly opposed. He tried to have me take another road, and not go to Kirtland, but I told him I was of age, and the case was an important one, of life, and death, existing between me and my God, and I must act for myself, for no one can act for me. I rode about three miles further and met another man of the same order,[212] I had about the same kind of discourse[213] with him and passed on" (*John Murdock Journal,* BYU Special Collections, 5).

JOHN MURDOCK MEETS THE MISSIONARIES

John Murdock continued his story, saying: "[I] arrived at father Isaac Morley's[214] about dark, and was soon introduced to those four men from New York, and presented with the Book of Mormon; I now said within myself, I have items placed before me that will prove to me whether it be of God or not: four men professing to be servants of the most high God, authorized to preach the gospel, and practice the ordinances thereof, and build up the Church after the ancient order;[215] and having a book professing to have come forth by the power of God, containing the fullness of the gospel;[216] I said if it be so their walk[217] will agree with their profession, and

the Holy Ghost will attend their ministration[218] of the ordinances, and the Book of Mormon will contain the same plan of salvation as the Bible. I was sensible[219] that such a work must come forth, but the question with me was, are these men that are to commence the work. I did not ask a sign of them by working a miracle, by healing a sick man, by raising a dead man, or, by casting out a devil; only I desired to know whether the Spirit would attend their ministration if the Book of Mormon was not true, neither if they were not sent forth by God. Accordingly, that night was held the first confirmation meeting[220] that was held in Ohio. And I said within myself it is a good time for me. For thought I, this night must prove it to be true, or false; I did not find out respecting the meeting till about ten o'clock at night. And at that time they had all left but three men; and I found they wanted to go to the meeting, and did not want those in, that had not been baptized. I said to them go, for if you wish to be alone, I do not blame you. The case is one of importance. They went and I stayed alone, and read the Book of Mormon.

"During the evening previous to the meeting, a Nathan Goodwell, a Campbellite came and conversed with Elder Oliver Cowdery for he was the principal one of the four, and I watched the Spirit of each one of them in their conversation, and I found

210. **stimulated**—moved or inspired

211. Early in U.S. history, *squire* often referred to a lawyer, judge, or city official

212. **order**—church

213. **discourse**—discussion

214. Isaac Morley was an early convert to the Church. His farm was used as a gathering place for Church members. Isaac Morley moved with the Saints to Missouri, Illinois, and Utah. He died as a faithful

member (see Susan Easton Black, *Who's Who in the Doctrine and Covenants,* 198–200).

215. This "ancient order" refers to the New Testament church organized by Jesus Christ during his mortal ministry. Paul gave a description of this church in Ephesians 4:11–12.

216. The Lord himself testified that the Book of Mormon contains "the fulness of the gospel of Jesus Christ" (D&C 20:9).

217. **walk**—conduct or behavior

218. **ministration**—performing

219. **sensible**—aware

220. In the early days of the Church special meetings were held to confirm those who had been baptized as members of the Church and to perform the ordinance or the laying on of hands for the gift of the Holy Ghost (see D&C 20:41; 33:15). This is now generally done in our regular sacrament meetings.

Isaac Morley

that Goodwell bore down with warmth,[221] whereas Cowdery wished not for contention, and endeavored to evade[222] controversy" (*John Murdock Journal,* BYU Special Collections, 5–6).

JOHN MURDOCK GAINS A TESTIMONY AND IS BAPTIZED

"I read till it was late and went into Father Morley's chamber[223] to bed and had not been long in bed, before they returned, and some half dozen or more came into the same house, and as soon as they came into the house, although I was in bed up [in the] chamber, the spirit of the Lord rested on me, witnessing to me of the truth of the work.[224] I could no longer rest in bed but got up and went down and found Elder Rigdon among the number, and he said to me I might go back to bed, for he would not talk to me that night, but I sat in a chair and conversed with them, and I found they appeared very tender in their feelings and I retired to bed again. I could not help secretly rejoicing on the occasion. The next morning I conversed with about half a dozen men separately who had been confirmed in the meetinghouse the night before. I found their testimony agreed on the subject that there was a manifestation of the spirit attended the ministration of the ordinance of laying on hands, and I found the items placed before me, that I before noticed, all testified that it was of God.

"About ten o'clock that morning, being November 5th, 1830, I told the servants of the Lord that I was ready to walk with them into the water of baptism. Accordingly, Elder [Parley] P. Pratt baptized me in the Chagrin River and the spirit of the Lord sensibly[225] attended the ministration, and I came out of the water rejoicing and singing praises to God, and the Lamb.[226] An impression sensibly rested on my mind that cannot, by me, be forgotten. It appeared to me that notwithstanding all the profession of religion that I had previously made and all that I had done, that by my act of now being baptized I had just escaped a horrible pit of destruction. This was the third time I had been immersed, but I never before felt the authority of the ordinance, but I felt it this time and felt as though my sins were forgiven. I continued with the brethren till Sunday at which time they preached in Mayfield and baptized a number, and on Sunday evening they confirmed about thirty. I was one of the number. Elder Oliver Cowdery was administrator.[227] I was also ordained an elder; and it was truly a time of the outpouring of the spirit. . . .

---

221. *bore down with warmth*—spoke with anger

222. *endeavored to evade*—tried to stay away from

223. *chamber*—bedroom

224. Have you felt the witness of the Spirit that the Church and the Book of Mormon are true? If so, how did your experience compare with Brother Murdock's? If not, what do you think you can do to receive a witness as he did? (See Moroni 10:3–5).

225. *sensibly*—noticeably

226. Brigham Young said this about the happiness people experience when they come unto the Church: "Where is happiness, real happiness? Nowhere but in God. . . . Every Latter-day Saint, who has experienced the love of God in his heart, after having received the remission of his sins, through baptism, and the laying on of hands, realizes that he is filled with joy, and happiness, and consolation. He may be in pain, in error, in poverty, or in prison, if necessity demands, still, he is joyful. This is our experience, and each and every

Latter-day Saint can bear witness to it" (*Discourses of Brigham Young*, 236).

227. *administrator*—[the] person performing the ordinance

The Chagrin River as it passes through Kirtland, Ohio. This was the site of many baptisms in the early Church

PHOTOGRAPH BY KENNETH MAYS

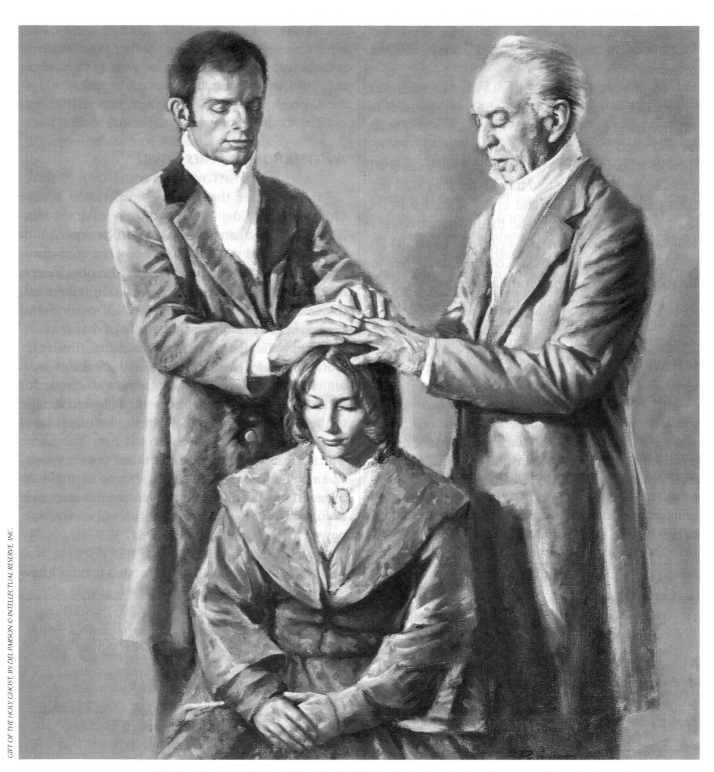

*The Lord promised James Covill and all faithful missionaries that they may give
the gift of the Holy Ghost to others by the laying on of hands*

his works and he knew him, and that at this particular time his heart was right and the Lord had placed great blessings upon him. He has seen great sorrow, and many times he had rejected the Lord because of his pride and the cares of the world [see D&C 39:7–9].

"He was promised that the day of his deliverance had come, if he would hearken unto the voice of the Lord [see D&C 39:10]. It seems from this commandment and promise that there had been times when Mr. Coville had received a desire to join the Church, but had weakened because of his pride and the love of the world. Now, however, he had come seeking the truth and the Lord informs him that is to him the day of deliverance from these worldly cares if he will now abide in the truth. The voice of the Spirit of the Lord had said to him on other occasions that he should rise and be baptized, and wash away his sins. This commandment was now renewed with the promise if he did so he would receive the Spirit as he had never had it before. 'If thou do this, I have prepared thee for a greater work,' the Lord said to him. He was to proclaim the Gospel in its fulness [see D&C 39:11]. . . . The power of the Lord would rest upon him and he would be given great faith, for the Lord would be with him and go before him.[20] He was called not to go to the 'eastern countries,' but to the Ohio, where the Lord had commanded his people to assemble, and where blessings had been kept in store such as had not been known among the children of men. And from thence[21] the blessings and the Gospel should go forth to all nations [see D&C 39:12–15]" (*Church History and Modern Revelation,* 1:158–59).

THE FALL OF JAMES COVILL

Joseph Fielding Smith continued, saying, "This man James Coville received a most wonderful revelation and blessing, provided he would turn to the Lord and in humility and faith seek to bring forth and establish Zion. 'And again,' the Lord said to him in conclusion, 'it shall come to pass, that on as many as ye shall baptize with water, ye shall lay your hands, and they shall receive the gift of the Holy Ghost, and shall be looking forth for the signs of my coming and shall know me. Behold, I come quickly. Even so. Amen.'

"We are led to believe that in this promised blessing, this foolish man was convinced of the truth, for it is clear that the Lord revealed to him things which he and the Lord alone knew to be the truth. However, when he withdrew from the influence of the Spirit of the Lord and had time to consider the fact that he would lose his place and position among his associates, he failed and rejected the promises and blessings which the Lord offered him.[22] In a revelation explaining why he failed the Lord said:

"'Behold, verily I say unto you, that the heart of my servant James Covill was right before me, for he covenanted with me that he would obey my word. And he received the word with gladness, but straightway[23] Satan tempted him; and the fear of persecution, and the cares of the world,[24] caused him to

---

20. The Lord promises his missionaries: "I will go before your face. I will be on your right hand and on your left, and my Spirit shall be in your hearts, and mine angels round about you, to bear you up" (D&C 84:88).

21. *thence*—that place

22. President Harold B. Lee taught, "The greatest responsibility that a member of Christ's church has ever had is to become truly converted—and it is just as important to stay converted" (*Stand Ye in Holy Places,* 91).

23. *straightway*—immediately

24. The "cares of the world" are anything that draws our love and affection away from God. The danger is that when you "let the cares of the world occupy your entire thoughts and attention," it leaves your "spiritual armor rusty and but little room found in [you] for the Holy Ghost to abide" (*Teachings of Lorenzo Snow,* 77).

Joseph Smith had a miraculous meeting with Newel K. Whitney in the Gilbert and Whitney store

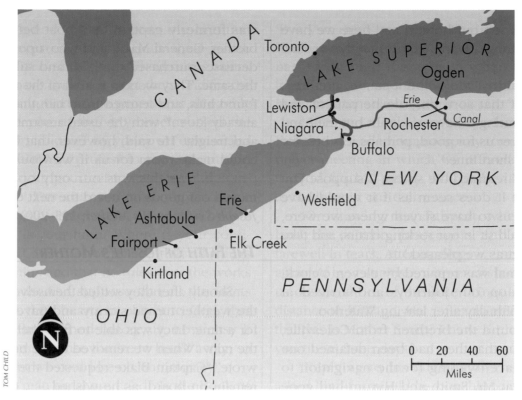

TOM CHILD

Many of the Saints traveled to Kirtland, Ohio, by way of the Erie Canal

came and bade us farewell, invoking[35] the blessing of heaven upon our heads. . . .

"Soon after this, we were pushed off and under fine headway.

"I then called the brethren and sisters together, and reminded them that we were traveling by the commandment of the Lord, as much as Father Lehi was, when he left Jerusalem;[36] and, if faithful, we had the same reasons to expect the blessings of God. I then desired them to be solemn,[37] and to lift their hearts to God continually in prayer, that we might be prospered. We then seated ourselves and sang a hymn. . . .

". . . The music sounded beautifully upon the water, . . . filling our souls with love and gratitude to God, for his manifold[38] goodness towards us. . . .

". . . On getting about half way to Buffalo, the canal broke.[39] This gave rise to much murmuring and discontentment,[40] which was expressed in terms like the following:

"'Well, the canal is broke now, and here we are, and here we are likely to be, for we can go no

---

35. 📖 *invoking*—praying

36. ☀️ The Lord commanded Lehi in a dream to take his family and depart into the wilderness, because the Jews sought to take away his life (see 1 Nephi 2:1–2).

37. 📖 *solemn*—serious or reverent

38. 📖 *manifold*—much

39. 🔍 A canal is a manmade waterway used for irrigation or water travel. Canals "broke" as silt or mud built up so high that barges were unable to pass (see Funk and Wagnalls *New Encyclopedia*, "Canal," 5:237).

40. 📖 *murmuring and discontentment*—complaining and unhappiness

Independence, Missouri, 1831

people, which are a remnant of Jacob, and those who are heirs according to the covenant.

"Wherefore, verily I say unto you, let my servants Joseph Smith, Jun., and Sidney Rigdon take their journey as soon as preparations can be made to leave their homes, and journey to the land of Missouri.

"And thus, even as I have said, if ye are faithful ye shall assemble[6] yourselves together to rejoice upon the land of Missouri, which is the land of your inheritance, which is now the land of your enemies.

"But, behold, I, the Lord, will hasten[7] the city in its time, and will crown the faithful with joy and with rejoicing" (vv. 1–3, 42–43).

The Mission to Missouri

And so, in the middle of June, the elders who were called of God began their missions to the west, traveling two by two. Among those who went were Thomas B. Marsh and his companion, Selah J. Griffin,[8] who went in the place of Ezra Thayre. Joseph Smith, Sidney Rigdon, Martin Harris, Edward Partridge, William W. Phelps, Joseph Coe, and Algernon Sidney Gilbert also embarked, leaving on June 19, 1831. The missionaries left with feelings of great anticipation,[9] knowing their destination was Zion, the "land of their inheritance."

Instructions for their travel had been revealed and included items such as "Preaching the word by

---

6. *assemble*—gather

7. *hasten*—prepare quickly

8. Selah J. Griffin was born March 17, 1799, in Redding, Connecticut. He lived in Morgan, Ohio, before moving to Kirtland, where he worked as a blacksmith and served the community as a supervisor

of highways. He was ordained an elder in the Church on June 6, 1831, by the Prophet Joseph. The next day he was called to serve as a missionary to Missouri accompanying Thomas B. Marsh (see Susan Easton Black, *Who's Who in the Doctrine and Covenants,* 109–13).

9. *anticipation*—hope

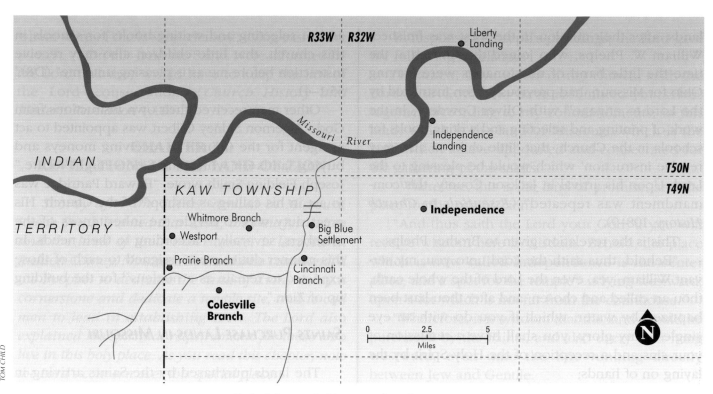

Early Saints settled in parts of southern Missouri

the way, saying none other things than that which the prophets and apostles have written," going "two by two," and remembering "in all things the poor and the needy, the sick and the afflicted" (see D&C 52:9–10, 40).[10]

THE LAND OF ZION

The elders began arriving in western Missouri in the middle of July. They were met with "tears of joy by their brethren there," wrote Joseph Fielding Smith. For there, "on the borders of the United States, had gathered renegades[11] from the east; lawless and vile[12] outcasts, who had been forced to flee to the west for safety. . . .

"The first Sabbath (July 17, 1831), the elders spent in Jackson County. William W. Phelps preached a public discourse. His congregation was composed of 'specimens[13] of all the families of the earth.' After this meeting two persons, who had previously believed, were baptized.

"A few days later the members of the Colesville branch,[14] from Thompson, Ohio, arrived in Missouri and were located on lands in Kaw township, where a portion of Kansas City is now built.

"The duty devolved[15] on the Prophet to assign the labors to the several elders who were to remain in the land. Some of them were called by revelation to make their permanent settlement in Missouri, while others were instructed to return to the eastern

10. Similar instructions are given to missionaries in our day. Do you know someone who has served or is serving a mission? What stories have you heard about missionaries that show they are following these "three instructions" from the Lord?

11. *renegades*—traitors or rebels

12. *vile*—wicked

13. *specimens*—samples

14. "The Church at Thompson," said John Whitmer, "made all possible haste to leave for Missouri, and left, and none of their enemies harmed them" (John Whitmer's *History of the Church,* chapter 8). Newel Knight was appointed the leader of this company, which was made up of the Colesville branch, and under his leadership they made the entire journey from Thompson to Missouri.

15. *devolved*—fell

will that my saints should be assembled upon the land of Zion; . . .

"Behold, I, the Lord, will give unto my servant Joseph Smith, Jun., power that he shall be enabled to discern by the Spirit those who shall go up unto the land of Zion, and those of my disciples who shall tarry"[87] (vv. 24, 36, 41).

Joseph Fielding Smith explained, "The reason for this advice is apparent, for haste would lead to confusion, unsatisfactory conditions and pestilence, and then, also, it creates consternation[88] and fear in the hearts of their enemies and arouses greater opposition. Satan desired to destroy them and in his anger endeavored[89] to stir them up to strife[90] and contention as well as the older settlers in Missouri" (*Church History and Modern Revelation*, 2:6).

MOVING TO ZION REQUIRES PURCHASING LAND

In section 63, we also learn that the land in Zion was to be purchased, that the Saints were warned not to create antagonism,[91] and that the land should not be obtained by shedding blood:

"Wherefore, I the Lord will that you should purchase the lands, that you may have advantage of the world, that you may have claim on the world, that they may not be stirred up unto anger"[92] (v. 27).

"And let all the moneys which can be spared, it mattereth not unto me whether it be little or much, be sent up unto the land of Zion, unto them whom I have appointed to receive"[93] (v. 40).

THE MAKING OF A ZION PEOPLE

In addition to instructions on the physical purchase of the land for Zion, the Lord taught the Saints how to become a Zion people. Joseph Fielding Smith explained, "The Lord has given instruction repeatedly that all who go to Zion shall obey His law—the celestial law on which Zion was to be built. Those who were weak in the faith, or indifferent to[94] the commandments, were warned that they would not be made welcome in that land unless they repented. . . . The Lord endeavored to impress upon the minds of the Saints that all who inherit Zion must keep his commandments. Great promises are made to those who will be obedient. The mysteries of the kingdom[95] are to be theirs . . . Why is it that so many members of the Church—in fact all of us to some extent—are so short-sighted that we fail to comprehend[96] these things?" (*Church History and Modern Revelation*, 2:3, 6).

In many revelations the Lord explains ways the Saints can become righteous, pure, and a Zion people:

Develop "faith" and do the will of the Lord
    (D&C 63:20)
Share the gospel with "the inhabitants[97] of the earth"
    (D&C 63:37)
"Forgive one another" (D&C 64:9)
Pay "tithing" (D&C 64:23)
Do not "get in debt" (D&C 64:27)
"Be not weary in well-doing" (D&C 64:33)

---

87. The Lord explained that the prophet has special gifts. "Unto such as God shall appoint and ordain to watch over the church and to be elders unto the church, are to have it given unto them to discern all those gifts. . . . That unto some it may be given to have all those gifts, that there may be a head, in order that every member may be profited thereby" (D&C 46:27, 29).

88. *consternation*—worry

89. *endeavored*—tried

90. *strife*—arguing and bitter feelings

91. *antagonism*—hard feelings

92. As members of the Church we believe in honoring and obeying the laws of the land (see Articles of Faith 1:12). The "advantage" and "claim on the world"

spoken of here may refer to the fact that if the Saints buy the property, others cannot legally take it away.

93. Even small amounts of money can help build the kingdom of God (see Mark 12:42–44). How can the money we give help build the Church today? What are some donations you have made to help build up the Church?

94. *indifferent to*—did not care about

95. "The mysteries of the kingdom, [are] things that are 'only to be seen and understood by the power of the Holy Spirit'" (Bruce R. McConkie, *The Mortal Messiah*, 1:409).

96. *comprehend*—understand

97. *inhabitants*—people

Charity is a quality of a Zion people

THE FIRST SAINTS IN THE LAND OF ZION WERE THE MISSIONARIES AND THEIR NEW CONVERTS

As you learned in chapter 25, several brethren, including Parley P. Pratt, Oliver Cowdery, and Peter Whitmer, were among the first Saints to arrive in Missouri. These brethren had been called to serve a mission to the Lamanites and started out on their journey in the middle of a bitter-cold winter. "After much fatigue[109] and some suffering," wrote Parley P. Pratt, "we all arrived in Independence, in the county of Jackson, on the extreme western frontiers of Missouri, and of the United States"[110] (*Autobiography of Parley P. Pratt,* 40).

The missionaries' gospel message—particularly that of the Book of Mormon—was well received by a number of Lamanites the missionaries met. Parley P. Pratt wrote that "some began to rejoice exceedingly, and took great pains to tell the news to others, in their own language." The news quickly spread about the missionaries' arrival. "The excitement now reached the frontier settlements in Missouri," Parley wrote, "and stirred up the jealousy and envy of the Indian agents and sectarian[111] missionaries to that degree that we were soon ordered out of the Indian country as disturbers of the peace; and even threatened with the military in case of non-compliance.[112] We accordingly departed from the Indian country, and came over the line, and commenced laboring in Jackson County, Missouri, among the whites. We were well received, and listened to by many; and some were baptized and added to the Church" (*Autobiography of Parley P. Pratt,* 44).

THE COLESVILLE BRANCH COMES TO ZION

Parley P. Pratt and the others labored for a time in Missouri. Brother Pratt eventually returned to Kirtland to report on their missionary labors. It wasn't until after Joseph Smith went to Missouri and dedicated the site for the temple that Parley returned to the land of his first mission. Upon his return, he reported:

"On our arrival we found a considerable settlement of the brethren from Ohio, who had immigrated[113] during the summer and taken up their residence in Jackson County. President Smith, and many of the Elders, had been there and held a conference, and, having organized a Stake of Zion, pointed out and consecrated certain grounds for a city and temple, they had again returned to the East. With them, the brethren whom I had left there the previous winter, had also returned.

"I tarried[114] mostly with a branch of the Church commonly called the Colesville branch. . . . They consisted of about sixty souls, and were under the presidency of a faithful and zealous Elder by the name of Newel Knight.

"This Colesville branch was among the first organized by Joseph Smith, and constituted[115] the first settlers of the members of the Church in Missouri. They had arrived late in the summer, and cut some hay for their cattle, sowed a little grain, and prepared some ground for cultivation, and were engaged during the fall and winter in building log cabins, etc. The winter was cold, and for some time about ten families lived in one log cabin, which was open and unfinished, while the frozen ground served for a floor. Our food consisted of beef and a little bread made of corn, which had been grated into coarse meal[116] by rubbing the ears on a tin

---

109. *fatigue*—extreme tiredness

110. "In the fourth year of Independence's existence—during the early months of 1831—four men representing a new religious group appeared on the ungraded, ungraveled streets of the thriving frontier town. They were missionaries sent by Joseph Smith, prophet and president of the recently restored church of Christ, to preach the gospel and bring the message of the Book of Mormon to Indians beyond the frontier of America" (T. Edgar Lyon, "Independence, Missouri, and the

Mormons, 1827–1833," *BYU Studies* 13 [Autumn 1972], 14).

111. *sectarian*—religious

112. *non-compliance*—disobedience

113. *immigrated*—traveled to Missouri

114. *tarried*—stayed

115. *constituted*—made up

116. *coarse meal*—rough grain

DANDELION FIELDS, BY JAMES T. HARWOOD © INTELLECTUAL RESERVE, INC.

" . . . a growth of flowers so gorgeous and grand as to exceed description . . ."

grater. This was rather an inconvenient way of living for a sick person; but it was for the gospel's sake, and all were very cheerful and happy.[117]

"We enjoyed many happy seasons in our prayer and other meetings, and the Spirit of the Lord was poured out upon us, and even on the little children, insomuch that many of eight, ten or twelve years of age spake, and prayed, and prophesied[118] in our meetings and in our family worship. There was a spirit of peace and union, and love and good will manifested in this little Church in the wilderness, the memory of which will be ever dear to my heart" (*Autobiography of Parley P. Pratt*, 53–54, 56).

A Description of the Land of Zion

When Joseph Smith arrived in Jackson County with his party in the summer of 1831, he provided this description of the land of Zion: "The country is unlike the timbered states of the East. As far as the eye can reach the beautiful rolling prairies lie spread out like a sea of meadows; and are decorated with a growth of flowers so gorgeous and grand as to exceed description; and nothing is more fruitful, or a richer stockholder in the blooming prairie than the honey bee. Only on the water courses is timber to be found. There in strips from one to three miles in width, and following faithfully the meanderings[119] of

117. The Lord counseled the Saints in Missouri to have a cheerful attitude: "And inasmuch as ye do these things with thanksgiving, with cheerful hearts and countenances, not with much laughter, for this is sin, but with a glad heart and a cheerful countenance—Verily I say, that inasmuch as ye do this, the fulness of the earth is yours" (D&C 59:15–16). Can you imagine being asked to sell all and move to a new home? Why is it important to have a cheerful attitude even while experiencing trials in life?

118. When we bear our testimonies of Christ, it is the act of prophesying, because John taught that "the testimony of Jesus is the spirit of prophecy" (Revelation 19:10).

119. *meanderings*—winding

"Verily I say unto you, that it is my will that an house should be built unto me in the land of Zion, like unto the pattern which I have given you;

"Yea, let it be built speedily by the tithing of my people.[130]

"Behold, this is the tithing and the sacrifice which I, the Lord, require at their hands; that there may be an house built unto me for the salvation of Zion, . . .

"And inasmuch as my people build a house unto me in the name of the Lord, and do not suffer[131] any unclean thing to come into it, that it be not defiled,[132] my glory shall rest upon it"[133] (vv. 1, 10–12, 15).

Brother Pratt later wrote that "this revelation was not complied with by the leaders and Church in Missouri, as a whole; notwithstanding many were humble and faithful. Therefore, the threatened judgment was poured out to the uttermost,[134] as the history of the five following years will show.[135]

"That portion of the inhabitants of Jackson County which did not belong to the Church, became jealous of our growing influence and numbers. Political demagogues[136] were afraid we should rule the county; and religious priests and bigots felt that we were powerful rivals, and about to excel all other societies in the State in numbers, and in power and influence" (*Autobiography of Parley P. Pratt,* 77–78).

---

130. President Thomas S. Monson taught that temples "are built with stone, glass, wood, and metal. But they are also a product of faith and an example of sacrifice. The funds to build temples come from all tithe payers and consist of the widow's mite, children's pennies, and workmen's dollars—all sanctified by faith" ("Days Never to Be Forgotten," *Ensign,* November 1990, 69).

131. *suffer*—allow

132. *defiled*—corrupted

133. President Gordon B. Hinckley said, "Every man who holds the Melchizedek Priesthood has an obligation to see that the House of the Lord is kept sacred and free of any defilement. . . . Additionally, each of us has an obligation—first, as to his own personal worthiness, and secondly, as to the worthiness of those whom he may encourage or assist in going to the House of the Lord" ("Keeping the Temple Holy," *Ensign,* May 1990, 50).

134. *uttermost*—fullest degree

135. President Marion G. Romney taught, "In this last dispensation, the Lord has taught the importance of complete dedication to his service and strict obedience to his commandments as emphatically as he did during his earthly ministry. For example, in 1831, the first year after the Church was organized, the Lord revealed through the Prophet Joseph Smith, who was visiting the Saints then assembled in Jackson County, Missouri, that they were in 'the land of promise, . . . the place for the city of Zion' (D&C 57:2). . . . The Lord was reminding the Saints there that there was some tribulation ahead before they could enjoy the promised blessings of Zion as it will be in its glory" ("A Disciple of Christ," *Ensign,* November 1978, 38–39).

136. *demagogues*—leaders

DEVELOPMENTS IN OHIO, 1831–1834

The years 1831 to 1834 were a time of growth and revelation for the Church. The Saints were living mainly in two states, Ohio and Missouri. The Prophet Joseph Smith and other leaders did their best to lead these two groups of Church members. In addition, the Lord revealed many truths from heaven to help guide the Church and its faithful Saints.

CHAPTER 38: APOSTASY AND PERSECUTION WITHIN THE CHURCH

From the time of Adam to the time of the Prophet Joseph Smith, living prophets and members of the true Church have been persecuted. Soon after the Prophet arrived in Ohio, he experienced persecution. Sadly, many of Joseph's enemies were former Church members who had apostatized.[1] As you read this chapter, think of some things you can do to strengthen rather than hurt the Church?

SYMONDS RYDER IS CONVERTED

In the early spring of 1831 a great earthquake hit China, killing many people. Some newspaper writers in Ohio wrote stories blaming the earthquake on the Church (see chapter 29 for more information on this topic).

Historian B. H. Roberts explained that that "earthquake in China is a matter of some interest in connection with the history of the church, since it was the means of bringing [Symonds] Ryder, a somewhat noted preacher of the Campbellite faith, into the Church. According to *Hayden's History of the Disciples on the Western Reserve* (a Campbellite book), Mr. Ryder was much perplexed[2] over 'Mormonism,' and for a time was undecided whether to join the Church or not. 'In the month of June,' (1831) writes Mr. Hayden, 'he read in a newspaper an account of the destruction of Pekin in China, and he remembered that six weeks before, a young 'Mormon' girl had predicted the destruction of that city.' J. H. Kennedy, in his *Early Days of Mormonism* (Scribner's & Sons, 1888), refers to the same thing, and adds: 'This appeal to the superstitious part of [Symonds Ryder's] nature was the final weight in the balance and he threw the whole power of his influence upon the side of 'Mormonism'" (in *History of the Church*, 1:158n).

SYMONDS RYDER APOSTATIZES FROM THE CHURCH

Like some who joined the Church in the early days, Symonds Ryder did not remain faithful. B. H. Roberts wrote that Ryder's initial reason for apostatizing was just as interesting as his reason for baptism:

"It appears that some time after [Symonds Ryder's] baptism he was ordained an Elder of the Church . . . and somewhat later informed by a communication[3] signed by the Prophet Joseph and Sidney Rigdon, that it was the will of the Lord, made known by the spirit that he should preach the Gospel. Both in the letter he received and in the official commission[4] to preach, however, his name was spelled R-i-d-e-r, instead of R-y-d-e-r, and is soberly[5] stated in the *History of the Disciples on the*

NOTES FOR CHAPTER 38

1.  **apostatized**—left the Church

2. **perplexed**—confused

3. **communication**—letter or mission call

4. **commission**—calling or assignment

5. **soberly**—seriously

 = Word Help	🔍 = A Closer Look
= More Light	= Ponder This

Words in pink are explained in the Glossary.

On the night of March 24, 1832, a mob of wicked men took Joseph
out of his house and tarred and feathered him

Simonds Ryder,[42]) 'pull up his drawers, pull up his drawers, he will take cold.' Another replied: '*Ain't ye going to kill 'im? ain't ye going to kill 'im?* when a group of mobbers collected a little way off, and said: 'Simonds, Simonds, come here;' and 'Simonds' charged those who had hold of me to keep me from touching the ground (as they had done all the time), lest I should get a spring upon them. They held a council, and as I could occasionally overhear a word, I supposed it was to know whether or not it was best to kill me. They returned after a while, when I learned that they had concluded not to kill me, but to beat and scratch me well, tear off my shirt and drawers, and leave me naked. One cried, 'Simonds, Simonds, *where's the tar bucket?* . . . They ran back and fetched the bucket of tar, when one exclaimed, . . . '*Let us tar up his mouth;*' and they tried to force the tar-paddle into my mouth; I twisted my head around, so that they could not; . . . They then tried to force a vial[43] into my mouth, and broke it in my teeth.[44] All my clothes were torn off me except my shirt collar; and one man fell on me and scratched my body with his nails like a mad cat.

---

42. The Book of Mormon explains why Symonds Ryder would be a part of this mob and why Ezra Booth would try to destroy the Church with his letters. "And thus we can plainly discern, that after a people have been once enlightened by the Spirit of God, and have had great knowledge of things pertaining to righteousness, and then have fallen away into sin and transgression, they become more hardened, and thus their state becomes worse than though they had never known these things" (Alma 24:30).

43. *vial*—bottle

44. "The mob ridiculed him, choked him, stripped him, and tried to force a vial of acid into his mouth, which chipped one of his teeth, causing him thereafter to speak with a slight whistle" (*Church History in the Fulness of Times,* 115).

Joseph and Emma suffered the loss of several of their children

Joseph had to be in tune with the Spirit in order to receive revelation

fulness at the time of which we write [2nd Feb., 1833]"[87] (in *History of the Church*, 1:324n).

CHAPTER 41:
THE BOOK OF COMMANDMENTS

Members of the newly restored Church so cherished the divine revelations received through the Prophet Joseph Smith that they wanted their own personal copies. Soon after the organization of the Church, the Prophet Joseph Smith and others began copying and arranging the revelations. Though these were shared with those close to the Prophet, most members did not have easy access to the revelations. At a special conference of the Church in November of 1831, the decision to publish these revelations was made. The Lord gave immediate approval to the publication. The revelations were compiled and called the Book of Commandments. The compilation of revelations later became known as the Doctrine and Covenants. As you read this chapter, consider how blessed we are to have the Doctrine and Covenants today.

THE LORD GIVES THE PREFACE TO THE BOOK OF COMMANDMENTS

At a conference on November 1, 1831, the elders of the Church met in Hiram, Ohio, and decided that the revelations received by the Prophet during the preceding years should be compiled[88] and published. The Lord blessed those at the conference by approving the elders' plan and giving a revelation, which he called his "preface[89] unto the book of my commandments:"[90]

"Behold, this is mine authority, and the authority of my servants, and my preface[91] unto the book of my commandments, which I have given them to publish unto you, O inhabitants of the earth.

"Wherefore, I, the Lord, knowing the calamity[92] which should come upon the inhabitants of the earth, called upon my servant, Joseph Smith, Jun., and spake unto him from heaven[93] and gave him commandments"[94] (D&C 1:6, 17).

This, of course, was not the first revelation given to Joseph Smith, but, wrote Joseph Fielding Smith,

---

87. From July 1833 until the Prophet's death in June 1844, "the Prophet and his scribes—usually Sidney Rigdon and Frederick G. Williams . . . , reviewed and revised the manuscript, preparing it for the press. In the review process additional revelations were received on some points over and beyond what had been done the first time" (Robert J. Matthews, *A Bible! A Bible!* 90).

The Book of Commandments contained early revelations to Joseph Smith, similar to what is found today in the Doctrine and Covenants sections 1 through 64

NOTES FOR CHAPTER 41

88. *compiled*—put together

89. *preface*—introduction

90. "Martin Harris (1783–1875), a New York farmer, was one of the Three Witnesses to the divine origin of the Book of Mormon. He also financed the first publication of the Book of Mormon in 1830 at a cost of $3,000 and later helped finance publication of the Book of Commandments" (*Encyclopedia of Mormonism*, 574). The first print run consisted of 3,000 copies.

91. "Section one in the Doctrine and Covenants is not the first revelation received, but it is so placed in the book because the Lord gave it as the preface to the book of his commandments. The Doctrine and Covenants is distinctively peculiar and interesting to all who believe in it that it is the only book in existence which bears the honor of a preface given by the Lord himself" (Joseph Fielding Smith, *Church History and Modern Revelation*, 2:24).

92. *calamity*—trouble

93. Heavenly Father and Jesus Christ spoke to Joseph Smith in the sacred grove (see JS—H 1:15–20).

94. Why do you think the Lord restored his glorious gospel through a young unlearned farm boy?

THE BOOK OF COMMANDMENTS IS SAVED FROM THE MISSOURI MOB

The Prophet Joseph decided that the manuscript pages for the Book of Commandments should be taken to Missouri for printing. By the summer of 1833 most of these revelations had been printed, but not all. Many of the Missourians objected to having the Church own a printing press in their midst and formed a committee that demanded the Church stop publishing their newspaper and all the revelations.

The members of the Church in Jackson County, Missouri, asked for some time to discuss the demands with the Church leaders in Ohio, but they were refused. A meeting of the Missourians quickly became an unruly mob that attacked the printing office and home of Brother William W. Phelps, the printer. During the attack on the printing office, nearly all of the printed copies of the revelations were destroyed.

Mary Elizabeth Rollins and her sister, Caroline, were both eyewitness of the mob attacks against the members of the Church. They were also both near the printing office when it was destroyed. Thanks to their faith, courage, and quick thinking, copies of the revelations were saved. Mary Elizabeth later recalled the event:

"The mob renewed their efforts again by tearing down the printing office, a two story building, and driving Brother Phelps' family out of the lower part of the house and putting their things in the street. They brought out some large sheets of paper, and said, 'Here are the Mormon Commandments.' My sister Caroline and myself were in a corner of a fence watching them; when they spoke of the commandments I was determined to have some of them. Sister said if I went to get any of them she would go too, but said 'They will kill us.' While their backs were turned, prying out the gable end of the house, we went, and got our arms full, and were turning away, when some of the mob saw us and called on us to stop, but we ran as fast as we could. Two of them started after us. Seeing a gap in a fence, we entered into a large cornfield, laid the papers on the ground, and hid them with our persons. The corn was from five to six feet high, and very thick; they hunted around considerable, and came very near us but did not find us. After we satisfied ourselves that they had given up the search for us, we tried to find our way out of the field, the corn was so high we could not see where to go, looking up I saw trees that had been girdled[112] to kill them. Soon we came to an old log stable which looked as though it had not been used for years. Sister Phelps and children were carrying in brush and piling it up at one side of the barn to lay her beds on. She asked me what I had. I told her. She then took them from us, which made us feel very bad. They got them bound in small books and sent me one, which I prized very highly" (*Utah Genealogical and Historical Magazine* 17 [1926], 196).[113]

THE BOOK OF COMMANDMENTS BECOMES THE DOCTRINE AND COVENANTS

In 1834, the presidency of the Church and a few others met to prepare the revelations again and have them published a second time. On August 17, 1835, the selection was presented to those gathered at a conference of the Church. Of this selection, Joseph stated that he prized these revelations beyond the wealth of this whole earth.[114]

The updated and enlarged collection of revelations was published two years later in Kirtland, Ohio, under the title *Doctrine and Covenants of The Church of Jesus Christ of Latter Day Saints.*

---

112. **been girdled**—bark cut off around them

113. These girls showed great faith and courage. Are there times when you have to show great faith and courage in your life?

114. The change in name from "Book of Commandments" to "Doctrine and Covenants" probably reflects a change in the content of the book. The Book of Commandments contained revelations only, whereas the Doctrine and Covenants contained the doctrine (originally there were seven "Lectures on Faith" included) and the Covenants (one hundred-three revelations). There have since been additional revelations added to the book, with the latest publication being in 1981.

Mary Elizabeth Rollins and her sister Caroline saved pages of the
original manuscript of the Book of Commandments

CHAPTER 44:
KIRTLAND: THE FIRST MISSION TRAINING CENTER

As the headquarters of the Church from 1831 to 1834, Kirtland was also the center of missionary activity. The Lord's charge to "teach all nations, baptizing them in the name of the Father, and of the Son, and of the Holy Ghost" (Matthew 28:19) was taken seriously by most Church members. The School of the Prophets and the School of the Elders, as described in chapter 42, provided some of the earliest training for these missionaries. From the winter through the summer of 1832 several people received mission calls to preach the gospel in parts of the United States and Canada. These missions ranged in length from a few days to a year or more, most of them being of the shorter time. As you study this chapter, consider the needs of early Church missionaries and think of ways in which you could prepare to share the gospel with others as a missionary.

MANY ARE CALLED TO MISSIONARY SERVICE

Throughout the early history of the restored Church, the Lord continually reminded the Saints that they should be missionaries of his gospel. The command to be missionaries was no different than it was in New Testament times. He told his leaders then to "Go ye into all the world, and preach the gospel to every creature" (Mark 16:15).

Today, divinely appointed Church leaders counsel that every young man should prepare spiritually, physically, emotionally, financially, and in every other way to serve a successful mission. Elder M. Russell Ballard, of the Quorum of the Twelve Apostles, stated:

"What we need now is the greatest generation of missionaries in the history of the Church. We need worthy, qualified, spiritually energized missionaries who, like Helaman's 2,000 stripling warriors, are 'exceedingly valiant for courage, and also for strength and activity' and who are 'true at all times in whatsoever thing they [are] entrusted' (Alma 53:20).

"Listen to those words, my young brethren: *valiant, courage, strength, active, true.* We don't need spiritually weak and semicommitted young men. We don't need you to just fill a position; we need your whole heart and soul. We need vibrant, thinking, passionate missionaries who know how to listen to and respond to the whisperings of the Holy Spirit. This isn't a time for spiritual weaklings. We cannot send you on a mission to be reactivated, reformed, or to receive a testimony. We just don't have time for that. We need you to be filled with 'faith, hope, charity and love, with an eye single to the glory of God' (D&C 4:5).

"As an Apostle of the Lord Jesus Christ, I call upon you to begin right now—tonight—to be fully and completely worthy. Resolve[174] and commit to yourselves and to God that from this moment forward you will strive diligently to keep your hearts, hands, and minds pure and unsullied[175] from any kind of moral transgression. Resolve to avoid pornography[176] as you would avoid the most insidious[177] disease, for that is precisely what it is. Resolve to completely abstain from tobacco, alcohol, and illegal drugs. Resolve to be honest. Resolve to be good citizens and to abide by the laws of the land in which you live. Resolve that from this night forward you will never defile your body or use language that is vulgar[178] and unbecoming to a bearer of the priesthood.

NOTES FOR CHAPTER 44

174. *Resolve*—Decide

175. *unsullied*—not stained

176. President Hinckley taught all youth, "The Church expects you to be chaste and virtuous. You know what this means. I am satisfied I need not repeat it here. But I do urge you, with all of the capacity of which I am capable, to avoid the corrosive, destructive forces of evil found in pornography. Pornography is the literature of the devil. Shun it. Stay away from it. Lift your sights and your minds to the higher and nobler things of life. Remember, 'wickedness never was happiness' (Alma 41:10). Sin never brought happiness. Transgression never brought happiness. Disobedience never brought happiness" (Brigham Young University Devotional, October 17, 1995, 53).

177. *insidious*—dangerous

178. *vulgar*—filthy; dirty

SPREADING TRUTH AND LIGHT, BY LARRY WADE

Missionaries are called to serve by the Lord through his prophets

"And that is not all we expect of you, my young brethren. We expect you to have an understanding and a solid testimony of the restored gospel of Jesus Christ. We expect you to work hard. We expect you to be covenant makers and covenant keepers. We expect you to be missionaries to match our glorious message" (M. Russell Ballard, "The Greatest Generation of Missionaries," *Ensign*, November 2002, 47).

During the early days of the Church in Kirtland, Ohio, many prepared for and answered the call to missionary service.[179] Notice the Lord's counsel and promises to these two early missionaries:

"Verily I say unto you, that it is my will that my servant Jared Carter should go again into the eastern countries, from place to place . . . proclaiming glad tidings of great joy, even the everlasting gospel.[180]

"And I will send upon him the Comforter, which shall teach him the truth and the way whither he shall go;[181]

---

179. Many verses in the scriptures remind us that we all have a duty to proclaim the gospel. "Every man should . . . lift a warning voice unto the inhabitants of the earth" (D&C 63:37). "It becometh every man who hath been warned to warn his neighbor" (D&C 88:81). There is much we can do before and after serving a full-time mission. Have you taken the opportunity to share the gospel with a friend? Who could you share the gospel with now? What can you do now to prepare to serve a full-time mission in the future?

180. The message of the gospel is the greatest source of joy in the world. "Ye should consider on the blessed and happy state of those that keep the commandments of God. For behold, they are blessed in all things, both temporal and spiritual" (Mosiah 2:41).

181. President Ezra Taft Benson emphasized the importance of the Holy Ghost in missionary work when he said, "The Spirit is the most important matter in this glorious work" (*Teachings of Ezra Taft Benson*, 198).

THE LORD REVEALS THE BUILDINGS HE REQUIRES IN KIRTLAND

In December of 1832 the Lord revealed to the Prophet Joseph Smith that the Saints were to build a temple[195] in Kirtland. That same revelation explained that other buildings would be required as well. The following is a portion of the revelation:

"Organize yourselves; prepare every needful thing; and establish a house, even a house of prayer, a house of fasting, a house of faith, a house of learning, a house of glory, a house of order, a house of God.

"And again, the order of the house prepared for the presidency of the school of the prophets, established for their instruction in all things that are expedient[196] for them, even for all the officers of the church, or in other words, those who are called to the ministry in the church, beginning at the high priests, even down to the deacons"[197] (D&C 88:119, 127).

President Joseph Fielding Smith described why the Lord commanded the Saints in Kirtland to turn their focus to building up the city at this time:

"It was necessary for the Elders who had been out preaching to return to Kirtland to receive instruction and endowment[198] so that they would be prepared to go forth to preach the Gospel to the world, 'for the last time.' It was for the purpose of gaining knowledge of the doctrines of the Kingdom, and also of countries, the perplexities[199] of the nations, and the judgments which are on the land, that the Elders were called in from their labors to Kirtland" (*Church History and Modern Revelation,* 2:135–36). The temple and the meeting place for the School of the Prophets were important buildings in which the leaders of the Church received the type of instructions needed to fulfill their callings.

THE LORD AGAIN DIRECTS HIS PEOPLE ON THE BUILDING OF KIRTLAND

The Saints who gathered to Kirtland were not wealthy people, and getting settled in this new area was their first concern. For two months very little was done to begin the buildings the Lord had commanded in Doctrine and Covenants section 88. Therefore, in May 1833, the Lord again reminded the

---

NOTES FOR CHAPTER 45

195. The Prophet Joseph Smith described the importance of temples in the Lord's kingdom on June 11, 1843, when he said, "What was the object of gathering . . . the people of God in any age of the world? . . . The main object was to build unto the Lord a house whereby He could reveal unto His people the ordinances of His house and the glories of His kingdom" (*History of the Church,* 5:423).

196. *expedient*—necessary; essential; or good

COURTESY CHURCH ARCHIVES, THE CHURCH OF JESUS CHRIST OF LATTER-DAY SAINTS

Heber C. Kimball

197. The members of the Church at this time were very poor; therefore, three months after this revelation was received, a committee was formed to organize the saving of money for the construction of the buildings. "At a conference held March 23rd, 1833, a committee was appointed to purchase land in Kirtland, upon which to build up a Stake of Zion. Several large farms were bought, and among these was the French farm, so called after its owner. This had an excellent stone quarry and good material for brick-making" (Hyrum M. Smith and Janne M. Sjodahl, *Doctrine and Covenants Commentary,* 600).

198. An endowment is a gift. "Certain special, spiritual blessings given worthy and faithful saints in the temples are called endowments, because in and through them the recipients are endowed with power from on high" (Bruce R. McConkie, *Mormon Doctrine,* 226).

199. *perplexities*—confusion

Saints of his desires for them to build Zion by constructing buildings for his purposes.

"And again, verily I say unto you, my friends, a commandment I give unto you, that ye shall commence a work of laying out and preparing a beginning and foundation of the city of the stake of Zion, here in the land of Kirtland, beginning at my house. . . .

"And let the first lot on the south be consecrated unto me for the building of a house for the presidency. . . .

"And again, verily I say unto you, the second lot on the south shall be dedicated unto me for the building of a house unto me, for the work of the printing of the translation of my scriptures, and all things whatsoever I shall command you" (D&C 94:1, 3, 10).

President Joseph Fielding Smith gave the following explanation of these verses:

"The Lord gave a revelation with directions for the building of this house. He declared that it should be built according to his pattern and not according to the pattern of the world. A lot was set apart for the building of a house for the use of the First Presidency and where revelation could be given and all matters pertaining to the progress of the Church could receive proper attention. . . .

"The second lot south of this building was to be dedicated for the building of another house where the printing for the Church could be done and the translation of the Scriptures, on which the Prophet had been working off and on for many months, could be published. . . . This house also was to be dedicated to the service of the Lord, and set apart for the printing, 'in all things whatsoever I shall command you, to be holy, undefiled[200] according to the pattern in all things, as it shall be given unto you'" (*Church History and Modern Revelation,* 2:165).

As a result of this revelation, the building committee went to work. "The committee," Joseph Fielding Smith explained, "issued a circular[201] and sent it forth among the members of the Church in the different branches asking that they bring about the fulfillment of the command of the Lord concerning the establishing, or the preparation of a house, 'wherein the elders, who have been commanded of the Lord so to do, may gather themselves together, and prepare all things, . . . and treasure up words of wisdom, that they may go forth to the Gentiles for the last time.' This appeal[202] went forth to the whole Church. It was a strong appeal and in their pleading they said: 'And unless we fulfill this command, viz.: establish an house, and prepare all things necessary that the elders may gather into a school, called the School of the Prophets, and receive the instruction which the Lord designs they should receive, we may despair of obtaining[203] the great blessing that God had promised to the faithful of the Church of Christ; therefore it is as important, as our salvation, that we obey this above-mentioned command, as well as all

PHOTOGRAPH BY SHAUNA GIBBY

Every temple bears the inscription: "The House of the Lord. Holiness to the Lord"

200. *undefiled*—free from sin

201. *issued a circular*—sent a letter

202. *appeal*—request

203. *despair of obtaining*—give up hope of receiving

Book of Mormon, and obey it; read the commandments that are printed, and obey them; yea, humble yourselves under the mighty hand of God, that peradventure[42] He may turn away His anger from you. Tell them that they have not come up to Zion to sit down in idleness, neglecting the things of God, but they are to be diligent and faithful in obeying the new covenant" (*History of the Church*, 1:319–20).

Conflict between the Mormons and the Missourians

In addition to those who were causing tensions because of their disobedience, the Saints in Jackson County began to feel tension with those who were already settled in Missouri. The Missourians' lifestyle was very different from the Mormons' lifestyle. Some of the old settlers felt that their lifestyle would be threatened by the Mormons who continued to move into Jackson County.[43]

Historian B. H. Roberts explained some of these differences: "The 'old settlers' were principally from the mountainous portions of the southern states," he wrote. "They had settled along the water courses in the forests which lined their banks, instead of out on the broad and fertile prairies, which only required fencing to prepare them for cultivation. It was the work of years to clear a few acres of the timber

lands, but with these small fields the 'old settlers' were content. They had no disposition[44] to beautify their homes, or even make them convenient or comfortable. They lived in their log cabins without windows, and very frequently without floors other than the ground; and the dingy, smoked log walls were unadorned by pictures or other ornaments. They were uneducated; those who could read or write being the exception; and they had an utter contempt[45] for the refinements of life. They were hospitable to the stranger, and even generous to an enemy in supplying him food and shelter when in need, yet they were narrow-minded, ferocious, and jealous of those who sought to obtain better homes, and who aspired to something better in life than had yet entered into the hearts of these people. . . .

"The saints could not join the Missourians in their way of life—in Sabbath-breaking, profanity, horse-racing, idleness, and in all too prevalent drunkenness.[46] They had been commanded to keep the Sabbath day holy, to keep themselves unspotted from the sins of the world.[47] The fact of people having so little in common with each other was of itself calculated to beget[48] a coldness and suspicion, which would soon ripen into dislike. The saints, too, for the most part, had come from the northern and New England states, and the dislike and suspicion that existed at that time between the people of the

---

42. *peradventure*—by chance

43. Joseph Fielding Smith explained, "Nearly all the Latter-day Saints were from the Eastern States while the Missourians were from the South. The Missourians feared that the 'Mormons' would increase and take from them their political domination. The question of slavery, even in that day, was quite keen, and the Missourians were determined to keep the state within the control of the slave holders. Above all else, however, was their extreme hatred for the 'Mormons' because of their industry and belief. Some of the latter had also failed to show the proper discretion and wisdom, for they openly stated that the Lord had given them the land for their eternal inheritance, and although they were to purchase the lands, yet in time there the city Zion would be built unto which none but the faithful would be privileged to come. Such expressions aroused the Missourians to fever heat, for they naturally hated the doctrines of the Church, and to be informed that the lands would ultimately be

taken from them, was adding fuel to the flame" (*Essentials in Church History*, 132).

44. *disposition*—desire

45. *utter contempt*—complete hatred

46. "Western Missouri . . . was on the frontiers of the United States, and therefore a place of refuge for those who had outraged the laws of society elsewhere. Here they were near the boundary line of the United States, and if pursued by the officers of the law, in a few hours they could cross the line out of their reach. These outcasts helped to give a more desperate complexion to the already reckless population of western Missouri" (B. H. Roberts, *Comprehensive History of the Church*, 321–22).

47. The Lord had given his law concerning the Sabbath while Joseph Smith visited Jackson County in 1831 (see D&C 59).

48. *calculated to beget*—sure to produce

SAINTS DRIVEN FROM JACKSON COUNTY, MISSOURI, BY C. A. CHRISTENSEN, COURTESY BRIGHAM YOUNG UNIVERSITY MUSEUM OF ART

The Saints lived under a constant threat of persecution

slaveholding and free states, was manifested toward the saints by their 'southern' neighbors. Moreover, the 'old settlers' were dear lovers of office,[49] and the honors and emoluments[50] growing out of it; and they greatly feared that the rapidly increasing Latter-day Saint population would soon out-number them, and that the offices would be wrested[51] from them" (*Comprehensive History of the Church*, 1:321–2).

THE SAINTS SUFFER PERSECUTIONS

Persecution began soon after the Saints arrived in Missouri, becoming very serious by the summer of 1833. "As early as the spring of 1832 there began to appear signs of an approaching storm," B. H. Roberts wrote. "In the deadly hours of the night the houses of some of the saints were stoned, the windows broken, and the inmates disturbed. In the fall of the same year a large quantity of hay in the stack belonging to the saints was burned, houses were shot into, and the people insulted with abusive language. In the month of April, 1833, the 'old settlers' to the number of some three hundred met at Independence, to consult upon a plan for the destruction, or immediate removal, of the 'Mormons' from Jackson county. They were unable, however, to unite on any plan, and the mob becoming the worse for liquor, the affair broke up in a 'Missouri row.'[52]

"The sectarian[53] priests inhabiting Jackson and the surrounding counties were earnestly engaged in fanning the flames of prejudice,[54] already burning in

---

49. *lovers of office*—people who wanted position

50. *emoluments*—money

51. *wrested*—taken

52. *row*—quarrel or fight

53. *sectarian*—religious

54. *fanning the flames of prejudice*—increasing hate and unfairness

women, and children, who had been driven or frightened from their homes, by yells and threats, began to return from their hiding places in thickets, corn-fields, woods, and groves, and view with heavy hearts the scene of desolation and wo: and while they mourned over fallen man, they rejoiced with joy unspeakable that they were accounted worthy to suffer in the glorious cause of their Divine Master. There lay the printing office a heap of ruins; Elder Phelps's furniture strewed over the garden as common plunder; the revelations, book works, papers, and press in the hands of the mob, as the booty of highway robbers; there was Bishop Partridge, in the midst of his family, with a few friends, endeavoring to scrape off the tar which, from its eating his flesh, seemed to have been prepared with lime, pearl-ash, acid, or some flesh-eating substance, to destroy him; and there was Charles Allen in the same awful condition. The heart sickens at the recital, how much more at the picture! More than once, those people, in this boasted land of liberty, were brought into jeopardy, and threatened with expulsion or death, because they desired to worship God according to the revelations of heaven, the constitution of their country, and the dictates of their own consciences. Oh, liberty, how art thou fallen! Alas, cler-gymen, where is your charity!"[72] (*History of the Church,* 1:393).

THE SAINTS ARE COUNSELED TO BEAR THEIR PERSECUTIONS PATIENTLY

On August 6, 1833, the Prophet Joseph Smith received a revelation, which in part instructed the Saints in Zion how to act in the midst of these persecutions:

"Now, I speak unto you concerning your families—if men will smite[73] you, or your families, once, and ye bear it patiently and revile not[74] against them, neither seek revenge, ye shall be rewarded;[75]

"But if ye bear it not patiently, it shall be accounted unto you as being meted[76] out as a just measure unto you.[77]

"And again, if your enemy shall smite you the second time, and you revile not against your enemy, and bear it patiently, your reward shall be an hundredfold.

"And again, if he shall smite you the third time, and ye bear it patiently, your reward shall be doubled unto you four-fold;[78]

"And these three testimonies shall stand against your enemy if he repent not, and shall not be blotted out"[79] (D&C 98:23–27).

---

72. Sadly, the leaders of this mob "were the county officers—the county judge, the constables, clerks of the court and justices of the peace; while Lilburn W. Boggs, the lieutenant-governor, . . . was there quietly looking on and . . . secretly aiding every measure of the mob—who, walking among the ruins of the printing office and house of W. W. Phelps, remarked to some of the saints, 'You now know what our Jackson boys can do and you must leave the country!'" (B. H. Roberts, *The Missouri Persecutions,* 87.)

73. *smite*—hit; hurt

74. *revile not*—don't seek to get even

75. Why do you think the Lord wants us to learn to be patient and forgiving toward those who hurt us? How did Jesus set an example for us?

76. *meted*—given

77. President Spencer W. Kimball taught, "If we are merciful with those who injure us, [the Lord] will be merciful with us in our errors" (*The Miracle of Forgiveness,* 267).

78. According to Parley P. Pratt, the Saints at first followed the Lord's counsel: "The saints submitted to these outrages for a time in all patience, without defence or resistance of any kind, supposing that the public authorities would of course put a stop to them. But they were soon convinced to the contrary, and were compelled to take up arms for defence. . . . We assembled in small bodies in different neighborhoods, and stood on guard during the nights, being ready to march in a moment to any place of attack" (*Autobiography of Parley P. Pratt,* 117).

79. *blotted out*—removed

The Saints are driven from their homes in Jackson County, Missouri

CHAPTER 48:
THE SAINTS ARE FORCED TO LEAVE JACKSON COUNTY

The Saints' first days in Jackson County were filled with excitement about establishing Zion. However, it was also a time of extreme hardship and persecution. After a few short years, they were cruelly driven from their homes. The Lord revealed that, at least in part, these Church members had caused some of their own problems. As you read this chapter, ponder what the Saints were supposed to learn from this experience. Notice how the Lord, in his mercy, continued to bless his people in their trials.

PERSECUTIONS AND MIRACLES FOLLOW THE SAINTS

The persecution of the Saints in Jackson County, Missouri, increased throughout the summer of 1833. Then, wrote Joseph Fielding Smith, "On the night of October 31, a band of about fifty marauders[80] proceeded against a branch of the Church west of the Big Blue River, not far from Independence. There they unroofed and partly demolished a number of houses, whipped in a savage[81] manner several men and frightened the women and children, who were forced to flee for safety. On the first of November, another attack was made on a branch on the prairie,

---

NOTES FOR CHAPTER 48   81. 🔲 *savage*—violent

80. 🔲 *marauders*—mobbers

fourteen miles from Independence. The same night another party raided the homes of the Saints in Independence, where a number of houses were demolished and the goods in the store of Gilbert, Whitney and Co., were scattered in the street. One Richard McCarty was caught in the act of breaking into the store and demolishing property and was taken before Samuel Weston, justice of the peace, where a complaint was made against him; Judge Weston, however, refused to consider the complaint, and turned McCarty loose. The next day McCarty caused the arrest of the witnesses who had captured him in this unlawful act, and had them tried for false imprisonment. The same justice, on the testimony of this fellow alone, found the witnesses, Gilbert, Morley and Corrill, guilty and committed them to jail. 'Although we could not obtain a warrant against him for breaking open the store,' said John Corrill, 'yet he had gotten one for us for catching him at it'" (*Essentials in Church History,* 137).

During this terrible time, there were also miraculous stories of the Lord's protecting and healing power among the Saints. One such miracle happened after the battle near the Big Blue River:

"At first the Latter-day Saints attempted to avoid direct conflict," one historical account retells; "however, the beatings of members and the destruction of property eventually led to a battle near the Big Blue River. Two members of the mob were killed, and the Saints lost Andrew Barber. Philo Dibble was shot three times in the stomach. Newel Knight was called to administer to[82] him, with miraculous results. Brother Dibble related:

"'Brother Newel Knight came to see me, and sat down on the side on my bed. . . . I felt the Spirit resting upon me at the crown of my head before his hand touched me, and I knew immediately that I was going to be healed. . . . I immediately arose and discharged[83] three quarts of blood or more, with some pieces of clothes that had been driven into my body by the bullets. I then dressed myself and went out doors. . . . From that time not a drop of blood came from me and I never afterwards felt the slightest pain or inconvenience from my wounds, except that I was somewhat weak from the loss of blood'" (*Our Heritage,* 42–43).

THE SAINTS CAMP ALONG THE MISSOURI RIVER

With their lives in jeopardy, many Saints began to flee north to escape persecution, camping along the banks of the Missouri River. Lyman Wight, who saw some of the Saints being driven from Jackson County, later said, "I saw one hundred and ninety women and children driven thirty miles across the prairie with three decrepit[84] men only in their company, in the month of November, the ground thinly crusted with sleet; and I could easily follow on their trail by the blood that flowed from their lacerated[85] feet on the stubble[86] of the burnt prairie" (in *History of the Church,* 3:439).

Parley P. Pratt described the camp at the Missouri River and the continuing persecution of the Saints in Jackson County:

"When night again overtook us we were on the bank of the Missouri River, which divided between Jackson and Clay Counties. Here we camped for the night, as we could not cross the ferry[87] till morning. Next morning we crossed the river, and formed an encampment amid the cottonwoods on its bank.

"While we thus made our escape companies of ruffians[88] were ranging[89] the county in every direction; bursting into houses without fear, knowing that the people were disarmed; frightening women and children, and threatening to kill them if they did not flee immediately. At the head of one of these parties appeared the Rev. Isaac McCoy (a noted Baptist missionary to the Indians), with gun in hand, ordering the people to leave their homes immediately and surrender everything in the shape of arms.[90]

---

82. *administer to*—bless

83. *discharged*—released

84. *decrepit*—tired and weak

85. *lacerated*—cut

86. *stubble*—dried stocks of grain

87. *the ferry*—on a boat

88. *ruffians*—angry enemies

89. *ranging*—riding around

90. *everything in the shape of arms*—all of their weapons

"Other pretended preachers of the gospel took part in the persecution—speaking of the Church as the common enemies of mankind, and exulting[91] in their afflictions. On Tuesday and Wednesday nights, the 5th and 6th of November, women and children fled in every direction. One party of about one hundred and fifty fled to the prairie, where they wandered for several days, mostly without food; and nothing but the open firmament[92] for their shelter. Other parties fled towards the Missouri River. During the dispersion[93] of women and children, parties were hunting the men, firing upon some, tying up and whipping others, and some they pursued[94] several miles.

"Thursday, November 7. The shore began to be lined on both sides of the ferry with men, women and children; goods, wagons, boxes, provisions, etc., while the ferry was constantly employed;[95] and when night again closed upon us the cottonwood bottom had much the appearance of a camp meeting. Hundreds of people were seen in every direction, some in tents and some in the open air around their fires, while the rain descended in torrents.[96] Husbands were inquiring[97] for their wives, wives for their husbands; parents for children, and children for parents. Some had the good fortune to escape with their families, household goods, and some provisions; while others knew not the fate of their friends, and had lost all their goods.[98] The scene was indescribable, and, I am sure, would have melted the hearts of any people on the earth, except our blind oppressors,[99] and a blind and ignorant[100] community" (*Autobiography of Parley P. Pratt*, 82).

THE LORD BLESSES THE SAINTS WITH SIGNS IN THE HEAVENS

Parley P. Pratt wrote about a miraculous experience, which was a sign to the Saints that the Lord had not forgotten them:

"About two o'clock the next morning we were called up by the cry of signs in the heavens. We arose, and to our great astonishment all the firmament seemed enveloped[101] in splendid fireworks, as if every star in the broad expanse[102] had been hurled from its course, and sent lawless through the wilds of ether.[103] Thousands of bright meteors were shooting through space in every direction, with long

91. *exulting*—celebrating

92. *firmament*—sky

93. *dispersion*—scattering

94. *pursued*—chased

95. *employed*—carrying people across the river

96. *torrents*—large amounts

97. *inquiring*—asking

98. Brigham Young prophetically spoke about scenes like this, "You may calculate, when this people are called to go through scenes of affliction and suffering, are driven from their homes, and cast down, and scattered, and smitten, and peeled, the Almighty is rolling on his work with greater rapidity" (*Discourses of Brigham Young*, 351).

99. *oppressors*—enemies

100. *ignorant*—uneducated

101. *enveloped*—surrounded on all sides

102. *broad expanse*—heavens

103. *ether*—space

ADVENTIS HERITAGE CENTER

Several Saints witnessed and wrote about the meteor shower

Zion's Camp

ZION'S CAMP, BY C. C. A. CHRISTENSEN, COURTESY BRIGHAM YOUNG UNIVERSITY MUSEUM OF ART

transgressors, therefore they must needs be chastened"[122] (vv. 1–3, 6–8, 41).

CHAPTER 49:
ZION'S CAMP

From the summer of 1833 to the spring of 1834, the Saints who had been driven from their homes in Jackson County, Missouri, made several attempts to get the government's help to take back their homes and lands. In the spring of 1834, after the efforts with the government had not produced any results, the Lord authorized the members of the Church in the East to gather an army and march to the aid of the scattered Missouri Saints. This army of a little over 200 men was called Zion's Camp. They traveled over 900 miles to Missouri in May and June of 1834 in spite of continuous threats and attempts by mobs to stop them. Although this army did not have to fight and were not able to help the Missouri Saints get back their homes and property, much good came from their willingness to go.

THE LORD REVEALS WHY THE SAINTS IN JACKSON COUNTY WERE DRIVEN FROM THEIR HOMES

The Saints in Jackson County, Missouri, had been driven from their homes in November and December of 1833. In Doctrine and Covenants section 103, the Lord explained why the Saints were driven out of Zion. In this same revelation, the Lord also called upon the leaders of the Church in Ohio to organize an army called Zion's Camp and march to Missouri to aid their brothers and sisters.

122. **chastened**—corrected

TOM CHILD

The Zion's Camp volunteers marched over 900 miles to defend the Saints in Missouri

"Verily I say unto you, my friends, behold, I will give unto you a revelation and commandment, that you may know how to act in the discharge of[123] your duties concerning the salvation and redemption of your brethren, who have been scattered on the land of Zion;

"Being driven and smitten[124] by the hands of mine enemies, on whom I will pour out my wrath without measure in mine own time. . . .

"And that those who call themselves after my name might be chastened for a little season with a sore and grievous chastisement,[125] because they did not hearken altogether unto the precepts[126] and commandments which I gave unto them. . . .

"For after much tribulation,[127] as I have said unto you in a former commandment, cometh the blessing.[128] . . .

"Therefore let my servant Joseph Smith, Jun., say unto the strength of my house, my young men and the middle aged—Gather yourselves together unto the land of Zion, upon the land which I have

bought with money that has been consecrated[129] unto me" (vv. 1–2, 4, 12, 22).

VOLUNTEERS FOR ZION'S CAMP ARE WILLING TO GIVE THEIR LIVES FOR THE LORD

In following the commandments of the Lord, Joseph sent out a call for volunteers to go to Zion. The Lord had asked for five hundred men, but said, "If you cannot obtain five hundred, seek diligently that peradventure[130] ye may obtain three hundred. And if ye cannot obtain three hundred, seek diligently that peradventure ye may obtain one hundred" (D&C 103:32–33). By May 5, 1834, an appropriate number of volunteers started out for Missouri.

In the journal of Heber C. Kimball we get a glimpse of the sacrifices that were made and the courage of the Zion's Camp volunteers. Brother Kimball wrote, "I took leave of my wife and children and friends, not knowing whether I would see them again in the flesh, as myself and brethren were

---

NOTES FOR CHAPTER 49

123. *in the discharge of*—in doing

124. *smitten*—beaten

125. *chastisement*—punishment

126. *precepts*—teachings

127. *tribulation*—trouble, trials

128. How are people blessed who are faithful in tribulation? Who do you know that has been faithful in trials and troubles? How do you think Jesus feels about them?

129. *consecrated*—dedicated, given

130. *peradventure*—perhaps

THE LORD REVEALS MORE ABOUT THE DUTIES OF THE QUORUM OF THE TWELVE APOSTLES

On March 28, 1835, the "Twelve met in council, confessing their individual weaknesses and short-comings, expressing repentance, and seeking the further guidance of the Lord" (D&C 107, introductory note). The Twelve had likely not understood the importance of their calling previous to this time and wanted the Lord's help in understanding what it was they should do. The result was section 107 of the Doctrine and Covenants, which outlined their responsibilities as well as the duty of all priesthood holders.

THE GREAT REVELATION ON THE PRIESTHOOD

Elder John A. Widtsoe explained:

"[A great] evidence of God's guiding hand over his Church, occurred on March 28th, 1835. . . . On that day the Church of Jesus Christ of Latter-day Saints received a revelation which is one of the most remarkable documents in the possession of man. It stands absolutely unique; there is none like it. . . . It sets forth, in plainness and simplicity, the organization of the quorums of the priesthood; the mutual relations of the quorums to one another; the judicial system of the Church is foreshadowed[20] and outlined; and there is a wonderful picture of the early history of the priesthood. I doubt whether any other such document, of the same small extent, the same few number of words, lies at the foundation of any other great human institution.

"This revelation, now known as Section 107, together with two or three other revelations, forms, as it were, the constitution of the Church of Jesus Christ of Latter-day Saints, upon which we are building today, and upon which we will build until the Lord comes. It is so comprehensive in its brevity,[21] so magnificent in its simplicity, that we have found no occasion, up to the present, to wish that it might

have been more complete" (in Conference Report, April 1935, 79).

A small portion of that revelation reads as follows:

"Of the Melchizedek Priesthood, three Presiding High Priests, chosen by the body, appointed, and ordained to that office, and upheld by the confidence, faith, and prayer of the church, form a quorum of the Presidency of the Church.[22]

"The twelve traveling councilors are called to be the Twelve Apostles, or special witnesses of the name of Christ in all the world—thus differing from other officers in the church in the duties of their callings.[23]

"And they form a quorum, equal in authority and power to the three presidents previously mentioned. . . .

"The Twelve are a Traveling Presiding High Council, to officiate[24] in the name of the Lord, under the direction of the Presidency of the Church, agreeable to the institution of heaven; to build up the church, and regulate all the affairs of the same in all nations, first unto the Gentiles and secondly unto the Jews (vv. 22–24, 33).

CHAPTER 51:
A DECLARATION ON GOVERNMENTS AND LAWS

In 1835 Oliver Cowdery wrote a declaration on governments and laws, much of it driven by the Saints' bitter experience with Missouri officials and mobs. During a conference of the Church in August 1835, this declaration was sustained by Church members and is now contained in Doctrine and Covenants section 134. As you study this chapter, think about the important role government plays in our world and consider whether your government's leaders follow the important principles contained in Doctrine and Covenants section 134.

---

20. *foreshadowed*—seen

21. *comprehensive in its brevity*—complete in its brief and simple words

22. What can you do to uphold or support the prophet and his counselors?

23. An apostle is called to bear "special witness" of Jesus Christ. Luke described this when he said, "with great power gave the apostles witness of the resurrection of the Lord Jesus" (Acts 4:33).

24. *officiate*—act

THE MISSOURI SAINTS PLEAD FOR HELP IN A LETTER TO THE GOVERNMENT

"In the month of July 1834," wrote Joseph Fielding Smith, "the brethren residing in Missouri, wrote a lengthy appeal[25] to . . . the constitutional authorities of the United States, . . . setting forth their difficulties in Missouri and how they had been robbed and driven from their homes.[26] In this appeal they declared that they had settled in that country in the spirit of peace, purchasing legitimately[27] the property which they acquired, with the intent of making it their homes and building 'a holy city' according to the command of the Lord, a New Jerusalem, a place they called Zion. . . . However, when they began to gather and take possession of their lands, the ire[28] of the older inhabitants of Jackson County was kindled against them. They had settled in peace desiring to live in peace with all men, but they had been beaten, scourged,[29] some of their number killed, and all driven from their homes; their property had been destroyed and many of their homes burned to the ground. They had petitioned[30] the governor of the State of Missouri and the courts of that state without avail.[31] They had thereupon petitioned the President of the United States for help, that they might be reinstated on[32] their lands,

and be given protection against mob violence that they might possess their lands without molestation.[33] All of these appeals had fallen on ears that were deaf, or that had refused to hear. Their arms[34] had been taken from them by order of the state and thus they were left at the mercy of their enemies, and all law had been put to defiance[35] in Jackson County, and no redress[36] was obtainable from the state the officers of which were in sympathy with the mob.[37]

"Citations were made from the Bible showing that the Lord had revealed to his prophets in ancient times that such a city should be built . . . and that they had gathered for this purpose at the command of the Lord. They had established a printing plant for the purpose of proclaiming to the world these purposes and inviting the honest everywhere to come and assist in the building of a temple and the city that the word of the Lord might be fulfilled. 'The inhabitants of Jackson County arrayed[38] themselves against us because of our faith and belief, and destroyed our printing establishment to prevent the spread of the work, and drove men, women and children from their lands, houses, and homes, to perish in the approaching winter. Every blast carried the wailing of women and the shrieks of children across the widespread prairies, sufficiently horrible

---

NOTES FOR CHAPTER 51

25. 📖 *appeal*—request

26. ☀ It is appropriate for Church members to take an active role in government. Elder L. Tom Perry taught: "Through our understanding and study of the scriptures, we have a knowledge of the laws of the Lord by which we should govern our earthly conduct. With this great blessing comes an obligation to be a part of the communities in which we live. Our influence should be felt to safeguard the moral standards in the villages, in the towns, and in the cities where our homes are located in all parts of the world. I challenge you to become involved in lifting the moral standards of the communities where your homes are" ("But Be Ye Doers of the Word," *Ensign*, May 1977, 61).

27. 📖 *legitimately*—legally

28. 📖 *ire*—anger

29. 📖 *scourged*—whipped

30. 📖 *petitioned*—written

31. 📖 *avail*—success

32. 📖 *reinstated on*—returned to

33. 📖 *molestation*—being annoyed or disturbed

34. 📖 *arms*—weapons

35. 📖 *put to defiance*—ignored

36. 📖 *redress*—relief from wrongs

37. ☀ Even when others do not obey or follow the laws, "we believe in being subject to kings, presidents, rulers, and magistrates, in obeying, honoring, and sustaining the law" (Articles of Faith 1:12).

38. 📖 *arrayed*—organized and set

them in[55] their opinions, so long as a regard and reverence are shown to the laws. . . ."[56]

"We believe that all religious societies have a right to deal with their members for disorderly conduct, according to the rules and regulations of such societies; provided that such dealings be for fellowship and good standing; but we do not believe that any religious society has authority to try men on the right of property or life, to take from them this world's goods, or to put them in jeopardy of either life or limb; or to inflict any physical punishment upon them; they can only excommunicate them from their society, and withdraw from them their fellowship.[57]

"We believe that men should appeal to the civil law for redress of all wrongs and grievances; . . . but we believe that all men are justified in defending themselves, their friends and property, and the government from the unlawful assaults and encroachments[58] of all persons in times of exigency[59] when immediate appeal cannot be made to the laws, and relief afforded" (D&C 134: introductory note, 1–5, 7, 10–11).[60]

CHAPTER 52:
JOSEPH SMITH AND THE BOOK OF ABRAHAM

One of the special callings of the Prophet Joseph Smith was to bring forth ancient scriptures.[61] Through a series of unusual events Joseph Smith purchased some ancient Egyptian objects, which included old writings on material called papyrus, that led to his translating and publishing the Book of Abraham. Notice how the Lord watches over his work to bring about his purposes.

THE PROPHET OBTAINS ANCIENT EGYPTIAN OBJECTS

In December 1835, the Prophet explained how he received ancient writings of Abraham and Moses: "The public mind has been excited of late, by reports which have been circulated[62] concerning certain Egyptian mummies and ancient records, which were purchased by certain gentlemen of Kirtland, last July. . . . The record of Abraham[63] and

---

55. *proscribe them in*—rule out

56. Elder James E. Talmage taught: "Now, the Lord has provided that those in his Church shall live according to the law, and he makes a distinction between the law pertaining to the Church and what we call the secular law, or the law of the land, but he requires obedience to each" (in Conference Report, October 1920, 63).

57. Priesthood leaders in disciplinary councils decide appropriate discipline for those who break the most serious commandments of God. You can learn more about such a council in Doctrine and Covenants section 102. Elder John A. Widtsoe wrote, "No officer in the Church has authority beyond matters pertaining to the Church" (*Priesthood and Church Government*, 62).

Oliver Cowdery wrote the declaration on government now known as Doctrine and Covenants section 134

58. *encroachments*—trespassing

59. *exigency*—emergency

60. As you think about the beliefs expressed in this declaration on government, how many of them appear to have grown out of the Church's experience in Missouri? What reasons can you give for the Saints' desire to have these beliefs accepted by others? Finally, how many of these beliefs would benefit many living in the world today?

NOTES FOR CHAPTER 52

61. Elder LeGrand Richards taught: "The Prophet Joseph Smith brought us the Book of Mormon, the Doctrine and Covenants, the Pearl of Great Price, and many other writings. As far as the records show, he has given us more revealed truth than any prophet who has ever lived upon the face of the earth" ("Call of the Prophets," *Ensign*, May 1981, 33).

62. *circulated*—passed from person to person

63. The prophet Abraham traveled to Egypt from the land of Ur. The Bible records his journey and experiences in Genesis 11:26–13:2.

Joseph,[64] found with the mummies, is beautifully written on papyrus,[65] with black, and a small part red, ink or paint, in perfect preservation.[66] The characters are such as you find upon the coffins of mummies—hieroglyphics,[67] etc.; with many characters of letters like the present (though probably not quite so square) form of the Hebrew without points.[68] The records were obtained from one of the catacombs in Egypt, near the place where once stood the renowned city of Thebes,[69] by the celebrated French traveler, Antonio Lebolo"[70] (*History of the Church*, 2:348).

After the death of Antonio Lebolo, the papyrus, along with eleven mummies, were sent to Italy and eventually America in 1833, where they ended up in the possession of Michael H. Chandler. Chandler picked up the Egyptian materials in New York in April.

"Up to this time," wrote the Prophet Joseph, "they had not been taken out of the coffins, nor the coffins opened. On opening the coffins, he discovered that in connection with two of the bodies, was something rolled up with the same kind of linen, saturated[71] with the same bitumen,[72] which, when examined, proved to be two rolls of papyrus, previously mentioned. Two or three other small pieces of papyrus, with astronomical calculations,[73] epitaphs,[74] &c., were found with others of the mummies. When Mr. Chandler discovered that there was something with the mummies, he supposed or hoped it might be some diamonds or valuable metal, and was no little chagrined[75] when he saw his disappointment. 'He was immediately told, while yet in the custom house, that there was no man in that city who could translate his roll: but was referred, by the same gentleman, (a stranger,) to Mr. Joseph Smith, Jun., who, continued he, possesses some kind of power or gifts, by which he had previously translated similar characters.' I was then unknown to Mr. Chandler, neither did he know that such a book or work as the record of the Nephites [the Book of Mormon], had been brought before the public. From

---

64. Gospel scholar Daniel Ludlow wrote, "The record of Abraham translated by the Prophet was subsequently printed, and it is now known as the book of Abraham in the Pearl of Great Price. However, the translation of the book of Joseph has not yet been published. Evidently the record of Joseph was translated by the Prophet, but perhaps the reason it was not published was because the great prophecies therein were 'too great' for the people of this day" (*A Companion to Your Study of the Book of Mormon*, 131).

65. Papyrus is "an Egyptian plant, a kind of reed, of which the ancients made paper" (Noah Webster, *An American Dictionary of the English Language*, 1828).

66. *in perfect preservation*—still in good condition

67. *hieroglyphics*—Egyptian writing done with pictures

68. Hebrew letters have dots and lines underneath them, which are the vowels, to help readers pronounce the words. These markings are called points.

69. The city of Thebes was the capitol of Upper Egypt where many treasures were stored. Antonio Lebolo was known to have been working in this area from 1817 to 1821. The early Saints were told by Michael Chandler that the papyrus and mummies were discovered in 1831, but it is now known that Antonio Lebolo died 19 February 1830. There seems to be a discrepancy with some of the dates pertaining to Lebolo's life and death (see H. Donl Peterson, *The Pearl of Great Price: A History and Commentary*, 38–39).

70. "Lebolo, who was born in 1781 in present day Italy, close to the French and Swiss borders, served as a gendarme [a police officer] under Napoleon. After Napoleon's defeat, Lebolo and many of his comrades-in-arms were forced to leave their homes or face certain imprisonment. By 1817, the exiled soldier was residing in Egypt, employed by Bernardino Drovetti, the former French consul general, to supervise the work of several hundred laborers in his excavations in Upper Egypt" (H. Donl Peterson, *The Pearl of Great Price: A History and Commentary*, 38).

71. *saturated*—soaked

72. *bitumen*—strong smelling substance used to preserve papyrus

73. "Astronomical calculations" are an ancient method of determining the seasons and days of the year.

74. *epitaphs*—writings

75. *no little chagrined*—displeased

LAST DAYS. My soul has been much edified[88] of late from time to time in hearing Joseph the Seer converse about the mysteries of the Kingdom of God, truly God is with him and is making him mighty in wisdom and knowledge and I am convinced for myself that none of the Prophets Seers or Revelators of the Earth have ever accomplished a greater work than will be accomplished in the Last days through the mercy of God by JOSEPH THE SEER"[89] (Scott G. Kenney, ed., *Wilford Woodruff's Journal*, February 19, 1842, 2:155–56).

CHAPTER 53:
BUILDING THE HOUSE OF THE LORD

Temples are unique places of worship where the Lord can bless his people with special understanding and promises. In spite of the poverty of the Church and its members, the Lord commanded the Prophet Joseph Smith to build a temple so the Saints could receive the Lord's greatest blessings. As you read, see how the Lord blesses us when we do what he commands.

THE SAINTS ARE COMMANDED TO BUILD A TEMPLE

Between 1833 and 1836, construction of a temple[90] in Kirtland, Ohio, became the Church's top priority.[91] The Saints at the time were quite poor and didn't have many people who could help in building the temple. This presented many challenges for the Saints. One early Saint, Eliza R. Snow, wrote, "At that time the Saints were few in number, and most of them very poor; and, had it not been for the assurance[92] that God had spoken, and had commanded that a house should be built to his name, of which he not only revealed the form,[93] but also designated the dimensions,[94] an attempt towards building that temple, under the then existing circumstances, would have been, by all concerned, pronounced preposterous"[95] (in Edward Tullidge, *Women of Mormondom*, 80).[96]

THE LORD REVEALS THE KIRTLAND TEMPLE DESIGN

On June 1, 1833, Joseph Smith received the following instructions from the Lord about the building of the Kirtland Temple:

"Yea, verily I say unto you, I gave unto you a commandment that you should build a house, in the which house I design to endow[97] those whom I have chosen with power from on high;[98] . . .

"Now here is wisdom, and the mind of the Lord—let the house be built, not after the manner of the world, for I give not unto you that ye shall live after the manner of the world;

---

88. *edified*—instructed

89. What impresses you about Wilford Woodruff's testimony of the Prophet Joseph Smith? What testimony could you bear about the Prophet?

NOTES FOR CHAPTER 53

90. President Gordon B. Hinckley taught that temples "represent the ultimate in our worship and the ultimate in blessings offered" ("Welcome to Conference," *Ensign*, November 1999, 6).

91. To read more about the Lord's commandment to build the temple, see chapter 45, "Sacred Places for Strengthening the Saints."

92. *assurance*—knowledge

93. *form*—plan and features

94. *designated the dimensions*—chose the size and shape

95. *pronounced preposterous*—said to be ridiculous

96. Because the Saints were very poor, the Lord's command to build the Kirtland Temple was difficult to obey. Yet somehow they completed the temple and the building still stands today. What people from the scriptures have been commanded to do something very difficult and yet were able to complete their task with the Lord's help? What is the most difficult commandment you have kept?

97. *design to endow*—plan to give or provide

98. The Lord revealed that "there were certain endowments and blessings to be given to the elders, before they could go forth fully prepared to preach the Gospel in the world, which could only be obtained in the temple of the Lord. For this cause the Lord commanded that the temple be built at once, for the preaching of the Gospel was urgent, and the laborers

THE KIRTLAND TEMPLE, BY CHAD HAWKINS

The Kirtland Temple was the first temple built in this dispensation

"Therefore, let it be built after the manner which I shall show unto three of you,[99] whom ye shall appoint and ordain unto this power" (D&C 95:8, 13–14).

Soon thereafter Joseph met in council with many of the leading brethren of the Church. They discussed the building of the house of the Lord. The Prophet's mother, Lucy Mack Smith, gave this account:

"In this council, Joseph requested that each of the brethren should give his views with regard to the house; and when they had all got through, he would give his opinion concerning the matter. They

all complied with[100] his request. Some were in favor of building a frame house, but others were of a mind to put up a log house. Joseph reminded them that they were not building a house for a man, but for God; 'and shall we, brethren,' said he, 'build a house for our God, of logs? No, I have a better plan than that. I have a plan of the house of the Lord, given by himself; and you will soon see by this, the difference between our calculations[101] and his idea of things.'

"He then gave them a full pattern of the house of the Lord at Kirtland, with which the brethren were highly delighted,[102] particularly Hyrum [Smith],

were few" (Joseph Fielding Smith, *Essentials in Church History*, 129).

99. Truman O. Angell, one of the architects of the temple, wrote in his journal how the temple plan was revealed: "Joseph received the word of the Lord for him to take his two counsellors Williams and Rigdon and come before the Lord, and He would show them the plan or model of the House to be built. We went upon our knees, called on the Lord, and the Building appeared within viewing distance: I being the first to

discover it. Then all of us viewed it together. After we had taken a good look at the exterior, the building seemed to come right over us, and the Makeup of this Hall seemed to coincide with what I there saw to a minutia" (Truman O. Angell, "Journal of Truman O. Angell" [typescript], Brigham Young University Special Collections, Harold B. Lee Library, Provo, Utah).

100. *complied with*—completed or obeyed

101. *calculations*—ideas

mortgage[118] on the farm upon which the temple was being built.

"The day after his arrival in Kirtland, . . . [he was] informed that the mortgage of the before mentioned farm was about to be foreclosed. Whereupon he loaned the prophet two thousand dollars and took his note on interest, with which amount the farm was redeemed"[119] (*Scraps of Biography: Faith-Promoting Series,* no. 10, 12–13).

Many years later, while the Saints were living in Nauvoo, John Tanner was preparing to leave on a mission to the Eastern States.

"Before starting, . . . he saw the Prophet Joseph, and, meeting him on the street, gave him his note of hand for the two thousand dollars loaned in Kirtland, January 1835, to redeem the temple land. The Prophet asked him what he wanted done with the note. Elder Tanner replied, 'Brother Joseph, you are welcome to it.'[120] The Prophet then laid his right hand heavily on Elder Tanner's shoulder, saying, 'God bless you, Father Tanner; your children shall never beg bread'"[121] (*Scraps of Biography: Faith-Promoting Series,* no. 10, 16).

CHAPTER 54: REMARKABLE REVELATIONS

The year 1836 began with difficult trials for both the Smith family and the Church. Satan was determined to destroy the Lord's Church right from the beginning. But five years earlier, in January 1831, the Lord promised the Saints that if they would gather in Ohio, "there you shall be endowed with power from on high" (D&C 38:32). Now that the Kirtland Temple was nearing completion, the promised spiritual blessings began to show forth. During this time the Lord blessed the Saints with increased visions and revelations that continued even after the Prophet dedicated the temple on March 27, 1836. As you read, look for important gospel principles that brought joy to the Saints.

SATAN TRIES TO DESTROY THE SMITH FAMILY AND THE CHURCH

As 1836 began, the Prophet Joseph Smith reflected in his writings about the trials and difficulties his family and the Church had endured during the past several months:

"My heart is filled with gratitude to God, that He has preserved my life and the lives of my family while another year has rolled away. We have been sustained and upheld in the midst[122] of a wicked and perverse[123] generation, although exposed to all the afflictions, temptations, and misery that are incident to[124] human life; for this I feel to humble myself in dust and ashes as it were before the Lord.[125] . . . My heart is pained within me because of the difficulty

God, for his complete restoration to health" (*Scraps of Biography: Faith-Promoting Series,* no. 10, 16).

118. **lift the mortgage**—pay the money owed

119. When a mortgage is foreclosed it means that those who own the land or building being purchased may legally take it away from those trying to buy it. John Tanner came just in time and paid the debt with his own money. Legally this made him the new owner of the farmland upon which the temple was built.

120. This action meant that John Tanner was giving the land upon which the temple was built to the Prophet Joseph Smith. The Church no longer had to pay Brother Tanner back for the land he had earlier bought. "It is estimated that at various times John Tanner gave or loaned over fifty thousand dollars to Joseph Smith and the Church" (Karl Ricks Anderson, *Joseph Smith's Kirtland,* 17).

121. Historian Leonard Arrington discovered that "when the family moved west after the martyrdom of the Prophet, John Tanner . . . had time to see his family settled and thriving . . . before his death in 1850. His ten children who came west fulfilled the Prophet's prediction, as they participated in the colonization, not only of South Cottonwood, [Utah], but of San Bernardino, California; of such Utah communities as Beaver, Fillmore, Payson, and North Ogden; and of Arizona. . . . Consistently devoted and hard-working, they gave their families economic and spiritual security and left an honorable legacy of commitment that has not decreased with time" (Leonard J. Arrington, "The John Tanner Family," *Ensign,* March 1979, 48–49).

NOTES FOR CHAPTER 54

122. **midst**—middle

123. **perverse**—stubborn

124. **are incident to**—happen in

125. Going before the Lord in "dust and ashes" is a symbol of humility. It was in this manner that Abraham

that exists in my father's family. The devil has made a violent attack on my brother, William[126] . . . and the powers of darkness . . . cast a gloomy shade over the minds of my parents and some of brethren and sisters, which prevents them from seeing things as they really are; and the powers of earth and hell seem combined to overthrow us and the Church, by causing a division in the family; and indeed the adversary[127] is bringing into requisition[128] all his subtlety[129] to prevent the Saints from being endowed, by causing division among the Twelve, also among the Seventy, and bickerings and jealousies among the Elders and official members of the Church" (*History of the Church*, 2:352).

THE SPIRIT OF THE LORD BRINGS HEALING TO THE CHURCH

Soon after the organization of the Quorum of the Twelve Apostles in March 1835, the Twelve were called to serve missions in the eastern states. They were to teach the gospel and strengthen the branches of the Church. While serving their mission, certain lies and accusations were spread about them. As a result of these lies, misunderstandings developed between the Twelve and members of the Presidency. A meeting was held on January 16, 1836, to settle their differences. Insight and understanding of the affair is contained in Elder

Orson F. Whitney's biography of Elder Heber C. Kimball:

"While the Apostles were absent upon this mission, the 'accuser of the brethren'[130] had been busy sowing discord,[131] with a view to causing coldness and estrangement[132] between the First Presidency and the Twelve. . . .[133]

"The accusations against the Twelve were . . . serious. It was said that they had sought to be independent of the presiding quorum of the Church,[134] and had failed to fulfill their mission, in not preaching . . . the gathering to Zion, or the collection of means for the Kirtland Temple and the purchase of lands in Missouri. Both charges were proved to be groundless.[135]

"At the council, where the Apostles laid their grievances before the Presidency [January 16, 1836], and 'all things were reconciled,[136] the Prophet Joseph . . . made a covenant with the Twelve that never again would he entertain a charge against them on one-sided testimony, or pass judgment upon them even in thought, without first giving them an opportunity of being heard in their own defense.

"If this noble, just, and charitable resolve had always been adhered to[137] by the Saints of God, . . . how many bitter heart-burnings might have been spared! . . . Are we not too prone to heed[138] the tale-bearer,[139] the secret enemy, who . . . seeks to build

---

asked Jehovah to spare Sodom and Gomorrah from destruction (see Genesis 18:27).

126. William Smith, the Prophet's brother, was a member of the Quorum of the Twelve Apostles. Unfortunately, he did not live with the spirit of this holy calling. His pride and temper seemed to influence his behavior, and he physically attacked Joseph Smith several times. He eventually left the Church a little over a year after the Prophet was martyred (see Hoyt W. Brewster Jr., *Doctrine and Covenants Encyclopedia*, 536–37).

127. *the adversary*—Satan

128. *bringing into requisition*—using

129. *subtlety*—sneakiness

130. Brigham Young once explained: "As it has always been, and will be yet for some time, when the sons of God assemble together, Satan will be on hand as an accuser of the brethren, to find fault with those who are trying to do good" (*Journal of Discourses*, 11:141).

131. *discord*—disagreement

132. *estrangement*—division

133. Why do you think Satan wanted to cause anger among the leaders of the Church? What is it like when your family has serious disagreements? How can you help keep it from happening?

134. It is against the Lord's plan for the Twelve Apostles to be "independent" of the First Presidency, for the Lord revealed that the First Presidency is "the highest council of the church of God" (D&C 107:80).

135. *groundless*—not true

136. *reconciled*—settled and forgiven

137. *adhered to*—followed or obeyed

138. *prone to heed*—tempted to listen to

139. *tale-bearer*—one who spreads rumors and lies

up his own, upon the ruins of his brother's reputation? . . . [140]

"'I will here remark,' says Heber, 'that every individual who used an influence against the Twelve on their mission, apostatized and went out of the Church;[141] and this should remain an everlasting warning to all others. In those days there was a continual itching in certain individuals to destroy the union existing between the Twelve and the First Presidency, . . . which thing they did at last effect, which broke up the Church for a time; for . . . six of the Twelve became disaffected,[142] and turned against Joseph and those of the Twelve who sustained him.'

"As, in the end, good comes of evil, . . . so from the unhappy event related, issued good and glad results. From the time the reconciliation took place between the Presidency and the Twelve, a reformation commenced[143] in the Church. 'Those meetings,' says Heber, 'of humiliation,[144] repentance, and confessing of sins, were truly the beginning of good days to us, and they continued through the endowment'"[145] (*Life of Heber C. Kimball,* 84–87).

THE SAINTS ARE BLESSED WITH A SEASON OF SPIRITUAL MANIFESTATIONS

As these difficulties were overcome through prayer and humility, the Lord poured out his Spirit in abundance, and rich spiritual experiences continued until after the dedication of the Kirtland temple.

"Much time was spent in January and February, 1836," wrote Joseph Fielding Smith, "in council meetings and the filling of vacancies in the various organizations of the Priesthood. . . . Thursday, January 21, the first of a number of meetings in the temple was held. These gatherings continued through several days, in which the faithful elders of the Church received blessings by the laying on of hands and anointing with oil.

"At this first meeting the presidency met, and Father Joseph Smith, the patriarch, was anointed and blessed. He then anointed and blessed each of the brethren of the presidency, beginning with the oldest, pronouncing such blessings upon them as the Spirit of the Lord revealed,[146] and many prophecies were uttered[147] by each of them.

"While thus engaged the heavens were opened and the Prophet received [a great] vision" (*Essentials in Church History,* 157).

That revelation is today found in Doctrine and Covenants section 137:

"The heavens were opened upon us, and I beheld the celestial kingdom of God, and the glory thereof, whether in the body or out I cannot tell.[148]

---

140. Do you have friends that tend to spread rumors about others? How can this hurt people? What can you do to help both your friends and others they might hurt?

141. Elder Russell M. Nelson taught: "Worthy servants of the Master . . . would not speak ill of the Lord's anointed nor provoke contention" because "contention is not of the Lord" (*Perfection Pending, and Other Favorite Discourses,* 59).

142. *disaffected*—unfriendly

143. *a reformation commenced*—improvement began

144. *humiliation*—humility

145. Humility and repentance invite the Holy Spirit. Why do you think this event was important for the Church? How have you been blessed by being worthy of the Spirit?

146. President Ezra Taft Benson taught that a patriarchal blessing is "personal scripture" to the person receiving it. "A patriarchal blessing is the inspired and prophetic statement of your life's mission together with the blessings, cautions, and admonitions as the patriarch may be prompted to give" (*The Teachings of Ezra Taft Benson,* 214).

147. *uttered*—spoken

148. The Apostle Paul had a similar experience and used nearly the same words to describe it (see 2 Corinthians 12:2–4). For a human to see a vision of celestial glory would require the influence of the Holy Ghost. As Moses learned, if he had seen God with his natural eyes, he would have "withered and died in his presence; but his glory was upon me" (Moses 1:11).

The Lord has provided a way for all of his children to hear the gospel

THE SAVIOR APPEARS

Once the temple was dedicated, ordinance work began. The Brethren held many meetings in the temple and learned much. At one such meeting, held Sunday, April 3, 1836, Joseph Smith and Oliver Cowdery knelt in prayer behind the temple veils. The two rose from their knees and witnessed a marvelous vision:

"The veil was taken from our minds, and the eyes of our understanding[190] were opened.

"We saw the Lord standing upon the breastwork of the pulpit, before us; and under his feet was a paved work of pure gold, in color like amber.[191]

"His eyes were as a flame of fire; the hair of his head was white like the pure snow; his countenance[192] shone above the brightness of the sun; and his voice was as the sound of the rushing of great waters, even the voice of Jehovah, saying:

"I am the first and the last;[193] I am he who liveth, I am he who was slain; I am your advocate[194] with the Father.

"Behold, your sins are forgiven you; you are clean before me; therefore, lift up your heads and rejoice.

"Let the hearts of your brethren rejoice, and let the hearts of all my people rejoice, who have, with their might, built this house to my name" (D&C 110:1–6).

MOSES, ELIAS AND ELIJAH RESTORE PRIESTHOOD KEYS

Historian B. H. Roberts explained what happened next: "The Savior appeared and proclaimed His acceptance of the temple and of the saints as His people; Moses appeared and restored the keys of the gathering of Israel;[195] Elias appeared[196] and committed[197] the dispensation of the gospel of Abraham;[198] Elijah came in fulfillment of the words of Malachi 'to turn[199] the hearts of the fathers to the children, and the hearts of the children to their fathers,'[200] preparatory to the coming of the great and dreadful day of the Lord.

---

190. The "eyes of understanding" are one's spiritual eyes or one's ability to understand spiritual ideas when one is "quickened by the Spirit of God" (D&C 67:10–12).

191. *amber*—yellowish-brown

192. *countenance*—appearance

193. The words "the first and the last" represent the eternal nature of God (see D&C 76:4; Revelation 1:8, 17).

194. An advocate is someone who helps, defends, and recommends another. In a revelation to Joseph Smith, the Lord described himself as our "advocate with the Father, who is pleading your cause before him" (D&C 45:3).

195. Moses returned with the keys of the gathering. Elder Bruce R. McConkie said, "The gathering of Israel is a reality. When the ten tribes return they will come at the direction of the President of The Church of Jesus Christ of Latter-day Saints, for he now holds and will then hold the keys of presidency and direction for this mighty work" ("The Final Glorious Gospel Dispensation," *Ensign*, April 1980, 22).

196. "A man called Elias apparently lived in mortality in the days of Abraham, who committed the dispensation of the gospel of Abraham to Joseph Smith" (Bible Dictionary, s.v. "Elias," 663). Through Abraham's children "shall all the families of the earth be blessed, even with the blessings of the Gospel, which are the blessings of salvation, even of eternal life" (Abraham 2:11).

197. *committed*—gave; delivered

198. According to Joseph Fielding Smith, Elias "held the keys of the gospel in the days of Abraham" and appeared to give these keys to Joseph Smith (see *Church History and Modern Revelation*, 2:49).

199. *turn*—bind or seal

200. The spirit of Elijah includes compiling family histories and personal journals, keeping books of remembrance, creating family organizations, and holding family reunions. What are you doing to help in this important work?

Elijah restored priesthood keys to bind families together

faithful and prominent elder in the church . . . in editing and publishing the *Times and Seasons,* states that the journey to Salem arose from these circumstances. There came to Kirtland a brother by the name of Burgess who stated that he had knowledge of a large amount of money secreted[24] in the cellar of a certain house in Salem, Massachusetts, which had belonged to a widow (then deceased), and thought he was the only person who had knowledge of it, or of the location of the house. The brethren accepting the representations[25] of Burgess as true made the journey to Salem to secure, if possible, the treasure. Burgess, according to Robinson, met the brethren in Salem, but claimed that time had wrought[26] such changes in the town that he could not for a certainty point out the house 'and soon left.'

"While in Salem the Prophet received a revelation in which the folly of this journey was sharply reproved"[27] (*Comprehensive History of the Church,* 410–11).

This revelation is now in Doctrine and Covenants section 111.

"I, the Lord your God, am not displeased with your coming this journey, notwithstanding your follies;[28]

"I have much treasure in the city for you,[29] for the benefit of Zion; and many people in this city whom I will gather out in due time for the benefit of Zion, through your instrumentality; . . .

"Concern not yourselves about your debts, for I will give you power to pay them. . . .

"For there are more treasures than one for you in this city"[30] (D&C 111:1–2, 5, 10).

Some time later, many converts to the Church were found in Salem and a branch of the Church was organized there.[31]

CHAPTER 57: PROBLEMS INCREASE—THE SAINTS BEGIN TO LEAVE KIRTLAND

Historian B. H. Roberts called the years 1837 and 1838 "the darkest days" for Kirtland. "The spirit of apostasy was rife,*"[32] he wrote. "No quorum of the church was free from it. Five of the quorum of the twelve at one time were* in league[33] *with the enemies of the Prophet, and it would seem that every evil power had combined to make an end of the New Dispensation so recently established" (A Comprehensive History of the Church, 1:396–97). The financial crisis of 1837 had tried the faith of many Church members (see chapter 56). Some Saints fell away from the Church, while others were greatly strengthened by those same trials and became great leaders in the kingdom of God. As you study this chapter, notice how the kind of "treasure" (see Matthew 6:24) a person sets his or her heart upon affects that person's choices and future.*

THE PROPHET RECEIVES A VISION AND A WARNING OF EVIL

After the completion of the Kirtland Temple, Joseph and several others went on a short mission

---

24. *secreted*—hidden

25. *representations*—statements

26. *wrought*—caused

27. *sharply reproved*—strongly criticized

28. *follies*—foolish mistakes

29. The greatest "treasure" we gain in doing missionary work is helping others find the gospel of Jesus Christ. The Lord taught: "How great is his joy in the soul that repenteth! . . . And if it so be that you should labor all your days in crying repentance unto this people, and bring, save it be one soul unto me, how great shall be your joy with him in the kingdom of my Father!" (D&C 18:13, 15).

30. What can we learn here from the way the Lord taught the Prophet Joseph? What do these verses teach us about what "treasures" are most important to the Lord? (see also D&C 18:10–16).

31. The Saints did not find financial treasure in Salem. Several years later, however, in 1843, Erastus Snow was called on a mission to Salem. He labored there for several years and baptized more than one hundred people.

NOTES FOR CHAPTER 57

32. *rife*—widespread

33. *in league*—planning and working together

Joseph Smith was a talented and articulate teacher

Northern Missouri

Northwest Missouri in the 1830s

TOM CHILD

"'Let us fix up a county expressly[6] for the Mormons,' exclaimed certain politicians and public men. Let us send all the Mormons in the state to that county and induce[7] all Gentiles[8] therein to sell out and leave. The proposition[9] suited everyone. The Gentiles said, 'If the Mormons are willing to go into that prairie country and settle, let them have it and welcome.' The Mormons said, 'If we may be allowed to remain peaceably and enjoy our religion, we will go into any country that may be set apart for us, no matter how wild and unbroken it may be, and we will make it to blossom as the rose.[10] If we obtain political control of a county we will honestly administer it and be loyal in all things to the state government over us.'[11]

"Arrangements were soon made. Every Gentile in the proposed new county that could be induced to sell his possessions at a reasonable price was bought out, and his place taken by a Mormon. The authorities of the church agreed that no Mormons should settle in any other county without the previous consent of the settlers already there" (as cited in B. H. Roberts, *Comprehensive History of the Church*, 1:417).

6. *expressly*—specifically

7. *induce*—persuade or make

8. At this time in history, the Saints sometimes referred to people who were not Church members as "Gentiles," especially those nonmembers who were hostile toward the Saints.

9. *proposition*—idea

10. The Prophet Isaiah used the term "blossom as a rose" (see Isaiah 35:1–2) to depict the day that Christ would return and Zion would be established.

11. Even though the Saints faced terrible persecution, they continued to be optimistic. President Gordon B. Hinckley wrote: "I have learned a secret. I have learned that when good men and good women face challenges with optimism, things will always work out!" (*Way to Be*, 84). Why do you think it is important to be optimistic? What did the Saints do to show optimism at this time? What can you learn from their example?

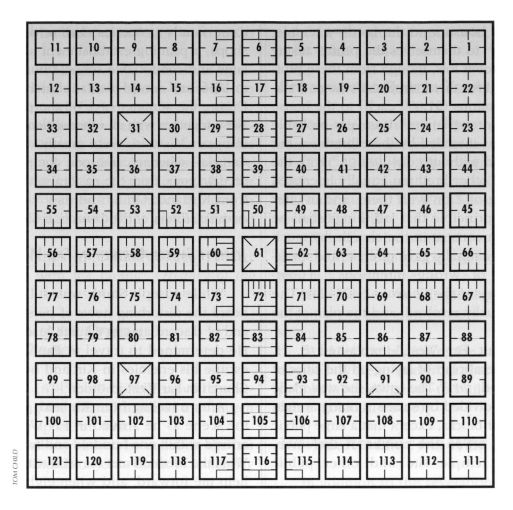

TOM CHILD

Plat map of Far West

MOVING FROM CLAY COUNTY TO THE NEW COUNTIES

With the new agreement in place, the Saints quickly left Clay County and began settling in Carroll, Daviess, and Caldwell Counties. The town of Far West became an important settlement at this time. Far West was located in Caldwell County, and was one mile south of Shoal Creek. Goose Creek, a tributary[12] of Shoal Creek, also ran through the county. Both streams provided waterpower to the Saints. Nearby, the town of Kingston, which later became the county seat of Caldwell County, sat above Far West on a high swell of land.[13]

FAR WEST GROWS

Although the selection of Far West as a home for the Saints was made with honorable intentions, the establishment of the city was not made with complete honesty. Historian B. H. Roberts wrote that "the site . . . was chosen by John Whitmer and W. W. Phelps in the summer of 1836, the entry being filed on the 8th of August of that year. The north half was entered in the name of W. W. Phelps, the south half in the name of John Whitmer; but both Phelps and Whitmer held the land in trust for the church. . . . They laid out the public square; they appointed and ordained a committee to supervise

12. *tributary*—branch or stream

13. *swell of land*—hill

but the sheriff would not allow them to fight on such unequal terms" (3:215n).[65]

FOUR NEW APOSTLES ARE CALLED

John Taylor, John E. Page, Wilford Woodruff,[66] and Willard Richards were called to the apostleship to take the places of the four who had fallen.[67] The call to Elders Taylor, Page, Woodruff, and Richards to serve as apostles came in a revelation given to the Prophet Joseph Smith[68] at Far West, Missouri, on July 8, 1838, and is recorded in Doctrine and Covenants section 118.

JOHN TAYLOR'S CALL TO THE QUORUM OF THE TWELVE APOSTLES

John Taylor was living in Canada in the fall of 1837 when he received a spiritual manifestation[69] that he would be called to serve as an apostle. He kept the knowledge to himself, waiting to receive the call from the Prophet. "His heart rejoiced," wrote his biographer, "at the thought that he was known of the Lord, and considered worthy by Him to stand in this exalted station[70] in the Church of Christ, he bore his new honors with becoming modesty.[71] Commenting upon the appointment, and the

prospect which now opened before him, he remarks:

"'The work seemed great, the duties arduous[72] and responsible. I felt my own weakness and littleness; but I felt determined, the Lord being my helper, to endeavor[73] to magnify it. When I first entered upon Mormonism, I did it with my eyes open. I counted the cost. I looked upon it as a life-long labor, and I considered that I was not only enlisted for time, but for eternity also, and did not wish to shrink now, although I felt my incompetency.'"[74] (B. H. Roberts, *Life of John Taylor*, 47–48).[75]

THE CALLING OF APOSTLE JOHN PAGE

John Page was a faithful missionary who served two missions in Canada, baptizing nearly six hundred people and traveling more than five thousand miles during this time. In 1838 he was moving his family and other Canadian Saints into DeWitt, Missouri, when a mob attacked the town and his group. He described the results: "We were attacked by an armed mob, and by them barbarously[76] treated for nearly two weeks. We then went to Far West, Caldwell county, where we united with the general body of the Church, and with them participated in all the grievous[77] persecutions practiced on

---

65. At one time these men were all very faithful and worthy enough to be called as special witnesses of the Lord (see D&C 107:23). But they began to become critical and say bad things about the Prophet and other Church leaders. Elder Dallin H. Oaks explained that those who start the habit of criticizing the Lord's servants soon give up "the guidance of the Spirit of the Lord. They drift from prayer, from the scriptures, from church activity, and from keeping the commandments. They inevitably lose spirituality and blessings" (*The Lord's Way*, 205).

66. Wilford Woodruff was a man who searched to know the truth, even in his youth. He studied the Bible as a young man and frequently offered sincere prayers to find the true church. After his baptism he spent many years as a very successful missionary. He served missions in both the southern and eastern part of the United States. Perhaps his most well-known missionary labors were in England, where he baptized well over one thousand converts. Wilford Woodruff served as an apostle for fifty years and as the president of the Church for nine years.

67. *fallen*—lost their Church membership

68. Apostles, like other Church leaders, are called by revelation from God (see Articles of Faith 1:5). Why do you think it is important for these calls to come by revelation?

69. *manifestation*— message

70. *exalted station*—important calling

71. *becoming modesty*—proper humility

72. *arduous*—difficult

73. *endeavor*—try

74. *incompetency*—lack of ability

75. Some of the responsibilities of apostles are outlined in D&C 107:23–24. When is the last time you were able to hear an apostle teach? What message or teachings did he have for you?

76. *barbarously*—cruelly

77. *grievous*—painful and hard

JOHN TAYLOR, BY LORUS PRATT

John Taylor (1808–1887) was ordained an apostle December 19, 1838. He eventually was sustained as the third president of the Church

the Church by means of[78] a furious mob, by which means I buried one wife and two children as martyrs to our holy religion, since they died through extreme suffering" (in *History of the Church,* 3:241n).[79]

On December 19, 1838, only a few weeks after the death of his wife and two children, John Page and John Taylor were ordained apostles under the hands of Brigham Young and Heber C. Kimball.[80]

WILFORD WOODRUFF RECEIVES A CALL TO THE QUORUM OF THE TWELVE APOSTLES

While serving a mission in the state of Maine, Elder Wilford Woodruff learned of his calls to both the Quorum of the Twelve Apostles and as a missionary to England. He wrote this about the calls:

"On the 9th of August, I received a letter from Elder Thomas B. Marsh, who was then President of the Twelve Apostles, informing me that the Prophet Joseph Smith had received a revelation from the Lord, naming as persons to be chosen to fill the places of those of the Twelve who had fallen. Those named were John E. Page, John Taylor, Wilford Woodruff and Willard Richards. In his letter President Marsh added: 'Know then, Brother Woodruff, by this, that you are appointed to fill the place of one of the Twelve Apostles, and that it is agreeable to the word of the Lord, given very lately, that you should come speedily to Far West, and, on the 26th of April next, take your leave of the Saints here and depart for other climes,[81] across the mighty deep.' The substance of this letter had been revealed

to me several weeks before, but I had not named it to any person"[82] (*Wilford Woodruff, His Life and Labors,* comp. Matthias F. Cowley, 93).

"It was on the 8th of July," wrote Elder Woodruff's biographer, "that this humble, faithful, diligent elder was called by the voice of God, through His prophet, to be one of the Twelve Apostles of the Lamb in this dispensation; and Wilford being at the time many hundreds of miles distant from the Prophet, the Lord then revealed to him the fact of that calling. Wilford had been true to the Lord as a teacher, priest, elder, and seventy in His Church, and thus was worthy of the higher call that had come, and to be trusted with its increased responsibility. He was prepared by the revelations of heaven to his own soul to be an apostle of the Lord Jesus Christ" (*Wilford Woodruff, His Life and Labors,* comp. Matthias F. Cowley, 93).

Wilford Woodruff was ordained on April 26, 1839, just before the apostles left Far West, Missouri, to begin their mission in England.[83]

WILLARD RICHARDS IS ORDAINED AN APOSTLE IN ENGLAND

Willard Richards was living in England and serving as a counselor to the mission president of the British mission when he learned of his call to the Quorum of the Twelve Apostles. He was ordained many months later when members of the Twelve arrived in England for their missions. Elder Joseph Fielding Smith described the circumstances:

---

78. *by means of*—through

79. Religious martyrs are people who die for their faith. It is not likely that you will lose your life because you believe in the Savior and his Church, but you may be required to face difficult trials and experiences. Are you willing to live your life as a testimony of your faith?

80. New apostles are called today whenever there is a vacancy in the quorum. Can you name any of today's members of the Quorum of the Twelve Apostles? Do

you remember when any of them were ordained and became part of that important quorum?

81. *climes*—far away places

82. The Lord, through the Spirit, let Wilford know he was going to be called as an apostle before notice of the call arrived. He did not speak about this personal revelation to anyone.

83. See chapter 67, "The Mission of the Twelve to England," for more information about Wilford Woodruff's mission.

Wilford Woodruff (1807–1898) was ordained an apostle April 26, 1839. He was sustained fifty years later, in 1889, as the fourth president of the Church

of the ranks and fell mortally wounded. Thus the work of death commenced. . . .

"The parties immediately came in contact, with their swords, and the mob were soon put to flight, crossing the river at the ford and such places as they could get a chance. In the pursuit, one of the mob fled from behind a tree, wheeled, and shot Captain Patten, who instantly fell, mortally wounded" (*History of the Church*, 3:170–71).

On October 27, 1838, Brother Patten was buried. Joseph wrote: "Before the funeral, I called at Brother Patten's house,[132] and while meditating on the scene before me in presence of his friends, I could not help pointing to his lifeless body and testifying, 'There lies a man that has done just as he said he would—he has laid down his life for his friends'"[133] (*History of the Church*, 3:175).

GOVERNOR BOGGS ORDERS THAT THE MORMONS BE EXTERMINATED

Lilburn W. Boggs, the governor of Missouri, received many false reports about the Mormons and decided to use the Missouri Militia to drive the Mormons out of the state or kill them.

On the day of the battle of Crooked River, Governor Boggs gave orders to General John B. Clark[134] to gather enough troops to force away the Saints and return the original settlers of Daviess County back to their land. He called for two thousand men to be made ready to fight.

"The first order to General Clark was followed by another the following day," explained Joseph Fielding Smith, "the report of the battle of Crooked River having reached the ear of the governor. When he discovered that the 'Mormons' were attempting to 'fight it out,' he had a change of heart and issued, . . . without provocation or due investigation, . . . by authority of the great office which he held, . . . an order to exterminate[135] or drive from Missouri twelve thousand defenseless citizens who had done no wrong. And the execution of this shameful and wicked order was to be carried out in the dead of winter, which would bring to pass exposure and death of delicate women and innocent children, against whom there could have been no charge.

132. "Heber C. Kimball informs us that . . . [Patten's] 'wound was such, that there was no hope entertained of his recovery; this he was perfectly aware of.' The wounded apostle . . . affirmed to those present his faith and testimony in the gospel restored through the instrumentality of Joseph Smith as well as his hope for eternal life. Patten spoke to his wife, Ann, counseling her, 'Whatever you do else, O, do not deny the faith!' Kimball further recorded Patten's last moments. 'A few minutes before he died he prayed as follows: "Father I ask thee, in the name of Jesus Christ, that thou wouldst release my spirit and receive it unto thyself:" and then said to those who surrounded his dying bed, "Brethren, you have held me by your faith, but do give me up and let me go I beseech you." We then committed him to God, and he soon breathed his last, and slept in Jesus without a groan.' . . . Some years prior, Wilford Woodruff reported David Patten had made it known to Joseph Smith that he had asked the Lord to let him die as a martyr. Joseph, deeply saddened, responded, 'When a man of your faith asks the Lord for anything, he generally gets it'" (Alexander Baugh, "The Battle Between Mormon and Missouri Militia at Crooked River," *Regional Studies in Latter-day Saint Church History Missouri*, 94–95).

133. The Lord revealed that he had received David Patten unto himself, and that David was with him at this time (see D&C 124:19).

134. Joseph Fielding Smith explained, "General John B. Clark, was a resident of Jackson County. So was General Samuel D. Lucas. Both assisted in driving the 'Mormons' from that county in 1833. Governor Lilburn W. Boggs was also from Jackson, and aided in that expulsion. . . . These three men hated the Latter-day Saints with a mortal hate. . . . Clark, who received the command, and Lucas who assisted him, were the two most fitted to carry out the order of extermination" (*Essentials in Church History*, 194).

135. *exterminate*—destroy

Governor Boggs's order opened the door to untold suffering by the Saints

"The Governor's orders soon became generally known and the mobbers looked upon it . . . as an approval of their unlawful course. Marauders sallied[136] forth, burning houses, driving off cattle, destroying property, ravishing[137] women and threatening with death any who dared resist their fiendish[138] deeds" (*Essentials in Church History,* 192–93).

The extermination order from Governor Boggs, given on October 27, 1838, included the following:

"The Mormons must be treated as enemies and *must be exterminated* or driven from the state, if necessary for the public good. Their outrages are beyond all description"[139] (in *History of the Church,* 3:175).

HAUN'S MILL MASSACRE

Just a few days after the extermination order, a tragic incident occurred at a place called Haun's Mill, a Latter-day Saint community built around a grist mill run by Jacob Haun. The Prophet Joseph had counseled the Saints living in all of the surrounding Mormon communities to come to Far West for protection because he feared for their lives. Those at Haun's Mill had chosen to stay.

"On 30 October 1838," according to one history, "some 200 men mounted a surprise attack against the small community of Saints at Haun's Mill on Shoal Creek, Caldwell County. The assailants, in an act of treachery, called for those men who wished to save themselves to run into the blacksmith shop. Then they took up positions around the building and fired into it until they thought all inside were dead. Others were shot as they tried to make their escape. In all, 17 men and boys were killed and 15 were wounded. . . .

" . . . Only a few able-bodied men remained, including Joseph Young, the brother of Brigham Young. Because they feared the return of the mob, there was no time to dig conventional graves. The bodies were thrown into a dry well, forming a mass grave" (*Our Heritage,* 47–48).

SURRENDER OF CHURCH LEADERS AT FAR WEST

The conflict between the Saints and the Missourians continued through October 1838. At this point Joseph Smith and other Church leaders were

Here at Haun's Mill, a mob massacred seventeen Saints and wounded fifteen others

HAUN'S MILL, BY C. C. A. CHRISTENSEN, COURTESY BRIGHAM YOUNG UNIVERSITY MUSEUM OF ART

136. *Marauders sallied*—Robbers rushed

137. *ravishing*—hurting and taking advantage of

138. *fiendish*—evil

139. President Spencer W. Kimball announced to the Church in 1976, "Since our last conference we have had a delightful message from Christopher S. Bond, Governor of the state of Missouri, who advised us that he has rescinded the 138-year-old Executive Order of Governor Lilburn W. Boggs calling for the extermination or expulsion of the Mormons from the state of Missouri. Governor Bond, present Missouri governor, wrote: 'Expressing on behalf of all Missourians our deep regret for the injustice and undue suffering which was caused by this 1838 order, I hereby rescind Executive Order No. 44 dated October 27, 1838, issued by Governor Lilburn W. Boggs.' . . . Thank you, Governor Bond" (Spencer W. Kimball, "A Report and a Challenge," *Ensign,* November 1976, 4).

THE ARREST OF MORMON LEADERS, BY C. A. CHRISTENSEN, COURTESY BRIGHAM YOUNG UNIVERSITY MUSEUM OF ART

Joseph and other leaders were betrayed and arrested

in Far West. George Hinkle,[140] who was leading the Saints in their march at Caldwell County, proved to be a traitor to Joseph Smith. He secretly arranged for the Mormon leaders to be captured. Joseph Fielding Smith described the scene:

"About eight o'clock, October 31, 1838, the enemy sent a flag of truce which was met by several brethren who hoped that a satisfactory arrangement could be made when they could present a true picture of the circumstances. Col. Hinkle, commander of the defending forces went to meet this flag. He was a coward who feared for his life. He made a secret agreement [Treaty of Far West] with this mob. . . .

"New forces of the enemies of the Church were hourly joining the ranks of this state militia. Towards the evening of the 31st the Prophet waited on Col. Hinkle who stated that the officers of the militia desired to have an interview with the Prophet Joseph Smith and some others, hoping that the difficulties might be settled without having occasion to carry into effect the exterminating order which had just been received from the governor. 'I immediately complied with the request,' said the Prophet, 'and in company with Elders Sidney Rigdon and Parley P. Pratt, Colonel Wight and George W. Robinson, went unto the camp of the militia. But judge of my surprise, when, instead of being treated with that respect which is due from one citizen to another, we were taken as prisoners of war, and treated with utmost contempt.[141] The officers would not converse

---

140. "George M. Hinkle (1801–61), born in Kentucky, joined the Church as early as 1832 and moved to Missouri. In Far West he operated a store. During the fall of Far West he allegedly turned Joseph Smith and other Church leaders over to General Lucas. Most of the Saints felt that he betrayed the Prophet. He was excommunicated in 1839" (Donald Q. Cannon and Lyndon W. Cook, *Far West Record*, 268).

141. ***contempt***—rudeness

to the wondering soldiers, who listened with almost breathless attention while I set forth the doctrine of faith in Jesus Christ, and repentance, and baptism for remission of sins, with the promise of the Holy Ghost, as recorded in the second chapter of the Acts of the Apostles.

"The woman was satisfied, and praised God in the hearing of the soldiers, and went away, praying that God would protect and deliver us. Thus was fulfilled a prophecy which had been spoken publicly by me, a few months previous—that a sermon should be preached in Jackson county by one of our Elders, before the close of 1838.

" . . . We proceeded on and arrived at Independence, past noon, in the midst of a great rain, and a multitude of spectators who had assembled to see us, and hear the bugles sound a blast of triumphant joy, which echoed through the camp" (*History of the Church,* 3:200–201).

THE PRISONERS ARE TAKEN TO RICHMOND, MISSOURI

Before being taken to Liberty, Missouri, Joseph Smith and the other prisoners were taken to a jail in Richmond. Parley P. Pratt, who was also a prisoner, relates an experience while there:

"I must not forget to state that when we arrived in Richmond as prisoners there were some fifty others, mostly heads of families, who had been marched from Caldwell on foot (distance 30 miles), and were now penned up[151] in a cold, open, unfinished court house, in which situation they remained for some weeks, while their families were suffering severe privations.[152] . . .

"The Court of Inquiry[153] now commenced, before Judge Austin A. King. This continued from the 11th to 28th of November. . . . It was a very severe time of snow and winter weather, and we suffered much. . . .

"These guards were composed generally of the most noisy, foul mouthed, vulgar,[154] disgraceful rabble[155] that ever defiled[156] the earth. . . .

"In one of those tedious[157] nights we had lain as if in sleep till the hour of midnight had passed, and our ears and hearts had been pained, while we had listened for hours to the obscene jests,[158] the horrid oaths, the dreadful blasphemies[159] and filthy language of our guards. . . .

"I had listened till I became so disgusted, shocked, horrified, and so filled with the spirit of indignant[160] justice that I could scarcely refrain from rising upon my feet and rebuking the guards; but had said nothing to Joseph, or any one else, although I lay next to him and knew he was awake. On a sudden he arose to his feet, and spoke in a voice of thunder, as the roaring lion, uttering, as near as I can recollect, the following words:

"'SILENCE, ye fiends[161] of the infernal pit.[162] In the name of Jesus Christ I rebuke you, and command you to be still; I will not live another minute and bear such language. Cease such talk, or you or I die THIS INSTANT!'

"He ceased to speak. He stood erect in terrible majesty. Chained, and without a weapon; calm, unruffled and dignified as an angel, he looked upon the quailing[163] guards, whose weapons were lowered or dropped to the ground; whose knees smote[164] together, and who, shrinking into a corner,

---

151. *penned up*—confined

152. *severe privations*—terrible poverty

153. A Court of Inquiry is where a judge seeks information by asking questions.

154. *vulgar*—rude and offensive

155. *disgraceful rabble*—shameful mob

156. *defiled*—polluted

157. *tedious*—long and difficult

158. *obscene jests*—offensive jokes

159. *blasphemies*—lack of reverence for God

160. *indignant*—angry

161. *fiends*—devils

162. *the infernal pit*—hell

163. *quailing*—trembling

164. *smote*—knocked

Joseph Smith rebuked the guards in Richmond

WINTER AT LIBERTY JAIL, BY AL ROUNDS

Joseph and his fellow prisoners were held in Liberty Jail through the winter

or crouching at his feet, begged his pardon, and remained quiet till a change of guards.[165]

"I have seen the ministers of justice, clothed in magisterial[166] robes, and criminals arraigned[167] before them, while life was suspended on a breath, in the courts of England; I have witnessed a Congress in solemn session to give laws to nations; I have tried to conceive of[168] kings, of royal courts, of thrones and crowns; and of emperors assembled to decide the fate of kingdoms; but dignity and majesty have I seen but once, as it stood in chains, at midnight, in a dungeon in an obscure[169] village of Missouri"[170] (*Parley P. Pratt Autobiography*, 178–80).

JOSEPH AND HIS COMPANIONS ARE TRANSFERRED TO LIBERTY, MISSOURI

At the end of their trial, Joseph Smith, Sidney Rigdon, Hyrum Smith, Lyman Wight, Caleb Baldwin, and Alexander McRae were taken to Liberty Jail. They remained there for six long months. Joseph Fielding Smith described the conditions of the jail:

"Here they suffered, during that time, many untold hardships. Much of the time they were bound in chains. Their food was often not fit to eat, and never wholesome or prepared with the thought of proper nourishment. Several times poison was administered to them in their food, which made

---

165. Joseph Smith, filled with the Holy Ghost, rebuked the guards, much like Nephi being filled with the power of God rebuked Laman and Lemuel (see 1 Nephi 17:48).

166. *magisterial*—official

167. *arraigned*—accused

168. *conceive of*—imagine

169. *obscure*—unknown

170. What does this account teach you about the Prophet? What does it teach you about standing up for what is right? What difficult experiences do you sometimes have?

While imprisoned in Liberty Jail, Joseph wrote an inspired letter to members of the Church

them sick nigh[171] unto death, and only the promised blessings of the Lord saved them. Their bed was on the floor, or on the flat side of a hewn[172] white oak log, and in this manner they were forced to suffer. Is it any wonder that they cried in the anguish[173] of their souls unto the Lord, for relief from such inhuman treatment?" (*Essentials in Church History,* 210).

THE PROPHET WRITES A LETTER TO THE CHURCH FROM LIBERTY JAIL

While imprisoned, Joseph Smith wrote a letter dated March 25, 1839. This letter was for all Church members. It shows the physical and emotional strain the Prophet and his companions were suffering after such a long time in this terrible condition. The letter also contains revelations from a merciful God to Joseph as he cried out in the anguish of his soul. Later, selections from it were used to make up Doctrine and Covenants sections 121, 122, and 123. The following are excerpts from his letter:

"To the Church of Latter-day Saints at Quincy, Illinois, and Scattered Abroad: . . .

"Your humble servant, Joseph Smith, Jun., prisoner for the Lord Jesus Christ's sake[174] and for the Saints, taken and held by the power of mobocracy.[175] . . . May the grace of God the Father, and of our Lord and Savior Jesus Christ, rest upon you all, and abide with you forever. . . .

---

171. *nigh*—near

172. *hewn*—cut

173. *anguish*—extreme pain

174. Paul shared similar feelings when he wrote to the Saints in his day that he was "a prisoner of Jesus Christ" (Ephesians 3:1; Philemon 1:1).

175. *mobocracy*—mob rule

JOSEPH'S VIEW FROM MONTROSE, BY AL ROUNDS

The name "Nauvoo" means "beautiful"

the saints, and no more eligible[30] place presenting itself, I considered it wisdom to make an attempt to build up a city'"[31] (*Comprehensive History of the Church*, 2:9).

JOSEPH AND HIS FAMILY MOVE TO COMMERCE

The Prophet Joseph was a commanding figure and brought immediate direction and leadership to the Saints. Within three weeks after his arrival, he had purchased lands for the gathering of the Saints and moved his family into a new home.

"[On] Friday, May 10, 1839, President Joseph Smith took up his residence[32] in a small log house on the bank of the Mississippi, . . . one mile south of Commerce,"[33] explained Joseph Fielding Smith. "The first house built by any of the Saints in that part was raised by Theodore Turley, in June, 1839. . . . Between Commerce and . . . the south front of the river there were four houses, three of which were log cabins, and into one of these the Prophet moved. . . . Notwithstanding the unhealthful condition, the Prophet felt that by draining the land . . . the place could be made a pleasant habitation[34] for the Saints, and he decided to build there. There was inspiration in this decision, for this was an excellent site for the building of a city, when the unfavorable conditions of the lowlands were removed" (*Essentials in Church History*, 221).

---

30. *more eligible*—other suitable

31. What does this teach you about the faith of the Prophet Joseph Smith? What do you think he knew about this area that others failed to see? How might knowing that the Lord can help a prophet understand the future bless your life?

32. *residence*—home

33. What kind of an example was Joseph's family setting for the rest of the Saints? In what ways do you find it a challenge to be an example of what you believe?

34. *habitation*—place to live

JOSEPH RENAMES THEIR NEW HOME NAUVOO

The Old Testament king, Solomon, taught, "where there is no vision, the people perish" (Proverbs 29:18). As the Lord's prophet, Joseph had a vision, which gave hope to the Saints. Though he understood that much of the area was a mosquito-infested swamp, Joseph envisioned a beautiful place for the Saints.

"The name 'Commerce' by which the little cluster of houses on the banks of the Mississippi was called, was early changed by Joseph Smith to 'Nauvoo,'" B. H. Roberts explained. "The word Nauvoo comes from the Hebrew, and signifies beautiful location; 'carrying with it also,' says Joseph Smith, 'the idea of rest.' And indeed, the location of the city is beautiful.[35] It stands on a bold point around which sweeps the placid,[36] but majestic 'Father of Waters'—the Mississippi. The city is nearly half encircled by that noble stream. From its banks the ground rises gradually for at least a mile where it reaches the common level of the prairie that stretches out to the eastward, farther than the eye can reach, in a beautifully undulating[37] surface, once covered by a luxuriant[38] growth of natural grasses and wild flowers, with here and there patches of timber; but now chequered[39] with an endless succession of meadows and cultivated fields" (*Comprehensive History of the Church*, 2:11).

A LETTER FROM THE QUORUM OF THE TWELVE APOSTLES TO THE SAINTS

Once the Saints were somewhat settled in their new wilderness home, the Church was quickly put in order again. The Twelve Apostles penned a letter of instruction and hope to the Saints, a part of which included this:

"Dear brethren, we would remind you . . . although you have had indignities,[40] insults and injuries heaped upon you till further suffering would seem to be no longer a virtue; we would say, be patient, dear brethren. . . . You have been tried in the furnace of affliction;[41] the time to exercise patience is now come; and we shall reap, brethren, in due time, if we faint not. Do not breathe vengeance upon your oppressors, but leave the case in the hands of God.[42] . . .

"We would say to the widow and the orphan, to the destitute[43] and to the diseased, who have been made so through persecution, be patient; you are not forgotten; the God of Jacob has His eye upon you; the heavens have been witness to your sufferings, and these are registered on high; angels have gazed upon the scene, and your tears, your groans, your sorrows, and anguish of heart, are had in remembrance before God"[44] (*History of the Church*, 3:393–94).

---

35. 🕮 When Heber C. Kimball first saw Commerce, Illinois, he wrote a prophetic entry in his journal: "It is a very pretty place, but not a long abiding home for the Saints" (in Orson F. Whitney, *The Life of Heber C. Kimball*, 256–57).

36. 📖 **placid**—peaceful

37. 📖 **undulating**—rolling

38. 📖 **luxuriant**—lush; thick

39. 📖 **chequered**—checkered; a patchwork

40. 📖 **had indignities**—been humiliated

41. 🕮 The "furnace of affliction" is a scriptural term (see 1 Nephi 20:10) and refers to the process of burning away imperfections and impurities. It had a positive effect among the Saints. Heber C. Kimball observed,

"Most of the members that remained were of the pure gold, refined by suffering, and throughout the community a better feeling prevailed than ever before" (in Orson F. Whitney, *The Life of Heber C. Kimball*, 256).

42. 🕮 The Saints were told not to try to "get even" with those who hurt them, but to leave it in the hands of the Lord. The Lord commands: "Man shall not smite, neither shall he judge; for judgment is mine, saith the Lord, and vengeance is mine also, and I will repay" (Mormon 8:20). Only the Lord has the ability to look "on the heart" (1 Samuel 16:7) and judge perfectly.

43. 📖 **destitute**—poor

44. 💬 In what ways do you think this message gives hope? Why do we gain strength when we realize we're not alone?

A DAY OF GOD'S POWER, BY LIZ LEMON SWINDLE

Many people were miraculously healed by the priesthood

raised the dead, he cried: 'BROTHER FORDHAM, IN THE NAME OF JESUS CHRIST, ARISE AND WALK.'[58] It was a voice which could be heard from house to house and nearly through the neighborhood. It was like the roaring of a lion, or the heavy thunderbolt. Brother Fordham leaped from his dying bed in an instant, shook the poultices and bandages from his feet, put on his clothes so quick that none got a chance to assist him, and taking . . . a little refreshment, he walked with us from house to house visiting other sick beds, and joining in prayer and ministrations for them, while the people followed us, and with joy and amazement gave glory to God.[59] Several more were called up in a similar manner

and were healed" (*Autobiography of Parley P. Pratt,* 254).

JOSEPH FINISHES HIS WORK OF HEALING FOR THE DAY

Elder Wilford Woodruff wrote in his journal the account of the Prophet's final healing for this miraculous day:

"As soon as we left Brother Fordham's house, we went into the home of Joseph B. Noble, who was very low.[60] When we entered the house, Brother Joseph took Brother Noble by the hand, and commanded him, in the name of Jesus Christ, to arise

---

58. In another description of the same healing, Joseph asked Elijah Fordham "if he had faith to be healed. He answered: 'I fear it is too late; if you had come sooner I think I would have been healed.' The Prophet said, 'Do you believe in Jesus Christ?' He answered in a feeble voice, 'I do'" (Joseph Fielding Smith, *Church*

History and Modern Revelation, 4:62–63). It was at this point that Joseph commanded his friend to rise.

59. Have you ever known or heard about someone who was miraculously healed? Why do you think it is important to give the glory to God in these instances?

60. *low*—weak

and be made whole. He did arise, and was healed immediately. . . .

"The case of Brother Noble was the last one of healing upon that day. It was the greatest day for the manifestation[61] of the power of God through the gift of healing since the organization of the Church. When we left Brother Noble's the Prophet Joseph, with those who had accompanied him from the other side, went to the bank of the river, to return home" (in *Wilford Woodruff, His Life and Labors,* comp. Matthias F. Cowley, 106).

JOSEPH SENDS WILFORD WOODRUFF TO HEAL THE SICK

Elder Wilford Woodruff was a part of another of the Prophet Joseph Smith's healing miracles:

"After healing the sick in Montrose, all the company followed Joseph to the bank of the river, where he was going to take the boat to return home," B. H. Roberts explained. "While waiting for the boat a man from the west, who had seen that the sick and dying were healed, asked Joseph if he would not go to his house and heal two of his children, who were very sick. They were twins and were three months old. Joseph told the man he could not go, but he would send someone to heal them. He told Elder Woodruff to go with the man and heal his children. At the same time he took from his pocket a bandana handkerchief,[62] and gave it to Brother Woodruff, telling him to wipe the faces of the children with it and they should be healed; and remarked at the same time: 'As long as you keep that handkerchief it shall remain a league[63] between you and me.' Elder Woodruff did as he was commanded, and the children were healed,[64] and he keeps the handkerchief to this day" (in *History of the Church,* 4:4–5n).

THE HEALING POWER IS SHARED WITH OTHERS

There were so many sick among the Saints that the work of healing continued for days. Joseph, seeing the great need before him, called others to assist in the labor.[65] Once again, grateful disciples of the Lord witnessed the divine calling of the Prophet Joseph Smith.

"To the saints who witnessed the remarkable manifestation of divine power in behalf of the sick," B. H. Roberts wrote, "it was a testimony that God was with them;[66] for they witnessed a fulfillment of His ancient promise to his people:

"'Is any sick among you? Let him call for the elders of the church; and let them pray over him, anointing him with oil, in the name of the Lord; and the prayer of faith shall save the sick, and the Lord shall raise him up'[67] (James 5:14–15). . . .

"The only mention that the Prophet himself makes in his journal of this notable experience is:—

"'*Monday* and *Tuesday,* 22nd and 23rd (July)— The sick were administered unto with great success, but many remained sick, and new cases are occurring daily.' . . .

"The modesty of the Prophet in making allusion to[68] an incident[69] so remarkable, and to which there were many witnesses, goes far towards correcting

---

61. *manifestation*—showing

62. Wilford Woodruff said the handkerchief was red and made from silk.

63. *league*—bond; symbol of friendship

64. In New Testament times the Apostle Paul also gave "handkerchiefs or aprons" to disciples to bless the sick "and the diseases departed from them, and the evil spirits went out of them" (Acts 19:12).

65. "There were many sick whom Joseph could not visit, so he counseled the Twelve to go and visit and heal them, and many were healed under their hands" (Wilford Woodruff, *Leaves from my Journal,* ch. 19).

66. Why do you think the Saints needed this show of divine power? If you had been there and witnessed this "day of healing," what would it have done for your hope and faith?

67. The Lord explained that "he that hath faith in me to be healed, and is not appointed unto death, shall be healed" (D&C 42:43–44).

68. *allusion to*—mention of

69. *incident*—experience

HURRAH, HURRAH FOR ISRAEL, BY ROBERT BARRETT

"Hurrah for Israel"

and then told the driver to go ahead. After this I felt a spirit of joy and gratitude, having had the satisfaction of seeing my wife standing upon her feet, instead of leaving her in bed, knowing well that I should not see them again for two or three years" (in Orson F. Whitney, *Life of Heber C. Kimball* 265–66).[90]

THE APOSTLES' MISSIONARY ACTIVITIES IN BRITAIN

The apostles endured long and dangerous travel across land and oceans, and most of them arrived in England sometime in April 1840, including Orson Hyde, who labored there for some months before leaving to serve a special mission to Palestine.[91]

Though the work was difficult, the blessings were great. Wilford Woodruff recorded this example:

"Mary Pitt . . . had not been able to walk a step for fourteen years, and [was] confined to[92] her bed nearly half that time. She had no strength in her feet and ankles and could only move about a little with a crutch or holding on to a chair. . . . On the day after she was baptized, Brother Richards and President Brigham Young came down to see me. We met at Brother Kington's. . . . I told President Young what Sister Pitt wished, . . . that she believed she had faith enough to be healed. We prayed for her and laid hands upon her. Brother Young was mouth, and commanded her to be made whole. She laid down her crutch and never used it after, and the next day

---

90. How do you think the Lord feels about his children who make such great sacrifices? What kind of sacrifices have you made for the Lord? What are you willing to sacrifice?

91. For more information about Orson Hyde's mission to Palestine, see chapter 68, "Orson Hyde Dedicates Palestine for the Return of the Jews."

92. *confined to*—had to stay in

John Benbow's farm was the site of many baptisms

she walked three miles"[93] (in *Journal of Discourses,* 15:344–45).

The apostles experienced great success. John Taylor labored in Liverpool. After a short time of preaching in the area, he baptized ten on one day, and many of those who watched the ceremony asked to be baptized.[94]

Wilford Woodruff and Willard Richards were assigned to labor in the south of England. Elder Woodruff described one of their missionary experiences this way:

"On the morning of the 4th I . . . walked a number of miles to Mr. John Benbow's, Hill Farm. . . .

"I . . . rejoiced greatly at the news Mr. Benbow gave me, that there was a company of men and women—over six hundred in number—who had broken off from the Wesleyan Methodists, and taken the name of United Brethren. . . . This body of United Brethren were searching for light and truth, . . . and were calling upon the Lord continually to open the way before them and send them light and knowledge. . . .

"I arose on the morning of the 5th, took breakfast, . . . and I preached my first gospel sermon in the house. I also preached at the same place on the following evening, and baptized six persons, including Mr. John Benbow, his wife, and four preachers

---

93. 🔎 What do the following verses suggest is necessary for miracles to be performed? "And whatsoever ye shall ask the Father in my name, which is right, believing that ye shall receive, behold it shall be given unto you" (3 Nephi 18:20). "There was not any man who could do a miracle in the name of Jesus save he were cleansed every whit from his iniquity" (3 Nephi 8:1).

94. 🔎 Among those baptized by John Taylor were members of the George Cannon family. One son, George Q. Cannon, later became an apostle and served as a member of the First Presidency with four Church presidents.

APOSTLE ORSON HYDE DEDICATES THE HOLY LAND, BY CLARK KELLEY PRICE

In 1840, Orson Hyde (1805–1878) and John E. Page (1799–1867) were called on a mission to Jerusalem

Previously, the Lord had revealed to the Prophet Joseph Smith that missionaries should go two by two. It is a great protection and source of strength for missionaries to be sent out in pairs as witnesses of the restored gospel (see D&C 42:6).

Joseph wished to obey this commandment, and thus felt impressed that Elder John E. Page should accompany Elder Hyde on his mission.[109]

JOHN E. PAGE FAILS TO FULFILL HIS MISSION

Because malaria was so common in Nauvoo at the time Orson Hyde and John Page were to depart, their mission was delayed. When they were finally able to leave, they traveled to the Eastern United States and stayed for some time in Pennsylvania.

The elders soon got word from the First Presidency that the Lord was not pleased with their delay. They were urged to leave soon and travel quickly.

Unfortunately, wrote Joseph Fielding Smith, "the enthusiasm[110] of John E. Page died out, he never left the shores of the United States. In June, 1841, he was still in Philadelphia gathering funds to enable him to sail with Orson Hyde. While in Philadelphia Elder George A. Smith met him and chided[111] him for his delay and requested that he be prepared to sail with Orson Hyde, two days after this interview. Although Elder Page had money in hand enough for his passage to Europe, he refused to go so Elder Hyde had to travel alone"[112] (*Church History and Modern Revelation,* 4:89–90).

---

109. Orson Hyde and John E. Page were called by a prophet to serve a mission. How have missionaries you know responded when called by a prophet to serve a mission?

110. *enthusiasm*—excitement

111. *chided*—scolded

112. Have you ever had to do something difficult alone? How do you think Orson Hyde felt as he made this long journey alone to a strange, faraway land?

ORSON HYDE LABORS IN EUROPE

After Elder Hyde landed in Europe, he immediately began preaching the gospel. In particular, he bore testimony to the leaders in the Jewish communities.

"In England," Joseph Fielding Smith explained, "Elder Hyde wrote to Rabbi[113] Solomon Hirschell, president of the Hebrew Society in England, stating the purpose of his mission abroad and his interest in the Jewish people. In the body of this communication[114] Elder Hyde said: 'About nine years ago, a young man [Joseph Smith] . . . laid his hand upon my head and pronounced these remarkable words—'In due time thou shalt go to Jerusalem, the land of thy fathers, and be a watchman unto the house of Israel; and by thy hands shall the Most High do a great work, which shall prepare the way and greatly facilitate[115] the gathering together of that people.' (D.H.C. 4:375.) He then bore testimony to this Jewish Rabbi, of the restoration of the Gospel and called on the Jews to repent and 'go out from among the Gentiles,' for 'Jerusalem is thy home'" (*Church History and Modern Revelation,* 4:90).

On June 20, 1841, Orson Hyde left London for Rotterdam, Holland. In a letter to Joseph Smith, Elder Hyde described the trip across the English Channel and on to Jerusalem. "The fine steamer[116] *Batavier* brought me safely over the billows[117] of a tremendous rough sea in about thirty hours. Never did I suffer more from sea sickness, than during this short voyage; but it was soon over, and we landed safely in Rotterdam. . . . Here I called on the Hebrew Rabbi, and proposed certain questions to him; . . . Do you believe in the restitution of your nation to the land of your fathers, called the land of *promise?* 'We hope it will be so,' was the reply. He then added, 'We believe that many Jews will return to Jerusalem and rebuild the city—rear a temple to the name of the Most High, and restore our ancient worship; Jerusalem shall be the capital of our nation.'

"After remaining here about one week, I took the coach for Amsterdam. . . .

"I remained in Amsterdam only one night and a part of two days. I called on the President Rabbi here, but he was gone from home. I left at his house a large number of the addresses for himself and his people,[118] and took coach for Arnhem on the Rhine. . . .

"It was my intention to have gone directly down the Danube to Constantinople, but having neglected to get my passport vised[119] by the Austrian Ambassador at Frankfort, I had to forward it to the Austrian Ambassador at Munich and procure[120] his permission, signature and seal[121] before I could enter the Austrian dominions.[122] This detained me five days, during which time I conceived[123] the idea of sitting down and learning the German language. . . . I have been engaged[124] eight days in this task. I have read one book through and part of another, and translated and written considerable. I can speak and write considerable German already"[125] (in *History of the Church,* 4:384–86).

---

113. A rabbi is a teacher in the Jewish religion.

114. *communication*—letter

115. *facilitate*—help

116. *steamer*—ship

117. *billows*—waves

118. How did Orson Hyde fulfill the following commandment? "Let them go . . . and thus let them preach by the way in every congregation" (D&C 52:10).

119. *vised*—signed

120. *procure*—obtain

121. *seal*—stamp

122. *dominions*—country

123. *conceived*—thought of

124. *engaged*—busy

125. Not only did Elder Hyde make good use of his time but he also was very smart and blessed by the Lord with the "gift of tongues" to learn a language so quickly (D&C 46:24–25). Do you know any missionaries who have learned another language? How long do you think it would take you to learn another language?

An early view of the city of Nauvoo

settlements surrounding Nauvoo. Beginning in tents and temporary shacks, energized members first built log cabins that eventually gave way to frame houses and finally brick. Nauvoo was transformed into a bustling city that eventually rivaled Chicago in size and importance. At this significant time, the Saints started construction on yet another temple. Think about what it might have been like to live in Nauvoo during this exciting time. How does it feel to belong to a church whose members are builders and doers?

THE PROPHET SEEKS JUSTICE FROM THE UNITED STATES GOVERNMENT

Joseph Smith, in company with others, attempted for several months to reclaim the possessions and lands owned by the Latter-day Saints that were stolen by organized mobs in Missouri. Their boldest move was paying a visit to the president of the United States in Washington, D.C., where they labored for several months for their cause.

"On Friday morning," Joseph wrote, "we proceeded to the house of the President.[136] We found a very large and splendid palace . . . decorated with all the fineries and elegancies[137] of this world. We went to the door and requested to see the President, when we were immediately introduced into an upper apartment, where we met the President, and . . . presented him with our letters of introduction. As soon as he had read one of them, he looked upon us with a half frown, and said, 'What can I do? I can do nothing for you! . . . '

"But we were not to be intimidated;[138] and demanded a hearing, and constitutional rights.

NOTES FOR CHAPTER 69

136. The president of the United States at this time was Martin Van Buren, who served from 1837 to 1841.

137. *fineries and elegancies*—expensive and beautiful things

138. *intimidated*—made afraid

Before we left him he promised to reconsider what he had said, and observed that he felt to sympathize with[139] us, on account of our sufferings.

"We have spent the remainder of our time in hunting up[140] the Representatives in order to get our case brought before the House; in giving them letters of introduction, etc., and in getting acquainted. A meeting of the delegation of the state of Illinois was appointed today, to consult for bringing our case before Congress. The gentlemen from Illinois are worthy men, and have treated us with the greatest kindness, and are ready to do all that is in their power" (*History of the Church*, 4:40).

Despite their hopes of receiving an apology and money for their lost property, the brethren left the nation's capital in disappointment. On February 6, 1840, the Prophet Joseph wrote:

"I had an interview with Martin Van Buren, the President, who treated me very insolently,[141] and it was with great reluctance he listened to our message,[142] which, when he had heard, he said: '*Gentlemen, your cause is just, but I can do nothing for you;*' and '*If I take up for you I shall lose the vote of Missouri.*' His whole course went to show that he was an office-seeker, that self-aggrandizement[143] was his ruling passion, and that justice and righteousness were no part of his composition.[144] I found him such a man as I could not conscientiously support at the head of our noble Republic. . . . I became satisfied

there was little use for me to tarry,[145] to press the just claims of the Saints"[146] (*History of the Church*, 4:80).

THE DEATH OF THE PATRIARCH, JOSEPH SMITH SR.

The Prophet Joseph returned to Nauvoo determined to make the best of their circumstances and resume building a city for the Saints. A few months later Joseph faced another challenge.

On September 14, 1840, Joseph Smith Sr., patriarch to the Church and father of the Prophet Joseph, died. Of Father Smith, B. H. Roberts wrote, "He endured many persecutions on account of the claims made by his son Joseph to being a prophet of God; for Joseph's declarations . . . not only brought down upon himself the wrath of bigoted[147] men, but involved his whole family in the persecutions which followed him throughout his life. Of these things, however, his father never complained, but endured all things patiently, and with true heroism. . . .

"Father Smith was a large man, ordinarily weighing two hundred pounds; he was six feet two inches in height, and well proportioned, strong and active; and almost up to the time of his death he stood unbowed beneath the accumulated sorrows and hardships he had experienced. . . . The exposure he suffered in the exodus from Missouri, however,

---

139. 📖 *sympathize with*—understand and feel sorry for

140. 📖 *hunting up*—finding

President Van Buren (1782–1862) refused to come to the aid of the Saints, saying: "Your cause is just, but I can do nothing for you"

141. 📖 *insolently*—rudely

142. 🔎 In what ways might it have been discouraging to find no help from the government? Why do you think the Saints still honored the laws of the land? What Article of Faith best describes the Church's feelings toward government?

143. 📖 *self-aggrandizement*—lifting himself in rank and honor

144. 📖 *composition*—character; personality

145. 📖 *tarry*—stay

146. ☀ Despite the president's refusing to help, Joseph knew the Constitution of the United States is an inspired document (see D&C 101:80; 109:54). He later wrote: "We believe in being subject to . . . presidents, . . . in obeying, honoring, and sustaining the law" (Articles of Faith 1:12).

147. 📖 *bigoted*—intolerant; prejudiced

"Another provision granted the city council the power to 'organize the inhabitants of said city, subject to military duty, into a body of independent military men, to be called the "Nauvoo Legion." . . . ' This legion was to perform the same amount of military duty as other bodies of the regular militia, and to be subject to the call of the mayor in executing the laws and ordinances of the city, and the governor for public defense"[160] (*Essentials in Church History,* 224–25).

THE PROPHET JOSEPH RECEIVES A NEW REVELATION

On January 19, 1841, the Prophet received a very important revelation. The revelation covered many subjects, explained Joseph Fielding Smith, but was concerned "particularly with the building of the temple and the ordinances to be performed therein. The Lord declared that the prayers of the Prophet

were acceptable to him, and he was called upon to make a solemn proclamation[161] of the Gospel to 'all the kings of the world, to the four corners thereof; to the honorable President-elect,[162] and the high-minded governors of the nation . . . and to all the nations of the earth' [D&C 124:3]. It was to be written in the spirit of meekness, yet of warning, for he was 'about to call on them to give heed[163] to the light and glory of Zion, for the set time has come to favor her' [D&C 124:6]. The Lord would visit the mighty and the rulers of the earth in the day of his visitation. Therefore, said he, 'Awake, O kings of the earth! Come ye, O, come ye, with your gold and your silver to the help of my people, to the house of the daughters of Zion'[164] [D&C 124:11]" (*Essentials in Church History,* 250–51).

The revelation spoken of was Doctrine and Covenants section 124, which in part told the Saints, "Come ye, with all your gold, and your silver, and your precious stones, and with all your antiquities;[165]

A banner used by the members of the Nauvoo Legion

160. Do you feel safe in your community? How does having a police force help you feel this way? What does it mean to you to know that there is a military to help protect your country?

161. A "solemn proclamation" is an official declaration or statement of belief. Joseph was killed before he could complete this request. "In 1845 the Quorum of the Twelve Apostles essentially fulfilled the instructions of section 124 by publishing their proclamation to the kings of the world" (Lyndon W. Cook, *The Revelations of the Prophet Joseph Smith,* 243).

162. The "honorable president-elect" was William Henry Harrison, newly elected president of the United States.

163. *give heed*—pay attention

164. The "daughters of Zion" refers to the righteous Saints who gather together to build Zion. In another revelation, the Lord said that "every man that will not take his sword against his neighbor must needs flee unto Zion for safety. . . . [They] shall be the only people that shall not be at war one with another" (D&C 45:68–69).

165. *antiquities*—ancient objects

TOM CHILD

As the Saints gathered in counties in
Illinois and Iowa, they eventually numbered
more than fifteen thousand

and with all who have knowledge of antiquities, that will come, may come, and bring the box tree, and the fir tree, and the pine tree, together with all the precious trees of the earth; and with iron, with copper, and with brass, and with zinc, and your precious things of the earth, and build a house to my name for the Most High to dwell therein"[166] (vv. 26–27).

HYRUM SMITH BECOMES THE PATRIARCH

Because of the death of the Prophet's father four months earlier, Hyrum was called to serve as Church patriarch and also as a prophet, seer, and revelator (see D&C 124:94).[167] The office of patriarch, Joseph Fielding Smith explained, "was [Hyrum's] by right of lineage,[168] . . . descended from father to son and was the right based on faithfulness of the first born. At the time of Hyrum Smith's call, he was serving as second counselor in the First Presidency" (*Essentials in Church History,* 254).

This call is found in section 124:

"And again, verily I say unto you, let my servant William [Law] be appointed, ordained, and anointed, as a counselor unto my servant Joseph [Smith] in the room of my servant Hyrum,[169] that my servant Hyrum may take the office of Priesthood and Patriarch, which was appointed unto him by his father, by blessing and also by right.[170]

"That from henceforth he shall hold the keys of the patriarchal blessing upon the heads of all my people" (vv. 91–92).

BUILDING ZARAHEMLA, IOWA

As the Saints obeyed the Prophet's call to gather, Church members settled on both sides of the Mississippi River. It became necessary to organize

---

166. This house is the Nauvoo Temple, begun on March 1, 1841, and dedicated on May 1, 1846, shortly after the Saints began the trek to the Salt Lake Valley.

167. After Oliver Cowdery left the Church, the Lord called Hyrum Smith to take his place. President Joseph Fielding Smith taught: "Had Oliver Cowdery remained true to his covenants and obligations as a witness with Joseph Smith, . . . he, and not Hyrum Smith, would have gone with Joseph Smith as a prisoner and to martyrdom [death] at Carthage" (*Doctrines of Salvation,* 1:219).

168. *lineage*—family line

169. When Hyrum Smith was ordained as Church patriarch, he was released as a counselor in the First Presidency. William Law replaced him and served from 1841 to 1844. William Law left the Church in April 1844.

170. Hyrum received the priesthood office of a patriarch from his father, Joseph Smith Sr., just prior to his death. In that blessing Father Smith promised: "I now seal upon your head the patriarchal power, and you shall bless the people. This is my dying blessing upon your head in the name of Jesus. Amen." Hyrum served in that office until his death on June 27, 1844 (see Hyrum M. Smith and Janne Sjodahl, *Doctrine and Covenants Commentary,* 786).

President of the Quorum of the Twelve, was given the following counsel:

"Dear and well beloved Brother Brigham Young, verily thus saith the Lord unto you: My servant Brigham, it is no more required at your hands to leave your family as in times past, for your offering[3] is acceptable to me;[4]

"I have seen your labor and toil in journeyings[5] for my name.

"I therefore command you to send my word abroad, and take special care of your family[6] from this time, henceforth[7] and forever. Amen"[8] (D&C 126:1–3).

THE FIRST WARDS IN THE CHURCH ARE CREATED IN NAUVOO

Thus far in the Church's history, the members of the Seventy, the Twelve, the First Presidency, and the high councils that presided over the stakes of the Church made up the majority of the young Church's leaders. Rapid growth made it impossible for these Church leaders to meet the needs of all the members. The Lord revealed to the Prophet Joseph several organizational changes that would provide local leadership of the Saints and help the high councils, and the Twelve, Seventy, and Presidency to carry their load.

One of these organizational changes was the creation of wards. According to the *Encyclopedia of Mormonism*, "The first wards were organized early in the history of the Church in the 1840s in Nauvoo, Illinois. By 1844 the city was divided into ten wards, with three more in the surrounding rural neighborhood.[9] The name 'ward' was borrowed from the term for political districts of the frontier municipality.[10] Joseph Smith, who was simultaneously[11] mayor of the city and President of the Church, assigned a bishop to preside over each ward. The bishop's chief responsibility to begin with was temporal[12] rather than spiritual leadership. To prevent hunger, he surveyed the physical needs of the members living within his ward boundaries. Second, the bishop organized his members for Church work assignments, particularly to serve one day in ten as laborers on the Nauvoo Temple. This was a form of paying tithing.

"Many of the Saints who fled Nauvoo under persecution in 1846 gathered at Winter Quarters, located near present-day Florence, Nebraska. There Brigham Young and other leaders again set up ward organizations. Their function was similar—to look

---

3. *offering*—sacrifice

4. The Lord called Brigham Young to remain in Nauvoo and direct the work as President of the Quorum of the Twelve. The wisdom of such a move was clearly seen in later years when Brigham Young was chosen by the Lord to succeed Joseph Smith. The Prophet Joseph was the leading inspiration of Brigham Young's life; no pain was too severe, no inconvenience too great for Brigham to be where Joseph was and learn from him. Speaking of the time he spent in the Prophet's presence, Brigham Young once said, "In the days of the Prophet Joseph, such moments were more precious to me than all the wealth of the world. No matter how great my poverty—if I had to borrow meal to feed my wife and children—I never let an opportunity pass of learning what the Prophet had to impart" (in Preston Nibley, *Brigham Young: The Man and His Work*, 28).

5. *toil in journeyings*—hard work in traveling

6. How does the Lord feel about Brigham Young and his family? What does this teach you about how well the Lord knows his children?

7. *henceforth*—from now on

8. "In order to grasp fully the significance of this Revelation, an incident from the first meeting, in 1832, between the Prophet Joseph and his successor [Brigham Young] should be recalled. They had spent the evening in conversation on the gospel, and when the time for parting had come, Brigham Young was invited to lead in prayer. While he was praying, the Spirit of the Lord came upon him, and he spoke in tongues—the first instance of the bestowal of that gift upon anyone in this dispensation. Afterwards, it is asserted, the Prophet said, 'A time will come when Brother Brigham will preside over this Church' . . . " (Leaun G. Otten and C. Max Caldwell, *Sacred Truths of the Doctrine and Covenants*, 2:322).

9. *rural neighborhood*—non-city area

10. *municipality*—town

11. *simultaneously*—at the same time

12. *temporal*—physical needs

Working on the Nauvoo Temple was a form of paying tithing

STRENGTH OF BODY AND MIND, BY LIZ LEMON SWINDLE

after the temporal Welfare of the people" (4:1541).[13] Wards were again established when Brigham Young and the Saints arrived in the Salt Lake Valley, and, eventually, the bishop's role grew to include the spiritual welfare of the members in addition to their temporal welfare.

THE RELIEF SOCIETY IS ORGANIZED

There is something in the very nature of women that inspires them to find joy and fulfillment in service to others. During the Nauvoo period the Lord revealed his plan for using the special gifts of women to build the kingdom of God. One history records the establishment of the Relief Society as follows:

"While the Nauvoo Temple was under construction, Sarah Granger Kimball, wife of Hiram Kimball, one of the city's wealthiest citizens, hired a seamstress named Margaret A. Cooke. Desiring to further the Lord's work, Sarah donated[14] cloth to make shirts for the men working on the temple, and Margaret agreed to do the sewing. Shortly thereafter, some of Sarah's neighbors also desired to participate in the shirt making. The sisters met in the Kimball parlor[15] and decided to formally organize. Eliza R. Snow[16] was asked to write a constitution and bylaws[17] for the new society.

---

13. As the Church grows, there are often changes that must take place. Have you ever been part of a ward or stake whose boundaries were changed? How did that change your life? As the Church grows, more and more local leaders are needed. What do you need to be doing right now so you will be ready to serve when you are needed?

14. **donated**—gave

15. **parlor**—family room

16. Eliza Roxey Snow (1804–1887) was called "Zion's poetess" by the Prophet Joseph Smith. She wrote many hymns for the Church, including ten that are in our present-day hymnal. One of those, "O My Father," has been a favorite since it was written in Nauvoo in 1845. In 1867, she was called to organize Relief Societies throughout the settlements of the Saints in the West. She also served faithfully in the Primary, with the youth, and in all that was asked of her.

17. **constitution and by-laws**—set of rules

"Eliza presented the completed document to the Prophet Joseph Smith, who declared it was the best constitution he had seen. But he felt impressed to enlarge the vision of the women concerning what they could accomplish.[18] He asked the women to attend another meeting, where he organized them into the Nauvoo Female Relief Society. Emma Smith, the Prophet's wife, became the society's first president.

"Joseph told the sisters that they would receive 'instruction through the order which God has established through the medium of those appointed to lead[19]—and I now turn the key to you in the name of God and this Society shall rejoice and knowledge and intelligence shall flow down from this time—this is the beginning of better days to this Society.'

"Soon after the society came into existence, a committee visited all of Nauvoo's poor, assessed their needs, and solicited[20] donations to help them. Cash donations and proceeds from the sale of food and bedding provided schooling for needy children. Flax, wool, yarn, shingles, soap, candles, tinware,[21] jewelry, baskets, quilts, blankets, onions, apples,

flour, bread, crackers, and meat were donated to help those in need.

"Besides helping the poor, Relief Society sisters worshiped together. Eliza R. Snow reported that in one meeting 'nearly all present arose and spoke, and the spirit of the Lord like a purifying stream, refreshed every heart.' These sisters prayed for each other, strengthened each other's faith, and consecrated their lives and resources to help further the cause of Zion" (*Our Heritage,* 61–62).

MANY REVELATIONS CONTAINED IN THE PEARL OF GREAT PRICE REVEALED

It was also during the Nauvoo period that a number of the writings found in the Pearl of Great Price were first published. Joseph had been working on translations of the book of Moses[22] and the book of Abraham[23] for quite some time. In 1842, selections from the Book of Abraham were printed in the *Times and Seasons* and the *Millennial Star.* The Articles of Faith, which Joseph had originally included in a letter to a Mr. John Wentworth as part

18. After hearing the proposed constitution that Eliza R. Snow had written, the Prophet Joseph praised her work: "'But,' he said, 'this is not what you want. Tell the sisters their offering is accepted of the Lord, and He has something better for them than a written constitution. Invite them all to meet me and a few of the brethren in the Masonic Hall over my store next Thursday afternoon, and I will organize the sisters under the priesthood after a pattern of the priesthood.' He further said, 'This Church was never perfectly organized until the women were thus organized'" (*Relief Society Magazine* 6 [March 1919]: 129).

19. **the medium of those appointed to lead**—the priesthood

20. **solicited**—asked for

21. **tinware**—cookware

22. "The Book of Moses is an extract of several chapters from Genesis in the Joseph Smith Translation of the Bible (JST) and constitutes one of the texts in the Pearl of Great Price. The Prophet Joseph Smith began an inspired revision of the Old Testament in June 1830 to restore and clarify vital points of history and doctrine missing from the Bible" (*Encyclopedia of Mormonism,* 1:216).

23. "The book of Abraham is linked to Joseph Smith's work on rolls of papyri that the Church obtained in 1835. Soon after he began studying the rolls, he produced a record of the life of the patriarch Abraham and a description of the creation of the world similar to that in Genesis and the Book of Moses. In 1842 the Nauvoo *Times and Seasons* and the *Millennial Star* in England printed the available text and facsimiles. It is certain that the materials incorporated into the books of Moses and Abraham were extracts and that more information was available than has ever been included in the printed editions of the Pearl of Great Price" (*Encyclopedia of Mormonism,* 3:1071).

Eliza R. Snow

Upon organizing the Relief society, the Prophet Joseph Smith said,
"I now turn the key to you in the name of God"

of a history of the Church, were also published in the *Times and Seasons*. Eventually, each of these publications, as well as an extract from the testimony of Matthew[24] and excerpts from Joseph Smith's history[25] became what we know today as the Pearl of Great Price.

CHAPTER 71: THE LORD REVEALS NEEDED DOCTRINE

By the summer of 1841, the little town of Commerce, Illinois, had grown to eight or nine thousand Latter-day Saints. Members had come from the eastern United States, Canada, Great Britain, and a large number from the state of Missouri following Governor Lilburn W. Boggs extermination order.[26] These dedicated Saints turned a swampland into a thriving city named Nauvoo. The Lord poured out his Spirit upon the Saints, and the Prophet Joseph received revelations concerning the doctrines and ordinances of the gospel.[27] As you read this chapter, watch for the important revelations and instructions the Lord gave to Joseph—and Joseph in turn gave to the Saints—while in Nauvoo.*

THE TEMPLE IN THE DAYS OF MOSES

Anciently Moses was commanded to build a portable temple, or tabernacle, that the children of Israel could use as they traveled in the wilderness. The importance of the temple was explained to the Saints in the Doctrine and Covenants:

"And again, verily I say unto you, how shall your washings[28] be acceptable unto me, except ye perform them in a house which you have built to my name?

"For, for this cause I commanded Moses that he should build a tabernacle,[29] that they should bear it with them in the wilderness, and to build a house in the land of promise, that those ordinances might be revealed which had been hid from before the world was" (124:37–38).

---

24. The excerpt from the testimony of Matthew is the Joseph Smith Translation of Matthew 23:39 through Matthew 24:51. It is now called Joseph Smith—Matthew.

25. Joseph Smith—History tells of the Prophet Joseph's experiences from his early years through May of 1829. It describes such events as the First Vision, the coming forth of the Book of Mormon, and the restoration of the Aaronic and Melchizedek Priesthoods, and is basically an excerpt of what eventually became the seven-volume *History of the Church.*

NOTES FOR CHAPTER 71

26. This was the order signed by the governor on October 27, 1838, that stated the Mormons must be driven from the state or exterminated. More information can be found in chapter 63, "Persecution and Fall of Far West."

27. In 1841, Joseph Smith had told the Saints that "the dispensation of the fullness of times will bring to light the things that have been revealed in all former dispensations; also other things that have not been before

revealed" (*History of the Church,* 4:426). The Saints had been given much doctrine up to this point, but it was not until the Nauvoo period that important ordinances to be performed in the temple were revealed.

28. A *washing* is a sacred ceremony performed in the Lord's temples which symbolizes one being made spiritually clean from the wickedness of the world.

29. Joseph F. Smith taught, "This tabernacle is the same temple where the boy Samuel heard the voice of the Lord. This sacred building was later replaced by Solomon's Temple. The question is often asked, 'What was the nature of the ordinances performed in these edifices in ancient times?' . . . It is true that in ancient Israel they did not have the fulness of ordinances as we do today, and most, if not all, of which they were privileged to receive, very likely pertained to the Aaronic Priesthood. (See D. & C. 84:21–26.) Neither did the ancients labor in their temples for the salvation of the dead. That work was reserved until after the Savior's visit to the spirit world where he unlocked the door to the prison and had the gospel carried to the spirits who had been confined" (*Church History and Modern Revelation,* 2:268).

The Lord commanded Moses to build a tabernacle in which to perform sacred ordinances. The tabernacle was a portable temple that the children of Israel carried with them as they traveled. They built a permanent temple when they settled in the Promised Land

THE TEMPLE ENDOWMENT IS INTRODUCED

One of the ordinances the Lord referred to when he explained the importance of the temple in section 124 is the endowment. On May 5, 1842, Joseph Smith presented the temple endowment for the first time to the brethren of the Church. He wrote:

"I spent the day in the upper part of the store, that is in my private office . . . with General James Adams, of Springfield, Patriarch Hyrum Smith, Bishops Newel K. Whitney and George Miller, and President Brigham Young and Elders Heber C. Kimball and Willard Richards, instructing them in the principles and order of the Priesthood, attending to washings, anointings, endowments[30] and the communication of keys pertaining to the Aaronic Priesthood, and so on to the highest order of the Melchi[z]edek Priesthood. . . . In this council was instituted the ancient order of things[31] for the first

---

30. Washings, anointings, and endowments are all sacred ordinances or ceremonies performed in the Lord's temples. The purpose of these ordinances is to teach and prepare God's children to come back into his presence.

31. Under the direction of the Lord, the Prophet Joseph brought back what he called "the ancient order of things." Robert Millet explained: "For the LDS prophet it was clear that the reestablishment of the kingdom of God entailed more than the reintroduction of saving truths or even of divine powers and authorities. The restoration of the gospel included the restoration of the 'ancient order of things,' both Old and New Testament principles and practices, especially those of the first-century Christian Church. He wrote in 1842, 'We believe in the same organization that existed in the Primitive Church, namely, apostles, prophets, pastors, teachers, evangelists, and so forth' . . . . " (*The Mormon Faith: Understanding Restored Christianity*, 94; emphasis added).

"He is a man like ourselves" (D&C 130:1)

unto in this life, it will rise with us in the resurrection.

"And if a person gains more knowledge and intelligence in this life through his diligence and obedience than another, he will have so much the advantage in the world to come.

"There is a law, irrevocably decreed[50] in heaven before the foundations of this world, upon which all blessings are predicated—[51]

"And when we obtain any blessing from God, it is by obedience to those laws upon which it is predicated" (vv. 18–21).

CHAPTER 72: BAPTISM FOR THE DEAD IS REVEALED

The Apostle John in the New Testament testified: "Except a man be born of the water and the Spirit, he cannot enter the kingdom of God" (John 3:5). There are many of Heavenly Father's children who die without the blessing of hearing the gospel and being baptized. But our loving Heavenly Father will not deny his children the opportunity to enter his kingdom. He, therefore, provides baptism for the dead, an ordinance that living members of the Church perform on behalf of those who have died without being baptized. This special ordinance is performed in temples. In this chapter you will read how the Lord revealed this important doctrine to the Prophet Joseph Smith. Ponder in your heart the comfort the doctrine of baptism for the dead can bring to the friends and relatives of those who die without being baptized.

DEATH AND TRAGEDY STRIKES THE SAINTS

The angel Moroni first appeared to Joseph Smith in 1823. Moroni promised that he would reveal the priesthood by the hand of Elijah.[52] Elijah[53] returned on April 3, 1836, in the Kirtland Temple, with priesthood keys that allowed the Saints to perform temple ordinances.

THE FIRST VISION, BY ROBERT BARRETT

The Prophet Joseph Smith taught that the Father and Son have physical bodies of flesh and bones, but the Holy Ghost is a spirit

50. 📖 **irrevocably decreed**—set and made unchangeable

51. 📖 **predicated**—based

NOTES FOR CHAPTER 72

52. 🕎 When Moroni appeared to Joseph Smith in September of 1823, he quoted many scriptures, including the following that is taken from Malachi 4:6: "Behold, I will reveal unto you the Priesthood, by the hand of Elijah the prophet, before the coming of the great and dreadful day of the Lord" (JS—H 1:38).

53. 🔍 Elijah was an Old Testament prophet who returned in the latter days to confer the keys of the sealing power on Joseph Smith and Oliver Cowdery. In his day, Elijah ministered in the Northern Kingdom of Israel. The Prophet Joseph Smith said that Elijah holds the sealing power of the Melchizedek Priesthood and was the last prophet with this power before the time of Jesus Christ (see *Guide to the Scriptures*, 72).

BUILDING THE NAUVOO TEMPLE, BY GLEN HOPKINSON

The Saints worked hard to build the Nauvoo Temple

rock cutters working on the temple in the bitter winter cold.

"Mary Fielding Smith, wife of Hyrum Smith, wrote to Latter-day Saint women in England, who within a year gathered 50,000 pennies, weighing 434 pounds, that were shipped to Nauvoo. Farmers donated teams and wagons; others sold some of their land and donated the money to the building committee. Many watches and guns were contributed. The Saints in Norway, Illinois, sent 100 sheep to Nauvoo to be used by the temple committee"[90] (*Our Heritage*, 59).

Brigham Young tells of the struggles and blessings the Saints experienced in building the temple:

"A few months after the martyrdom of Joseph the Prophet, in the autumn and winter of 1844 we did much hard labor on the Nauvoo temple, during which time it was difficult to get bread and other provisions[91] for the workmen to eat. I counseled the committee who had charge of the temple funds to deal out all the flour they had, and God would give them more; and they did so; and it was but a short time before Brother [Joseph] Toronto[92] came and brought me twenty-five hundred dollars in gold. The bishop and the committee met, and I met with them; and they said, that the law was to lay the gold at the apostles' feet. Yes, I said and I will lay it at the bishop's feet; so I opened the mouth of the bag and

90. Why did the Saints sacrifice so much in building the temple? What can you do to help with the work that goes on inside of the temples?

91. *provisions*—food

92. Joseph Toronto was a native of Sicily, who, wrote E. Cecil McGavin, "had served for years as a sailor in the Italian navy. This frugal man had carefully hoarded

his money for years, concealing his gold coins in his money belt.

"As he approached New York harbor, he became fearful that some rogue in the large city might rob him of his golden spoil—the earnings of a lifetime. In the midst of his concern about the safety of his money, he dreamed one night that a man came to him, requesting

took hold at the bottom end, and gave it a jerk . . . and strewed[93] the gold across the room and said, now go and buy flour for the workmen on the temple and do not distrust the Lord any more; for we will have what we need" (as quoted in B. H. Roberts, *Comprehensive History of the Church* 2:472).

THE FIRST ENDOWMENTS ARE GIVEN

Prior to the completion of the Nauvoo Temple, the Lord inspired the Prophet Joseph Smith to begin giving the blessings of the temple to some members of the Church. Joseph Fielding Smith wrote the following about the introduction of certain temple ordinances in Nauvoo:

"In the revelation of January 19, 1841, the Lord promised to reveal to Joseph Smith all things pertaining to the temple and the Priesthood thereof, which revelation and knowledge were necessary before the temple was erected.[94] Wednesday, May 4, 1842, the Prophet met with his brother, Patriarch Hyrum Smith, President Brigham Young, Elders Heber C. Kimball, Willard Richards, James Adams of Springfield, Bishops Newel K. Whitney and George Miller, and instructed them in the principles and orders[95] of the Priesthood that belong to the temple of the Lord" (*Essentials in Church History*, 263).

This was the first time the temple endowment had been given to any of God's children in this last dispensation. "After receiving the endowment, husbands and wives could be sealed together by the power of the priesthood for time and all eternity. Joseph Smith realized that his time on earth was short,[96] so while the temple was still under construction, he began giving the endowment to selected faithful followers in the upstairs room of his red brick store.

"Even after the murder of the Prophet Joseph Smith, when the Saints realized they must shortly leave Nauvoo, they increased their commitment to completing the temple. The attic of the unfinished temple was dedicated as a part of the structure where the endowment would be administered. The Saints were so anxious to receive this sacred ordinance that Brigham Young, Heber C. Kimball, and others of the Twelve Apostles remained in the temple both day and night, sleeping no more than about four hours a night. Mercy Fielding Thompson had charge of the washing and ironing of temple clothes, as well as overseeing the cooking. She too lived in the temple, sometimes working throughout the night to have everything ready for the next day. Other members were just as devoted" (*Our Heritage*, 60).

---

that he leave his money with 'Mormon Brigham' and he should be blessed.

"On reaching New York, he began to inquire about 'Mormon Brigham,' but no one knew him. Finally he met a person who told him that Brigham Young had recently become president of the Mormon Church, and was residing at Nauvoo, Illinois. Young Toronto left immediately for the city of the Saints. He arrived at the city of his desire during the April conference, at which President Young told how difficult it was to get enough bread for the workmen to eat, and made a strong appeal for assistance. At the close of the meeting, the twenty-seven year old Italian went to President Young's office where he removed his belt and placed

it on the President's desk, informing him that it contained twenty-five hundred dollars in gold" (*Nauvoo the Beautiful*, 26–27).

93. **strewed**—scattered

94. **erected**—built

95. **orders**—priesthood offices

96. Joseph Smith knew that he was not going to live very long, so he wanted to finish all that the Lord had given him to do. Wilford Woodruff records in his journal, "Elder [Lyman] Wight said that Joseph told him, while in Liberty jail, Missouri, in 1839, he would not live to see forty years, but he was not to reveal it till he was dead" (*History of the Church*, 7:212).

poverty—if I had to borrow meal to feed my wife and children, I never let an opportunity pass of learning what the Prophet had to impart" (Journal of Discourses, *12:270). Joseph gave nearly two hundred sermons during this time period (1840 to 1844), and what he taught helped the Saints to better understand the doctrines and gave the Church the direction that would be needed following his death. As you read this chapter, look for gospel truths that the Prophet Joseph received that are important to you.*

THE PROPHET WRITES A LETTER TO JOHN WENTWORTH ABOUT THE HISTORY AND TEACHINGS OF THE CHURCH

As the Saints settled in Nauvoo, Joseph began teaching and instructing them on many principles and doctrines of the gospel. Many in the state of Illinois who were not members of the Church also had an interest in learning more about the Mormons.

"At the request of Mr. John Wentworth, editor of the Chicago Democrat," explained Joseph Fielding Smith, "the Prophet prepared an article for publication giving a brief history of the Church. This history was published[110] in the *Times and Seasons* [the Church's newspaper in Nauvoo], March 1, 1842. . . . This article is one of the earliest documents giving a consecutive account of the history of the Church. It is concise and comprehensive,[111] yet covers only a few pages. The most important feature in this paper is the publication therein, for the first time, of the Articles of Faith. These articles, thirteen in number, were given by inspiration, and form a simple, comprehensive declaration[112] of many doctrines[113] of

the Church which have since been accepted by the vote of the Church as a standard . . . of belief"[114] (*Essentials in Church History*, 261).

THE PEARL OF GREAT PRICE

The Articles of Faith, the Book of Abraham, portions of Joseph Smith's history, and other important revelations and translations were first published in book form in England in 1851. Elder Franklin D. Richards, who was a member the Twelve and president of the British Mission, published them so that the Saints in Europe would have more of the inspired words of the Prophet Joseph Smith. Elder Richards called this publication the Pearl of Great Price. "The Pearl of Great Price received wide use and subsequently[115] became a standard work of the Church by action of the First Presidency and the general conference in Salt Lake City on October 10, 1880" (see Pearl of Great Price, Introductory Note).

THE PROPHET REVEALS COMFORTING TRUTHS AS HE SPEAKS TO THE SAINTS IN NAUVOO

In March 1842, Joseph gave very comforting words to all parents when he spoke at the funeral of the child of Windsor P. Lyon. In his sermon, Joseph said, "in my leisure[116] moments I have meditated[117] upon the subject, and asked the question, why it is that infants, innocent children, are taken away from us, especially those that seem to be the most intelligent and interesting. The strongest reasons that present themselves to my mind are these: This world is a very wicked world. . . . In the earlier ages of the world a righteous man, and a man of God and of

---

NOTES FOR CHAPTER 74

110. 📖 *published*—printed

111. 📖 *concise and comprehensive*—short and complete

112. 📖 *declaration*—statement

113. 📖 *doctrines*—teachings and beliefs

114. 🔥 Michaelene P. Grassli, a former Primary general president (1988–1994), explained one way we can use the Articles of Faith: "The Articles of Faith are a good way for us to share the gospel. While they don't tell all of our beliefs, they were written by a prophet of God,

Joseph Smith, and they are scripture. They have stood the test of time as a way to help us understand and tell others what we believe. But learning the Articles of Faith is only worthwhile to us as we let them be part of our lives. They are words and beliefs to plant firmly in our hearts and minds and actions" ("Using the Articles of Faith," *Friend*, January 1995, inside front cover).

115. 📖 *subsequently*—later

116. 📖 *leisure*—quiet

117. 📖 *meditated*—thought deeply

JOSEPH SMITH AT NAUVOO, BY TED GORKA © INTELLECTUAL RESERVE, INC.

Joseph took every opportunity he could to teach

intelligence, had a better chance to do good, to be believed and received than at the present day. . . . The Lord takes many away, even in infancy,[118] that they may escape the envy[119] of man, and the sorrows and evils of this present world; they were too pure, too lovely, to live on earth; therefore, if rightly considered, instead of mourning[120] we have reason to rejoice as they are delivered from evil, and we shall soon have them again. . . .

"The doctrine of baptizing children, or sprinkling them, or they must welter[121] in hell, is a doctrine not true, not supported in Holy Writ,[122] and is not consistent with the character of God. All children are redeemed by the blood of Jesus Christ, and the moment that children leave this world, they are taken to the bosom of Abraham.[123] The only difference between the old and young dying is, one lives longer in heaven and eternal light and glory than the other, and is freed a little sooner from this miserable, wicked world. Notwithstanding all this glory, we for a moment lose sight of it, and mourn the loss, but we do not mourn as those without hope" (*History of the Church,* 4:553–54).[124]

118. *in infancy*—while they are babies

119. *envy*—sinful jealousy

120. *mourning*—feeling sad at their death

121. *welter*—suffer

122. *Holy Writ*—scripture

123. *bosom of Abraham*—heaven

124. D&C 42:45–46 explains that because we love each other we feel sad when those whom we love die, but, "it shall come to pass that those that die in me shall not taste of death, for it shall be sweet unto them."

governor of Illinois to deliver Joseph Smith and O. P. Rockwell to a representative of the state of Missouri"[8] (*What of the Mormons?* 135).

MISSOURI AND ILLINOIS PLOT TOGETHER TO DESTROY THE PROPHET

Officials of the state of Missouri claimed that the Prophet Joseph fled to Illinois after attempting to kill former Governor Boggs. They made this claim because Joseph had not been in Missouri at the time of the crime so they could not require him to be brought to Missouri for trial.

Joseph Fielding Smith explained that "the foundation for this accusation[9] was perhaps based on the rumor circulated[10] at the time, and printed in the *Quincy Whig*[11] that Joseph Smith had prophesied that Boggs would die a violent death. As soon as the Prophet heard of this rumor he took occasion to deny it publicly, saying that he had made no such statement. Nevertheless, it gave occasion for an accusation, and it appears evident that Boggs and his fellow conspirators[12] thought it an opportunity, and an excuse, to get the Prophet within their clutches,[13] where they might kill him 'according to law.'

"Governor Carlin of Illinois appeared to be a party to this conspiracy. . . . He was thoroughly acquainted with the law and knew perfectly well that the Prophet was in Nauvoo on the 6th day of May, 1842, consequently was not subject to the requisition of Governor Reynolds of Missouri. He knew that President Smith was not a fugitive from justice;[14] . . . he knew the Prophet was entitled to a fair and legal trial in Illinois, not Missouri. Yet he would yield[15] to this unlawful and unrighteous demand against his knowledge of these facts" (*Essentials in Church History,* 267).

JOSEPH PROPHESIES THAT THE SAINTS WILL BE DRIVEN TO THE ROCKY MOUNTAINS

During these continued persecutions, the Prophet Joseph prophesied about the future of the Saints:

"I prophesied that the Saints would continue to suffer much affliction and would be driven to the Rocky Mountains, many would apostatize,[16] others would be put to death by our persecutors or lose their lives in consequence of exposure or disease, and some of you will live to go and assist in making settlements and build cities and see the Saints become a mighty people in the midst of the Rocky Mountains"[17] (*History of the Church,* 5:85).

JOSEPH GOES INTO HIDING TO AVOID BEING FALSELY ARRESTED

Occasionally, when the officers of the law were so corrupt that fair treatment was impossible, Joseph was forced to go into hiding.

Joseph Smith's pistol. Though innocent, Joseph was accused of firing a pistol at Governor Boggs

8. Why do you think ex-governor Boggs would blame the Saints for trying to kill him? Could hatred and guilt make a person angry enough to tell a lie? Have you ever done anything when you were angry that you were sorry for later?

9. **foundation for this accusation**—reason for the charges or blame

10. **rumor circulated**—lie spread around

11. Quincy was a town about 40 miles south of Nauvoo. The "Whig" was the name of their newspaper and also the name of a national political party.

12. **conspirators**—schemers, a group planning evil together

13. **clutches**—hands

14. **fugitive from justice**—someone running away from the law

15. **Yet he would yield**—Still he agreed

16. **apostatize**—lose faith and leave the Church

17. The Rocky Mountains is the area eventually settled by the Saints in Utah and surrounding states. Anson Call, who was with the Prophet Joseph when Joseph had the vision of the Rocky Mountains, wrote this:

Joseph Fielding Smith explained that "Because of the . . . fear that they would be unlawfully dragged to Missouri, Joseph and O. P. Rockwell retired to seclusion.[18] While in retirement the Prophet kept in touch with affairs in Nauvoo and wrote to the Saints from time to time. It was while thus confined[19] that he wrote the important letters which now appear as sections 127 and 128 in the Doctrine and Covenants, on baptism for the dead" (*Essentials in Church History,* 268).

CHARGES AGAINST THE PROPHET JOSEPH ARE DROPPED

The Prophet Joseph was advised by his lawyers to come out of hiding and surrender for trial at Springfield, Illinois, where they thought he could get a fair trial. This Joseph did the day after Christmas in 1842. Judge Pope, who tried the case, released the Prophet with these words:

"To authorize the arrest in this case . . . the affidavit should have stated distinctly—1st, that Smith had committed a crime; 2nd, that he committed it in Missouri. It must appear that he fled from Missouri to authorize the governor of Missouri to demand him. . . . It must appear that the crime was committed [by Joseph] in Missouri, to warrant the governor of Illinois in ordering him to be sent to Missouri for trial" (in Joseph Fielding Smith, *Essentials in Church History,* 272–73).

"On these grounds an order was entered discharging[20] the prisoner from arrest," Joseph Fielding Smith wrote. "Once again Missouri, persecutor of saints and prophets, was defeated; but her thirst for their blood was not satisfied" (*Essentials in Church History,* 273).

JOHN C. BENNETT'S RISE AND FALL

The Saints were on their guard against attacks by their Missouri enemies. However, other enemies

"I had before seen him in a vision, and now saw while he was talking his countenance change to white. . . . He seemed absorbed in gazing at something at a great distance, and said: 'I am gazing upon the valleys of those mountains.' . . .

"It is impossible to represent in words this scene which is still vivid in my mind. . . . There was a force and power in his exclamations . . . : 'Oh the beauty of those snow-capped mountains! The cool refreshing streams that are running down through those mountain gorges!' . . . 'Oh the scenes that this people will pass through! The dead that will lay between here and there.' . . . 'Oh the apostasy that will take place before my brethren reach that land!' 'But,' he continued, 'The priesthood shall prevail over its enemies, triumph over the devil and be established upon the earth, never more to be thrown down!'" (in *History of the Church,* 5:86n).

18. *retired to seclusion*—went into hiding

19. *confined*—hidden

20. *discharging*—releasing

The courtroom where Joseph was tried was on the second floor of this building above Abraham Lincoln's law office

John C. Bennett—great friend, bitter enemy

THE PROPHET REINED HIS HORSE; JUST ONE LAST LOOK, BY HAROLD HOPKINSON © INTELLECTUAL RESERVE, INC.

Joseph Smith was frequently pursued by the law

not to avoid arrest; for he feared that if he started for Nauvoo he might be apprehended en route[44] where he had no friends and be run over into Missouri among his bitterest enemies. A short time after . . . Wilson and Reynolds, appeared . . . and very brutally,[45] with oaths and threats and unnecessary violence, placed President Smith under arrest, and were for dragging him into Missouri. . . . By the activity and energy of his friends, however, President Smith succeeded in . . . delaying the haste of his captors" (*Comprehensive History of the Church*, 2:166–68).

JOSEPH SUCCEEDS IN BEING JUDGED BY A COURT IN NAUVOO

The rights granted by the Nauvoo charter protected the Saints many times from the unfair treatment they suffered in courts controlled by their enemies. Although the arresting officers didn't like it, the Prophet was able to get a hearing before the court in Nauvoo rather than being taken immediately to his enemies in Missouri.

"The same day they arrived in Nauvoo the municipal court convened,"[46] Joseph Fielding Smith wrote. "The summons was issued and Reynolds complied with the attachment[47] and delivered the Prophet into the hands of the marshal of the city. That afternoon President Smith addressed the people at great length, declaring that he would not peacefully submit again to such ill-treatment. While he was speaking Reynolds and Wilson with a lawyer named Davis, of Carthage, left for that place threatening to raise the militia and come again and take President Smith out of Nauvoo.

---

44. *apprehended en route*—caught or captured on the way

45. *brutally*—cruelly

46. *municipal court convened*—city court came together

47. *complied with the attachment*—obeyed the order

"Saturday, July 1, 1843, the court convened. . . . Cyrus Walker, Shepherd G. Patrick, Edward Southwick and a Mr. Backman, defended Joseph Smith while Attorney Mason was counselor for Reynolds. Witnesses were examined and the case tried on its merits, Hyrum Smith, Parley P. Pratt, Brigham Young, George W. Pitkin, Lyman Wight and Sidney Rigdon giving testimony, at the conclusion of which the prisoner was discharged. . . ."[48]

"The proceedings[49] of the municipal court of Nauvoo in this case were promptly forwarded to Governor Ford. . . . Judge James Adams came from Carthage with the information that Reynolds and Wilson were exciting the people there to mobocracy,[50] and petitioning the governor for a posse[51] forcibly to take Joseph Smith, on the grounds that he had been unlawfully taken out of their hands. . . .

"Governor Reynolds of Missouri requested [Governor Ford of Illinois] to call out the militia—a method they had of doing in Missouri—to retake Joseph Smith, Governor Ford replied that Joseph Smith had been tried . . . and discharged from arrest. He, as governor, had fully executed the duty which the laws imposed,[52] . . . and the constitution would not permit him to take such action as the Missouri official proposed"[53] (*Essentials in Church History,* 287–89).

CHAPTER 76:
THE MARTYRDOM OF JOSEPH AND HYRUM

The persecution the Church faced from its enemies made the Saints gather even more closely together to protect themselves. Unfortunately, it was this practice of sticking together that also caused fear and mistrust among their enemies. The Saints were different from the people who lived around them, not only in their religious beliefs but also in their views on government and how people should live together. Much more serious than any of these differences, however, was the trouble caused by those who once were members of the Church but, because of sin, became bitter enemies. Look for the ways the leaders of the Church did everything they could to obey the law.

THE PROPHET'S ENEMIES TURN TO MOB VIOLENCE

The attempt by Joseph Smith's enemies to use the law to take him to Missouri failed, and the Saints rejoiced that their beloved Prophet was free again. Sadly, it was only a temporary victory. Elder Joseph Fielding Smith wrote:

---

48.   It is interesting to notice how Joseph's persecutions are similar to the trials and persecutions Jesus Christ suffered. Their enemies tried to destroy them both many times, but they were both saved until their work on earth was finished. The Prophet Joseph declared: "This generation is as corrupt as the generation of the Jews that crucified Christ; and if He were here to-day, and should preach the same doctrine He did then, they would put Him to death. I defy all the world to destroy the work of God; and I prophesy they never will have power to kill me till my work is accomplished, and I am ready to die" (*History of the Church,* 6:58.) What does this teach you about God's ability to protect his servants? What does this teach you about the importance of being faithful servants?

49.   *proceedings*—results; decision

50.   *mobocracy*—mob violence

51.   *posse*—group of men

52.   *imposed*—required

53.   *proposed*—wanted

under the heavens; little do they know the trials that await them.'

"Further on he made another significant remark: 'I am going like a lamb to the slaughter; but I am calm as a summer's morning; I have a conscience void[107] of offense towards God, and towards all men. I shall die innocent, and it shall yet be said of me—he was murdered in cold blood.' . . .

"When they arrived in Carthage, they were arrested on a charge of *treason!* Then they were committed to jail. . . . When the illegality of this action was protested to Governor Ford, he replied that he did not think it his duty to interfere, as they were in the hands of the civil law. He therefore turned the matter over to the local magistrate,[108] who happened to be one of the leaders of the mob, and suggested that he use the Carthage Greys.[109] . . .

"Joseph Smith secured an interview with the governor who promised him that he would be protected from the mobs which by this time had gathered in Carthage. Moreover, the governor assured him that if he, the governor, went to Nauvoo to investigate matters for himself, as Joseph Smith had requested him to do, he would take the Prophet with him.

"Notwithstanding these promises, Governor Ford went to Nauvoo on the morning of June 27, leaving Joseph and Hyrum Smith, and Willard Richards and John Taylor incarcerated[110] in Carthage jail, with a mob militia[111] encamped on the town square" (Gordon B. Hinckley, *Truth Restored,* 74–76).

THE PROPHETS JOSEPH AND HYRUM ARE MARTYRED

Elder Hinckley continued: "The day [June 27, 1844] was spent by the prisoners in discussion and the writing of letters. To his wife Joseph wrote: 'I am very much resigned to my lot,[112] knowing I am justified,[113] and have done the best that could be done. Give my love to the children and all who inquire after me. May God bless you all. . . .' The letters were sent with visitors who left at one-thirty in the afternoon.

"As the day wore on a feeling of depression[114] came over the group. At the request of the Prophet, John Taylor sang 'A Poor Wayfaring Man of Grief.' . . .

"When the song was finished, 'there was a little rustling at the outer door of the jail, and a cry of surrender, and also a discharge[115] of three or four firearms followed instantly. The Doctor[116] glanced an eye by the curtains of the window, and saw about a hundred armed men around the door. . . . The mob encircled the building, and some of them rushed by

---

107. *void*—empty

108. The local magistrate was a city official with power to enforce the law.

109. The Carthage Greys were the Carthage military unit that was really just part of the mob.

110. *incarcerated*—locked up

111. *militia*—army

112. *resigned to my lot*—prepared to accept what is coming

113. *justified*—not guilty

114. *depression*—sadness

115. *discharge*—firing

116. The "Doctor" was Willard Richards. An hour or so before the martyrdom, Elder Richards said to Joseph, "Brother Joseph, you did not ask me to cross the river with you . . . you did not ask me to come to Carthage . . . you did not ask me to come to jail with you—and do you think I would forsake you now? But I will tell

you what I will do; if you are condemned to be hung for 'treason,' I will be hung in your stead, and you shall go free" (as quoted in B. H. Roberts, *Comprehensive History of the Church,* 2:283).

PHOTOGRAPH BY KENNETH MAYS

John Taylor's watch still bears the mark of the bullet

OH, MY POOR DEAR BROTHER HYRUM, BY LIZ LEMON SWINDLE

"Oh, dear brother Hyrum"

the guards up the flight of stairs, burst open the door, and began the work of death.'

"Hyrum was struck first, and he fell to the floor exclaiming, 'I am a dead man.' Joseph ran to him, exclaiming, 'Oh, dear brother Hyrum.' Then John Taylor was hit, and he fell to the floor seriously wounded. Fortunately, however, the impact[117] of one ball was broken by the watch in his vest pocket. This saved his life.

"With bullets bursting through the door, Joseph sprang to the window. Three balls struck him almost simultaneously,[118] two coming from the door and one from the window. Dying, he fell from the open window, exclaiming, 'O Lord, my God!'

"Dr. Richards escaped without injury. But the Church had lost its Prophet, and his brother, the Patriarch. The dastardly deed[119] was completed in a matter of seconds. They had sealed their testimonies with their blood" (*Truth Restored*, 82–85)

THE REACTION OF THE SAINTS IN NAUVOO

"When news of the murder of Joseph and Hyrum Smith reached Nauvoo a pall[120] of gloom settled over the city," Elder Hinckley wrote. "The next day the bodies of the dead were taken to Nauvoo. Thousands lined the streets as the cortege[121]

117. *impact*—force

118. *simultaneously*—at the same time

119. *dastardly deed*—shameful or cowardly act

120. *pall*—dark feeling

121. *cortege*—caskets and those walking by them

MARTYRDOM OF JOSEPH AND HYRUM SMITH, CARTHAGE, BY GARY SMITH © INTELLECTUAL RESERVE, INC.

The martyrdom of Joseph and Hyrum

passed. The brothers were buried on the following day.

"Meanwhile, the inhabitants of Carthage had fled from their homes in fear that the Mormons would rise en-masse and wreak vengeance.[122] But there was no disposition[123] to return evil for evil. . . .

"The mobocrats had thought that in killing Joseph Smith they had killed Mormonism. But in so doing they had understood neither the character of the people nor the organization of the Church" (*Truth Restored*, 85).

JOHN TAYLOR'S TESTIMONY OF JOSEPH SMITH

Elder John Taylor was shot four times but miraculously lived. In honor of the Prophet Joseph Smith and his brother Hyrum, he wrote what is now Doctrine and Covenants section 135. It reads in part:

"Joseph Smith, the Prophet and Seer of the Lord, has done more, save Jesus only, for the salvation of men in this world, than any other man that ever lived in it.[124] In the short space of twenty years, he has brought forth the Book of Mormon, which

---

122. **wreak vengeance**—take revenge

123. **disposition**—feeling

124. A Russian historian who visited the United States to study the lives of great Americans was boarding his ship to return home when reporters asked him, "'In your study of great Americans during this past year

which of them do you consider to be the greatest?' His answer is most startling. He said, 'You have only had one truly great American, one man who gave to the world ideas that could change the whole destiny of the human race—Joseph Smith the Mormon Prophet'" (in William E. Berrett, "The Life and Character of the Prophet Joseph Smith," *BYU Speeches of the Year*, 1964, 2).

he translated by the gift and power of God, and has been the means of publishing it on two continents; has sent the fulness of the everlasting gospel, which it contained, to the four quarters of the earth; has brought forth the revelations and commandments which compose[125] this book of Doctrine and Covenants, and many other wise documents and instructions for the benefit of the children of men; gathered many thousands of the Latter-day Saints, founded a great city, and left a fame and name that cannot be slain. He lived great, and he died great in the eyes of God and his people; and like most of the Lord's anointed in ancient times, has sealed his mission and his works with his own blood; and so has his brother Hyrum. In life they were not divided, and in death they were not separated! . . .

"Hyrum Smith was forty-four years old in February, 1844, and Joseph Smith was thirty-eight in December, 1843; and henceforward their names will be classed among the martyrs of religion; and the reader in every nation will be reminded that the Book of Mormon, and this book of Doctrine and Covenants of the church, cost the best blood of the nineteenth century to bring them forth for the salvation of a ruined world. . . . They lived for glory; they died for glory; and glory is their eternal reward"[126] (vv. 3, 6).

CHAPTER 77:
BRIGHAM YOUNG AND THE TWELVE
LEAD THE CHURCH

Following the death of the Prophet Joseph Smith and his brother Hyrum in Carthage Jail in June 1844, the members of the Church struggled with the death of their beloved leader and with concerns over who would now lead them. By August 8th, this matter was settled and Brigham Young and the Twelve began leading the Church into years of growth and success. As you read this chapter, look for what Brigham Young and the Quorum of the Twelve did for the Church with the help and guidance of the Lord.

THE LORD REVEALED WHO WOULD LEAD THE CHURCH IF THE PROPHET DIED

After the Prophet's death, the Church experienced a crisis:[127] the presiding quorum of the priesthood was now disorganized. Joseph Fielding Smith wrote that "very little thought had been given to the subject of succession in the Presidency,[128] even by the leading brethren. . . . The revelations were clear on that point, but there had been no occasion for consideration of[129] the subject. In the revelation on Priesthood, given to the apostles in 1835 (Doc. and Cov. Sec. 107), the Lord said that the council of the apostles was equal in authority with the First Presidency, and Joseph Smith stated that its place was second only to the presidency of the Church, and where there was no First Presidency, the apostles would preside"[130] (*Essentials in Church History*, 318).

JOSEPH GAVE THE TWELVE APOSTLES ALL THE AUTHORITY TO LEAD THE CHURCH

Elder Wilford Woodruff recorded the details of how the Prophet Joseph gave the authority to lead the Church to the Twelve Apostles:

"Before [Joseph] died he organized the Church with Apostles, Patriarchs, Pastors, Teachers, and the whole government of the Church of God; and that Priesthood he organized or laid the foundations of remained with the people after his death. . . . The Twelve Apostles stood next to the First Presidency of the Church; and I am a living witness to the testimony that Joseph gave to the Twelve Apostles when

---

125. *compose*—make up

126. Think about what you have learned about the Prophet Joseph Smith. What are some of the blessings you enjoy because he was faithful in fulfilling his calling to restore the gospel of Jesus Christ to the earth? How would your life be different without the gospel? If you could meet the Prophet Joseph face to face, what would you like to say to him?

NOTES FOR CHAPTER 77

127. *crisis*—trial

128. *succession in the Presidency*—who would become the next Church president

129. *occasion for consideration of*—reason to think about

130. *preside*—lead

"All that are in favor of this, in all the congregation[151] of the saints, manifest[152] it by holding up the right hand. (There was a universal vote[153]). If there are any of the contrary mind, every man and every woman who does not want the Twelve to preside, lift up your hands in like manner. (No hands up)" (in *History of the Church*, 7:240).

WHY DID BRIGHAM LOOK AND SOUND LIKE JOSEPH SMITH?

Wilford Woodruff gave the following explanation as to why Brigham Young looked and sounded like Joseph Smith.

"The question might be asked, why was the appearance of Joseph Smith given to Brigham Young? Because here was Sidney Rigdon and other men rising up and claiming to be the leaders of the Church, and men stood, as it were, on a pivot,[154] not knowing which way to turn. But just as quick as Brigham Young rose in that assembly, his face was that of Joseph Smith—the mantle[155] of Joseph had fallen upon him, the power of God that was upon Joseph Smith was upon him, he had the voice of Joseph, and it was the voice of the shepherd. There was not a person in that assembly, . . . but was

satisfied in his own mind that Brigham was the proper leader of the people. . . . There was a reason for this in the mind of God; it convinced the people"[156] (*Journal of Discourses*, 15:81).

THE TWELVE SET SOME IMPORTANT GOALS FOR THE CHURCH

"After the question of the presiding quorum[157] was decided," Joseph Fielding Smith explained, "the Saints settled down to their usual duties, and the progress of the Church continued with greater strides than ever before. At the October conference in 1844, a great deal of important business was transacted.[158] At that time . . . many brethren were ordained to the ministry,[159] a number of quorums of seventy were organized, and missionaries were called to go to various parts of the United States and abroad[160] with the message of salvation. The building of the temple was continued with renewed diligence and prosperity[161] was manifest in the settlements of the Saints. . . . Each room [of the temple] was dedicated separately as it was finished and ordinance work for the Saints, as well as baptisms for the dead, were performed" (*Essentials in Church History*, 323).[162]

---

151. *congregation*—group; gathering

152. *manifest*—show

153. *universal vote*—vote everyone agreed upon

154. *pivot*—turning point

155. *mantle*—authority

156. A similar account in the Old Testament tells how Elisha was given the mantle of Elijah. Soon after, Elisha parted the Jordan River as Elijah had done and the people knew he was God's chosen prophet (see 2 Kings 2:9–15).

157. *the presiding quorum*—who would lead the Church

158. *transacted*—completed

159. "President Brigham Young . . . proceeded to select men from the high priests' quorum, to go abroad in all the . . . United States, to preside over the branches of the church. . . .

"President Young explained the object for which these high priests were being sent out, and informed them that it was not the design to go and tarry six months and then return, but to go and settle down, . . . and build up a stake as large as this [Nauvoo]" (in *History of the Church*, 7:305–7).

160. *abroad*—to other countries

161. *prosperity*—growth and success

162. Elder John Taylor emphasized the need to continue building the temple when he said, "The first thing we have got to do is to build the Temple, where we can receive those blessings which we so much desire" (in *History of the Church*, 7:292).

The Lord and the members of the Church chose Brigham Young and the Twelve Apostles to lead the Church after the Prophet Joseph Smith was killed

Nauvoo Loses Its Freedom Charter

The one thing that gave the Saints an advantage over their enemies was the Nauvoo Charter. Knowing this, their enemies worked to have it overthrown. Joseph Fielding Smith explained:

"The city charter of Nauvoo[174] had . . . guaranteed safety against the plottings of the wicked. It was the aim of the Nauvoo conspirators[175] to cause its repeal.[176] . . . The charter was repealed by the legislature in January, 1845. Some of the murderers of Joseph and Hyrum Smith sat in that body[177] and violently denounced[178] the 'Mormons,' although it was well known that their hands were stained with innocent blood.[179] After the repeal of the charter, and without hope of protection from the officers of the state, the Saints were at the mercy of their enemies" (*Essentials in Church History*, 325).[180]

Mobs Attack Small Communities

Mob violence began in smaller communities outside of the heavily populated city of Nauvoo. Isaac Morley and others had settled and built a little city twenty-five miles south of Nauvoo.

According to one writer, "The mob continued organizing and gathering apostates[181] into their ranks and threatening to exterminate[182] the Mormons and on the 10th of September, 1845, they set fire to Morley's settlement and Green Plain, burned all the houses, barns and shops in the settlements and drove the sheriff of Hancock County from his home and tried to kill him, when Porter Rockwell, in defending him, killed a man by the name of Worrell who was a leader in the mob and took active part in killing the Prophet and Patriarch.[183] The persecution continued to rage and people left the small

---

174. 🔍 The Nauvoo Charter "granted the right to establish a local militia, a municipal court, and a university. Church leaders were elated . . . that government officials would no longer be able to take advantage of the Saints as they had in Missouri" (*Church History in the Fulness of Times*, 223).

175. 📖 ***Nauvoo Conspirators***—enemies of the Church

176. 📖 ***cause its repeal***—take it away

177. 📖 ***body***—group

178. 📖 ***denounced***—spoke against

THE BATTLE OF NAUVOO, BY C. C. A. CHRISTENSEN, COURTESY BRIGHAM YOUNG UNIVERSITY MUSEUM OF ART

The Battle of Nauvoo

179. 🔍 The desire of the mobs to destroy the Saints did not end with the deaths of Joseph and Hyrum. "The anti-Mormon leaders planned 'wolf-hunts' in 1844, where the wolves to be hunted were Mormons" (H. Dean Garrett, ed., *Regional Studies in Latter-day Saint History: Illinois*, 228).

180. 🔍 "Of this act [repealing the Nauvoo Charter] on the part of the state legislature, the state's attorney, Josiah Lamborn, in a letter to Brigham Young, . . . said: 'I have always considered that your enemies have been prompted by political and religious prejudices, and by a desire for plunder and blood, more than the common good. By the repeal of your charter, . . . our legislature has given a kind of sanction to the barbarous manner in which you have been treated" (B. H. Roberts, *Comprehensive History of the Church*, 2:468–69).

181. 📖 ***apostates***—wicked former members

182. 🐢 People "exterminate" unwanted bugs from their houses. What does this attitude say about how the mobbers felt about the Saints? Have you seen similar attitudes today? How should a good Latter-day Saint respond to these kinds of people?

183. 🔍 The Patriarch referred to here was Hyrum Smith, who was serving as Church Patriarch at the time of his death.

settlements and went to Nauvoo for protection and business was paralyzed.[184] We were kept on guard nearly all the time and many poor men were entirely destitute[185] of anything to eat at times" (George Morris, Autobiography, BYU Special Collections, Writings of Early Latter-day Saints, 27.)

CHURCH LEADERS STRENGTHEN THE MEMBERS

As fear of their enemies increased among the members of the Church, Heber C. Kimball of the Twelve told the Saints how they could continue to have the Lord's blessings and protection.

"I would exhort[186] the brethren to pay their tithing, and to pay the best of your substance,[187] and the Lord will sanctify the elements[188] for our good, . . . and you will have favor in the sight of God and angels. . . . I know that he hears our prayers; our enemies may organize wolf hunts; but what can they accomplish? for God has a power in this church, and their plans are frustrated"[189] (*Times and Seasons* 6 [July 15, 1845]: 973).

ENEMIES OF THE CHURCH HOLD A FATEFUL MEETING

On September 22, 1845, the enemies of the Church met together and formally decided that the Saints must leave Illinois. Their first action was to publish the following in a local newspaper:

"It is a settled thing that the public sentiment[190] of the State is against the 'Mormons,' and it will be in vain[191] for them to contend[192] against it; and to prevent bloodshed, and the sacrifice of many lives on both sides, it is their duty to obey the public will and leave the State as speedily as possible. That they will do this we have a confident hope and that too, before the next extreme is resorted to—that of force" (in Joseph Fielding Smith, *Essentials in Church History*, 326).

THE SAINTS ANSWER THE MOB'S ORDER

Brigham Young replied to this request from the enemies of the Church by letter on September 24, 1845. He told them that though the Saints had been persecuted, they had tried "to live in peace and desired to do so with all men." Even so, he wrote:

"We would say . . . that we propose to leave this country next spring. . . .

"That we will use all lawful means, in connection with others, to preserve[193] the public peace while we tarry;[194] and shall expect, decidedly, that we be no more molested[195] with house-burning, or any other depredations,[196] to waste our property and time, and hinder[197] our business" (as quoted in Joseph Fielding Smith, *Essentials in Church History*, 326–27).

THE SAINTS PREPARE FOR THEIR JOURNEY WEST

Between October 1845 and February 1846, the Saints worked very hard to be prepared to move west. They also finished the Nauvoo Temple, and many Saints received their temple ordinances.[198] Joseph Fielding Smith recorded:

---

184. *paralyzed*—stopped; discontinued

185. *destitute*—poor or needy

186. *exhort*—tell, encourage

187. *substance*—belongings, what you own

188. *sanctify the elements*—bless the weather

189. *are frustrated*—do not happen as they would like

190. *sentiment*—feeling

191. *in vain*—useless

192. *contend*—argue; fight

193. *preserve*—keep

194. *tarry*—stay

195. *molested*—hurt and persecuted

196. *depredations*—wicked acts

197. *hinder*—slow

198. "In December, the ordinance work in the temple was commenced, and thereafter the building was occupied both day and night to afford the Saints the opportunity to receive their endowments. This continued until most all of the Saints had departed on their westward journey. May 1, 1846, after the majority of the people had departed from the city, the temple was publicly dedicated in the presence of about three hundred persons" (Joseph Fielding Smith, *Essentials in Church History*, 329–30).

*Settlements were established by the pioneers all along the
westward trek to aid those who followed after them*

were slowly wending[219] their way seeking a haven[220] in the West" (*Essentials in Church History*, 333–34).

THE "CAMP OF ISRAEL" IS ORGANIZED

The lead pioneer companies learned much as they traveled west. The need for better organization was apparent.[221]

"While encamped near the Chariton River," Joseph Fielding Smith wrote, "the organization of the camps was reduced to a more systematic[222] order. They were divided into companies of hundreds, fifties and tens, with officers appointed to preside over each.[223] The apostles were appointed to take charge of divisions, and the camps were divided into two grand divisions. Over one of these President Brigham Young had command. He was also sustained as 'president over all the camps of Israel.' Elder Heber C. Kimball was appointed to the command of the other grand division. . . . Of necessity the regulations in the camps were strict, yet the freedom and rightful privileges of the Saints were

safely guaranteed" (*Essentials in Church History*, 334).

BRIGHAM YOUNG PRAISES THE SAINTS

Brigham said the following about these brave pioneers:

"I did not think there had ever been a body of people since the days of Enoch placed under the same unpleasant circumstances that this people have been, where there was so little grumbling;[224] and I was satisfied that the Lord was pleased with the majority of the 'Camp of Israel'" (*History of the Church*, 7:608).

AN ADVANCE COMPANY PREPARES THE WAY FOR OTHERS TO FOLLOW

As the Saints moved across Iowa, they wisely established settlements where those who followed could camp, rest, and replenish supplies. Joseph Fielding Smith explained:

---

219. *wending*—making

220. *haven*—place of safety and peace

221. "The main 'Camp of Israel' took 131 days to cover the 300 miles they traveled across Iowa. The Pioneer Company a year later took only 111 days to cover 1,050 miles from Winter Quarters to the Great Salt Lake Valley. Inadequate preparation, lack of knowledgeable guides, delays, miserable weather, and difficult terrain made the Iowa journey one of the most

trying in the Church history" (*Church History in the Fulness of Times*, 309).

222. *systematic*—logical

223. A similar order was given to Brigham Young in D&C 136:12–16.

224. If you had been a pioneer, would you have been tempted to grumble? Why? What can people do to keep from grumbling?

"At the beginning of the journey about one hundred men, under command of Colonel Stephen Markham, were selected as pioneers, to travel in advance of the companies to build and repair the roads; also to seek out temporary places for shelter where fields could be cultivated[225] and homes . . . might be provided for the exiles. The advance companies arrived at a place . . . some one hundred and forty-five miles west of Nauvoo, April 24, 1846. Here a temporary settlement was selected which they named Garden Grove. Two days later a council meeting was held and three hundred and fifty-nine laboring men were reported in the camp. From these one hundred were selected to cut trees and make rails; ten to build fences; forty-eight to build houses; twelve to dig wells and ten to build bridges. The remainder were employed[226] in clearing land and preparing it for cultivation. Every one was busy, and in a few days a respectable village, magic-like, had risen in the wilderness. . . . At this point President Young addressed the Saints saying it would be necessary to leave some of their number here, . . . while the main body would push on . . . until they could all gather at the place appointed, and 'build the house of the Lord in the tops of the mountains'" (*Essentials in Church History*, 335).[227]

THE SAINTS SETTLE MOUNT PISGAH

In May, a number of the apostles reached the middle fork of the Grand River, where they found Parley P. Pratt and his group. Parley had named the site Mount Pisgah. The brethren were pleased with the site and decided to make another settlement for the Saints at Mount Pisgah.

"At Mount Pisgah," wrote B. H. Roberts, "the scenes of Garden Grove were reenacted.[228] A farm of 'several thousand acres,' was inclosed[229] and planted, and the place became a permanent settlement, of which William Huntington was made president, with Ezra T. Benson and Charles C. Rich as his counselors" (*Comprehensive History of the Church*, 3:55).

BRIGHAM YOUNG'S CAMP CONTINUES WEST TO THE MISSOURI RIVER

As Brigham Young and the main group of Saints moved west from Mount Pisgah, they found traveling a little easier.

"The camps were now traveling through an Indian country," wrote Joseph Fielding Smith, "where there were no roads, no settlements and

The Saints decided to spend the winter of 1846–47 by the Missouri River and prepare for the journey to the Rocky Mountains in the spring

WINTER QUARTERS, BY C. C. A. CHRISTENSEN, COURTESY BRIGHAM YOUNG UNIVERSITY MUSEUM OF ART

225. *cultivated*—planted

226. *employed*—put to work

227. "'The camp was like a hive of bees,' says George Q. Cannon, 'every one was busy. And withal the people felt well and happy.' . . . The presidency of Garden Grove was instructed . . . to see that the crops were cared for and secured; that the people be taught the law of tithing—the payment of one-tenth of their increase to the church annually—and that the tithes be received and disbursed to the poor and sick among them" (in B. H. Roberts, *Comprehensive History of the Church*, 3:54–55).

228. *reenacted*—done again

229. *inclosed*—fenced

GLOSSARY

Aaronic Priesthood. The lesser priesthood. Its offices are bishop, deacon, teacher, and priest. It holds the keys of the ministering of angels, of the gospel of repentance, and of baptism (see D&C 13) and deals with the temporal or outward ordinances of the gospel. It was restored to the earth on May 15, 1829, when John the Baptist conferred it on Joseph Smith and Oliver Cowdery on the banks of the Susquehanna River near Harmony, Pennsylvania.

Amen. Firm or true. The word is used to show approval (Deuteronomy 27:15–26) or testify of the truthfulness of a statement or act (1 Kings 1:36).

Comforter. One of the titles for the Holy Ghost. The Holy Ghost can give comfort and peace to those who repent of sin.

Consecrate, Consecrated, Consecration, Law of Consecration. To dedicate, to make holy, or to become righteous. The law of consecration is a divine principle whereby men and women voluntarily dedicate their time, talents, and material wealth to the establishment and building up of God's kingdom.

Covenant. An agreement between two people. In the scriptures it is usually a sacred agreement between God and a person or a group of people. We promise to be obedient to God's commandments and he promises to bless us.

Cowdery, Oliver. (1806–1850) A schoolteacher who learned about the Prophet Joseph Smith while living with Joseph's parents in Palmyra, New York. He was the Prophet's scribe during most of the Book of Mormon translation. He was present when John the Baptist restored the Aaronic Priesthood and when Peter, James, and John brought back the Melchizedek Priesthood. He was also one of the Three Witnesses to the Book of Mormon. He had some difficulties and left the Church in 1838 but was rebaptized in 1848 shortly before his death.

Dispensation. A period of time. We live in the dispensation of the fulness of times, or the last dispensation before the coming of Jesus Christ.

Enoch. A great prophet of Old Testament times. Adam ordained him to the priesthood (see D&C 107:48). After Enoch ministered among wicked people for hundreds of years, some of them repented and became righteous. Over time, he and his people were taken up into heaven (see Moses 7:21). At Jesus Christ's Second Coming, Enoch and his city will joyfully return to the earth (see Moses 7:60–66).

Gentiles. The word *Gentiles* has several meanings in the scriptures. Sometimes it refers to those not of the family of Israel. Other times it refers to people who are not Jewish or who do not live in the Holy Land. It can also refer to people who do not believe in the God of Israel or to nations who are without the gospel. Since the restoration of the gospel the term *Gentile* has also been used to refer to people who are not members of the Church.

Gilbert, Algernon Sidney. (1789–1834) A business partner with Newel K. Whitney. Joined the Church in 1830. Because of his talent in business the Lord called Sidney to be an agent for the Church (see D&C 53:4). It was said of him: "The Lord had few more devoted servants in this dispensation" (*History of the Church,* 2:118). Brother Gilbert died of cholera only four years after his baptism in the Church.

Grace. Grace is divine help given by God through the atonement of Jesus Christ. It provides us with the power needed to repent, keep the commandments, and become like God.

Millennium" (*The Guide to the Scriptures,* s.v. "New Jerusalem," 177).

Only Begotten Son. "Ancient and modern scriptures use the title Only Begotten to emphasize the divine nature of Jesus Christ. Latter-day Saints recognize Jesus as literally the Only Begotten Son of God the Father in the flesh [mortality]. This title signifies that Jesus' physical body was the off-spring of a mortal mother and of the eternal Father" (*Encyclopedia of Mormonism,* s.v. "Only Begotten in the Flesh," 2:729).

Partridge, Edward. (1793–1840) Baptized on December 11, 1830. He served as the first bishop in the Church (see D&C 41:11). Bishop Partridge was a dedicated and faithful saint and was considered by the Prophet Joseph Smith to be "one of the Lord's great men" (*History of the Church,* 1:128). After his death, the Lord declared that He had received Edward unto Himself (see D&C 124:19).

Phelps, William Wines. (1792–1872) Baptized on June 10, 1831. The Lord commanded him to be a "printer unto the Church" (D&C 57:11), and Brother Phelps was instrumental in the printing of the Book of Commandments (Doctrine and Covenants). He also printed the first newspaper in the Church, helped prepare the first hymnbook, and wrote several hymns. Although W. W. Phelps left the Church for a time, he later repented and was a prominent figure in the Church throughout the rest of his life.

Pratt, Orson. (1811–1881) Baptized on his nineteenth birthday in 1830 by his older brother, Parley. Orson became one of the great leaders and teachers in the Church. He was a faithful missionary and loved sharing the Gospel—crossing the Atlantic Ocean sixteen times to preach in the British Isles. Orson was a great scholar of many subjects. He wrote pamphlets and articles defending the Church that are still studied today by students of the gospel. He also served as one of the original members of the Quorum of the Twelve Apostles in this dispensation.

Pratt, Parley P. (1807–1857) One of the great missionaries of the restored gospel of Jesus Christ. His own conversion came from following the promptings of the Spirit and reading the Book of Mormon. In 1835 he was called as one of the original members of the Quorum of the Twelve Apostles. He wrote many books, articles, and hymns that are beloved in the Church today. He was murdered while serving a mission to Arkansas in 1857.

Priesthood. The authority and power of God, by which all things were created. God has delegated the priesthood to man to act in his name on earth.

Redeem, Redeemed, Redeemer, Redemption. To buy back or to set free. Jesus Christ is our Redeemer because he willingly paid the price to buy us back and set us free from the effects of the fall of Adam, and the burden of our own sins (see 1 Corinthians 6:20; D&C 18:11). The price he paid was his own blood and his life (see 1 Peter 1:18–19).

Restoration of the gospel. "God's reestablishment of the truths and ordinances of his gospel among men on earth. The gospel of Jesus Christ was lost from the earth through apostasy that took place following the earthly ministry of Christ's apostles. That apostasy made necessary the restoration of the gospel. Through visions, the ministering of angels, and revelations to men on the earth, God restored the gospel. The Restoration started with the Prophet Joseph Smith (JS—H 1:1–75; D&C 128:20–21) and has continued to the present through the work of the Lord's living prophets" (*The Guide to the Scriptures,* s.v. "Restoration of the Gospel," 207).

Resurrect, Resurrection. At death, the body and the spirit separate. The spirit goes to the spirit world and the body returns to the dust from which it was made. In resurrection, the spirit joins together with the body to never separate again. All people will resurrect because Jesus Christ overcame death and made it possible. Resurrected people will never die again. They are immortal or not subject to death.

Richards, Willard. (1804–1854) "Served as the private secretary to Joseph Smith. He kept the Prophet's private journals and later served as Church Historian and Recorder. . . . He served a mission to England with members of the Twelve Apostles, and on July 8, 1838, was himself called to serve in that quorum of special witnesses. . . . He was one of the two survivors of the tragedy at Carthage, and the only one who was left physically unmarred from the attack. . . . On December 27, 1847, he was sustained as Second Counselor in the First Presidency, where he served faithfully until his death on March 11, 1854" (Hoyt W. Brewster Jr., *Doctrine and Covenants Encyclopedia*, 471–72).

Rigdon, Sidney. (1793–1876) A minister of another religion when he heard the Restoration message and was baptized. He was a man of many talents and became an important figure in Church history. He served as the Prophet's scribe and as a counselor in the First Presidency. He also spent time in Liberty Jail with Joseph Smith. He made many sacrifices for the gospel but eventually left the Church.

Rockwell, Orrin Porter. (1813–1878) Born in Belcher, Massachusetts, on June 28, 1813. A close friend of the Prophet Joseph Smith, Porter Rockwell was baptized in 1830, shortly after the organization of the Church. Hated by enemies of the Church, he was falsely charged with many crimes, including trying kill to ex-Governor Lilburn W. Boggs in 1842. Unable to convict him, the State of Missouri finally released him on December 13, 1843. A colorful personality, Porter Rockwell played an important role in the Mormon exodus to the Great Salt Lake Valley. He died June 9, 1878, in Salt Lake City.

Salvation. "To be saved from both physical and spiritual death. All people will be saved from physical death by the grace of God, through the death and resurrection of Jesus Christ. Each individual can also be saved from spiritual death as well by the grace of God, through faith in Jesus Christ. This faith is manifested in a life of obedience to the laws and ordinances of the gospel and service to Christ" (*The Guide to the Scriptures,* s.v. "Salvation," 216).

Sanctify, Sanctified, Sanctifies, Sanctification. To become clean, pure, and spotless. A person can become sanctified only through the atonement of Jesus Christ and by obedience to the laws, ordinances, and commandments of the gospel of Jesus Christ (see Articles of Faith, 1:3).

Seed. Descendants, meaning children, grandchildren, and so on.

Seer. Someone who can see "things which [are] not visible to the natural eye" (Moses 6:36).

Smith, Emma Hale. (1804–1879) Married the Prophet Joseph Smith on January 18, 1827. Together they had eight children and adopted two children. The Prophet's mother said of Emma, "I have never seen a woman in my life, who would endure every [type] of fatigue and hardship, from month to month, and from year to year, with [such steady] courage, zeal, and patience" (Lucy Mack Smith, *History of Joseph Smith by His Mother,* 191). During a time of trial and persecution, the Lord declared to Emma: "Thou art an elect lady, whom I have called" (D&C 25:3).

Smith, Hyrum. (1800–1844) The Prophet Joseph's older brother. He served faithfully in the gospel as one of the Eight Witnesses of the gold plates, as a missionary, as a patriarch to the Church, and as a trusted advisor to the Prophet. He gave his life, along with his brother, at Carthage Jail. The Lord said of Hyrum, "I, the Lord, love him because of the integrity of his heart, and because he loveth that which is right before me" (D&C 124:15).

Smith, Joseph Jr. (1805–1844) While praying to know which church to join, was visited by God the Father and Jesus Christ. They told him that the true Church was not upon the earth and that he would help restore it (see JS—H 1:16–20). Joseph eventually translated the Book of Mormon, received the priesthood, and organized the Church. He also preached the gospel and gathered the Saints to locations in Ohio, Missouri, and Illinois. On June 27, 1844, he was killed by mobs who opposed his work. He sealed his testimony with his blood.

Sources Cited

Anderson, Karl Ricks. *Joseph Smith's Kirtland.* Salt Lake City: Deseret Book, 1989.

Anderson, Richard Lloyd, "Reuben Miller, Recorder of Oliver Cowdery's Reaffirmations." *BYU Studies* 8, no. 3 (1968): 277–93.

Andrus, Hyrum L., and Helen Mae Andrus, comps. *They Knew the Prophet.* Salt Lake City: Bookcraft, 1974.

Angell, Truman O. "Journal of Truman O. Angell." Typescript copy. BYU Special Collections. Harold B. Lee Library, Provo, Utah.

Arrington, Leonard J. "The John Tanner Family." *Ensign* 9 (March 1979): 46–51.

Ashton, Marvin J. "Faith in Oneself." In *Faith.* Salt Lake City: Deseret Book, 1983.

Backman, Milton V. Jr. *The Heavens Resound: A History of Latter-day Saints in Ohio, 1830–1838.* Salt Lake City: Deseret Book, 1983.

Backman, Robert L. "They Were Awesome." *New Era* 13 (May 1983): 5–8.

Ballard, M. Russell "The Greatest Generation of Missionaries." *Ensign* 32 (November 2002): 46–49.

———. "The Legacy of Hyrum." *Ensign* 24 (September 1994): 55–58.

———. "Restored Truth." *Ensign* 24 (November 1994): 65–68.

Barrett, Ivan J. *Joseph Smith and the Restoration.* Rev. ed. Provo: Brigham Young University Press, 1973.

Baugh, Alexander. "The Battle Between Mormon and Missouri Militia at Crooked River." *Regional Studies in Latter-day Saint Church History: Missouri.* Provo: Department of Church History and Doctrine, Brigham Young University, 1994, 85–103.

Bell, James P., and James E. Faust. *In the Strength of the Lord: The Life and Teachings of James E. Faust.* Salt Lake City: Deseret Book, 1999.

Benson, Ezra Taft. "The Book of Mormon—Keystone of Our Religion." *Ensign* 16 (November 1986): 4–7.

———. "Cleansing the Inner Vessel." *Ensign* 16 (May 1986): 4–6.

———. *Come unto Christ.* Salt Lake City: Deseret Book, 1983.

———. Conference Reports. October 1967.

———. *God, Family, Country: Our Three Great Loyalties.* Salt Lake City: Deseret Book, 1974.

———. "I Testify." *Ensign* 18 (November 1988): 86–87.

———. "Ministering to Needs through the Lord's Storehouse System." *Ensign* 7 (May 1977): 82–84.

———. "Seek the Spirit of the Lord." *Ensign* 18 (April 1988): 2–6.

———. *The Teachings of Ezra Taft Benson.* Salt Lake City: Bookcraft, 1988.

Berrett, William E. *The Restored Church.* 7th ed. Salt Lake City: Deseret Book, 1953.

Black, Susan Easton. *Who's Who in the Doctrine and Covenants.* Salt Lake City: Bookcraft, 1997.

Brewster, Hoyt W., Jr. *Doctrine and Covenants Encyclopedia.* Salt Lake City: Bookcraft, 1988.

Bushman, Richard L. *Joseph Smith and the Beginnings of Mormonism.* Urbana: University of Illinois Press, 1984.

Cannon, Donald Q. "Topsfield Massachusetts: Ancestral Home of the Prophet Joseph." *BYU Studies* 14, no. 1 (1973): 56–75.

Cannon, Donald Q., and Lyndon W. Cook, eds. *Far West Record: Minutes of The Church of Jesus Christ of Latter-day Saints, 1830–1844.* Salt Lake City: Deseret Book, 1983.

Cannon, George Q. *Gospel Truth.* Edited by Jerreld L. Newquist. Salt Lake City: Deseret Book, 1987.

———. *The Life of Joseph Smith the Prophet.* Salt Lake City: Deseret Book, 1964.

Clark, James R., comp. *Messages of the First Presidency of The Church of Jesus Christ of Latter-day Saints.* 6 vols. Salt Lake City: Bookcraft, 1965–75.

Cook, Gene R. *Raising Up a Family to the Lord.* Salt Lake City: Deseret Book, 1993.

———. *Sermons and Writings of Bruce R. McConkie*. Edited by Mark L. McConkie. Salt Lake City: Bookcraft, 1998.

McConkie, Joseph Fielding, and Craig J. Ostler. *Revelations of the Restoration*. Salt Lake City: Deseret Book, 2000.

McGavin, E. Cecil. *The Family of Joseph Smith*. Salt Lake City: Bookcraft, 1963.

———. *Nauvoo the Beautiful*. Salt Lake City: Bookcraft, 1972.

McKay, David O. Conference Reports. April 1954.

———. *Steppingstones to an Abundant Life*. Salt Lake City: Deseret Book, 1971.

Merriam-Webster's Collegiate Dictionary. 10th ed. Springfield, Mass.: Merriam-Webster, Inc., 1999.

Millet, Robert L. *The Mormon Faith: A Modern Look at Christianity*. Salt Lake City: Shadow Mountain, 1998.

Millet, Robert L., and Joseph Fielding McConkie. *The Life Beyond*. Salt Lake City: Bookcraft, 1986.

Monson, Thomas S. "Days Never to Be Forgotten." *Ensign* 20 (November 1990): 67–69.

Morrell, Jeanette McKay, *Highlights in the Life of President David O. McKay*. Salt Lake City: Deseret Book, 1966.

Murdock, John. "John Murdock Journal." Typescript copy. BYU Special Collections. Harold B. Lee Library, Provo, Utah.

Nelson, Russell M. *Perfection Pending, and Other Favorite Discourses*. Salt Lake City: Deseret Book, 1998.

Nibley, Preston. *Brigham Young: The Man and His Work*. 4th ed. Salt Lake City: Deseret Book, 1960.

Oaks, Dallin H. "Apostasy and Restoration." *Ensign* 25 (May 1995): 84–86.

———. *The Lord's Way*. Salt Lake City: Deseret Book, 1991.

———. *Pure in Heart*. Salt Lake City: Bookcraft, 1988.

———. "Teaching and Learning by the Spirit." *Ensign* 27 (March 1997): 7–14.

———. "The Witness: Martin Harris." *Ensign* 29 (May 1999): 35–37.

Old Testament Student Manual: Genesis–2 Samuel. 2d ed. rev. Salt Lake City: The Church of Jesus Christ of Latter-day Saints, 1981.

Otten, Leaun G., and C. Max Caldwell. *Sacred Truths of the Doctrine and Covenants*. 2 vols. Salt Lake City: Deseret Book, 1982–83.

Our Heritage: A Brief History of The Church of Jesus Christ of Latter-day Saints. Salt Lake City: The Church of Jesus Christ of Latter-day Saints, 1996.

Packer, Boyd K. "Personal Revelation: The Gift, the Test, and the Promise." *Ensign* 24 (November 1994): 59–62.

———. *Things of the Soul*. Salt Lake City: Bookcraft, 1996.

———. "What Every Elder Should Know—and Every Sister as Well: A Primer on Principles of Priesthood Government." *Ensign* 23 (February 1993): 7–14.

Perry, L. Tom. "The Articles of Faith." *Ensign* 28 (May 1998): 22–24.

———. "But Be Ye Doers of the Word." *Ensign* 7 (May 1977): 59–61.

———. "By the Hands of His Prophets." *Ensign* 28 (August 1998): 49–55.

Petersen, Mark E. *The Great Prologue*. Salt Lake City: Deseret Book, 1975.

Peterson, H. Donl. *The Pearl of Great Price: A History and Commentary*. Salt Lake City: Deseret Book, 1987.

Porter, Larry C. "The Restoration of the Aaronic and Melchizedek Priesthoods." *Ensign* 26 (December 1996): 30–47.

Porter, Larry C., and Susan Easton Black, eds. *The Prophet Joseph: Essays on the Life and Mission of Joseph Smith*. Salt Lake City: Deseret Book, 1988.

Pratt, Orson. *Interesting Accounts of Several Remarkable Visions*. Pamphlet. Edinburgh. 1840.

Pratt, Parley P. *Autobiography of Parley P. Pratt*. Edited by Parley P. Pratt Jr. Salt Lake City: Deseret Book, 1985.

Providing in the Lord's Way: A Leader's Guide to Welfare. Salt Lake City: The Church of Jesus Christ of Latter-day Saints, 1990.

Richards, LeGrand. "Call of the Prophets." *Ensign* 11 (May 1981): 31–33.

Roberts, B. H. *A Comprehensive History of The Church of Jesus Christ of Latter-day Saints*. 6 vols. Salt Lake City: Deseret News, 1930.

———. *The Life of John Taylor*. Salt Lake City: George Q. Cannon and Sons, 1892.

————. *The Missouri Persecutions*. Salt Lake City: George Q. Cannon and Sons, 1900.

Robinson, Stephen E., and H. Dean Garrett. *A Commentary on the Doctrine and Covenants*. 4 vols. Salt Lake City: Deseret Book, 2000–2005.

Romney, Marion G. "A Disciple of Christ." *Ensign* 8 (November 1978): 38–39.

Scraps of Biography: Faith-Promoting Series, no. 10. Salt Lake City: Juvenile Instructor's Office, 1883.

Skousen, W. Cleon. *The Making of America*. Washington, D.C.: National Center for Constitutional Studies, 1985.

Smith, George Albert. *Sharing the Gospel with Others*. Compiled by Preston Nibley. Salt Lake City: Deseret News Press, 1948.

————. *The Teachings of George Albert Smith*. Edited by Robert McIntosh and Susan McIntosh. Salt Lake City: Bookcraft, 1996.

Smith, Hyrum M., and Janne M. Sjodahl. *Doctrine and Covenants Commentary*. Salt Lake City: Deseret Book, 1978.

Smith, Joseph. *History of The Church of Jesus Christ of Latter-day Saints*. Edited by B. H. Roberts. 2d ed. rev. 7 vols. Salt Lake City: The Church of Jesus Christ of Latter-day Saints, 1932–51.

————. *The Personal Writings of Joseph Smith*. Compiled and edited by Dean C. Jessee. Salt Lake City: Deseret Book, 1984.

————. *Teachings of the Prophet Joseph Smith*. Selected and arranged by Joseph Fielding Smith. Salt Lake City: Deseret Book, 1976.

Smith, Joseph F. *From Prophet to Son: Advice of Joseph F. Smith to His Missionary Sons*. Compiled by Hyrum M. Smith III and Scott G. Kenney. Salt Lake City: Deseret Book, 1981.

————. *Gospel Doctrine*. Salt Lake City: Deseret Book, 1939.

Smith, Joseph Fielding. *Church History and Modern Revelation*. 4 vols. Salt Lake City: The Church of Jesus Christ of Latter-day Saints, 1946–49.

————. Conference Reports. April 1970.

————. *Doctrines of Salvation*. Edited by Bruce R. McConkie. 3 vols. Salt Lake City: Bookcraft, 1954–1956.

————. *Essentials in Church History*. Classics in Mormon Literature edition. Salt Lake City: Deseret Book, 1979.

————. "Eternal Keys and the Right to Preside." *Ensign* 2 (July 1972): 87–88.

————. *The Restoration of All Things*. Salt Lake City: Deseret News Press, 1945.

————. *The Way to Perfection*. Salt Lake City: Genealogical Society of Utah, 1949.

Smith, Joseph III. "Last Testimony of Sister Emma." *Saints' Herald* 26, no. 19 (1 October 1879): 289–90.

Smith, Lucy Mack. *The History of Joseph Smith by His Mother*. Edited by Preston Nibley. Salt Lake City: Bookcraft, 1979.

Snow, Eliza R. *Biography and Family Record of Lorenzo Snow*. Salt Lake City: Deseret News, 1884.

Snow, Lorenzo. *The Teachings of Lorenzo Snow*. Edited by Clyde J. Williams. Salt Lake City: Bookcraft, 1984.

Stuy, Brian H., ed. *Collected Discourses*. 5 vols. Burbank Calif. and Woodland Hills, Utah: B. H. S. Publishing, 1987–92.

Talmage, James E. Conference Reports. October 1920.

————. *The Great Apostasy*. Salt Lake City: Deseret Book, 1958.

————. *The House of the Lord*. Salt Lake City: Deseret Book, 1968.

————. *Jesus the Christ*. Salt Lake City: Deseret Book, 1983.

Tanner, N. Eldon. "The Administration of the Church." *Ensign* 9 (November 1979): 42–47.

Times and Seasons (Nauvoo, Illinois). 1839–46.

Tullidge, Edward. *The Women of Mormondom*. New York: Tullidge & Crandall, 1877.

Webster, Noah. *An American Dictionary of the English Language*. 1828. Reprint, San Francisco: Foundation for American Christian Education, 1980.

Whitmer, John. *The Book of John Whitmer*. Typescript copy. BYU Special Collections. Harold B. Lee Library, Provo, Utah.

Whitney, Orson F. Conference Reports. October 1911, April 1912.

————. *Life of Heber C. Kimball*. Salt Lake City: Kimball Family, 1888.

Widstoe, John A. Conference Reports. April 1935.

———. *Evidences and Reconciliations.* Arranged by G. Homer Durham. Salt Lake City: Bookcraft, 1960.

———. *Joseph Smith—Seeker after Truth, Prophet of God.* Salt Lake City: Bookcraft, 1951.

———. *Message of the Doctrine and Covenants.* Salt Lake City: Bookcraft, 1969.

———. *Priesthood and Church Government.* Salt Lake City: Deseret Book, 1939.

———. *Program of The Church of Jesus Christ of Latter-day Saints.* Salt Lake City: Deseret Book, 1937.

Wirthlin, Joseph B. "Cultivating Divine Attributes." *Ensign* 28 (November 1998): 25–28.

———. "Seeking the Good." *Ensign* 22 (May 1992): 86–88.

———. "Windows of Light and Truth." *Ensign* 25 (November 1995): 75–78.

———. "Without Guile." *Ensign* 18 (May 1988): 80–82.

Woodruff, Wilford. *The Discourses of Wilford Woodruff.* Edited by G. Homer Durham. Salt Lake City: Bookcraft, 1969.

———. *Leaves from My Journal.* Salt Lake City: Juvenile Instructor's Office, 1881.

———. *Wilford Woodruff, His Life and Labors.* Compiled by Matthias F. Cowley. Salt Lake City: Deseret News, 1916.

———. *Wilford Woodruff's Journal: 1833–1898.* Edited by Scott G. Kenney. 9 vols. Midvale, Utah: Signature Books, 1983.

Young, Brigham. *Discourses of Brigham Young.* Compiled by John A. Widtsoe. Salt Lake City: Deseret Book Company, 1954.

———. *Manuscript History of Brigham Young.* Archives of The Church of Jesus Christ of Latter-day Saints, Salt Lake City, Utah.

ISBN 1-59038-327-3